Booking & Tour Management

for the

Performing Arts

Rena Shagan

ALLWORTH PRESS, NEW YORK

to Michael, Jillian, and Ethan Shagan with love

Published by Allworth Press, and imprint of Allworth Communications, Inc.
10 East 23rd Street, New York, NY 10010

Cover design by Douglas Design Associates, New York, NY

Book design by Sharp Des!gns, Lansing, MI

ISBN: 1-880559-36-6

Library of Congress Card Catalog Number: 95-76687

Contents
and List of Exhibits

LIST OF EXHIBITS

Acknowledgements

A number of people played major roles behind the scenes in both the original preparation of this book and in the present revision, and I would like to acknowledge their contributions.

Robert Porter, then at the American Council for the Arts, ably shepherded the writing and production of the first edition from the beginning stages of the manuscript and also worked with me on the revised version. Tad Crawford of Allworth Press took over the publishing of the present edition and has done an extraordinary job in making it possible for people who need it to once again purchase the book.

Three very knowledgeable people agreed to write chapters for the book in their special areas of expertise. Susan Farr was director of Cal Performances at the University of California, Berkeley, when she wrote "What Presenters Need from Artists." Shortly thereafter she became Executive Director of the Association of Performing Arts Presenters. She gives important insights into what the booking and tour management process looks like from the presenter's perspective. Her comments, as revised for this edition, are crucial to any company's understanding of what goes on, on the other side of the fence.

Art Becofsky, the author of the chapter on booking and touring abroad, was the executive director of the Cunningham Dance Foundation for more than twenty years. He brings to the chapter many years' experience in booking the engagements and managing the tours that have frequently taken the Cunningham company to Europe and Asia.

M. Kay Barrell has written the chapter on the technical end of touring. He is a lighting designer and production director for Ballet West and a theatre consultant. He draws on more than twenty years of production experience, both on tour and at home with a variety of performing arts companies, to offer updated insights into the kinds of information you need to know about facilities to give your best performance possible. In addition, he has kindly created a technical questionnaire especially for this book to aide companies in their efforts.

To update the book, I interviewed a group of leaders in the touring and presenting field—managers, presenters, and funders. Kim Chan, Janet Cowperthwaite, Jacqueline Z. Davis, John Gingrich, Joseph Gresser, Henry Moran, Mark Murphy, Irene Namkin, Neill Archer Roan, Ivan Sygoda, John Ullman, and Andrea Wagner were interviewed for the revised edition. Each is a valued colleague, and I thank them for their important contribution to *Booking and Tour Management for the Performing Arts*.

For the original edition of this book I interviewed four artists, Leon Bates, Richard Iglewski, Chris Komar, and Mary Shearer, who took time out of their busy schedules to participate in a series of interviews. Their points of view and feelings about touring are an invaluable contribution to the book's completeness.

Several organizations permitted me to use examples of their materials as examples in this book, the Association of Performing Arts Presenters, Mid-America Arts Alliance, Montana Repertory Theatre, The National Theatre of the Deaf, Susan Marshall & Company, and Western Alliance of Arts Administrators.

I am very fortunate to have had the privilege of working with a group of extraordinary artists in my more than twenty years in the field. Without naming each individually, I want to acknowledge their important role in my life and thank them for trusting me with their work.

This book could not have been written without the special help and support of my husband Michael Shagan, who acted as editor of "first recourse" throughout the book's preparation and who made valuable contributions to its form and style.

RENA SHAGAN

Editor's Notes

1. The principles set forth in this book are applicable to the booking and touring process for both solo artists and large companies. For simplicity, both individual performers and performing arts organizations are referred to throughout the text as *companies*.

2. To simplify the text, masculine pronouns have been used throughout, instead of the more cumbersome him/her or he/she. This is in no way meant to imply that women do not hold important roles in the performing arts as artists, administrators, board members, booking managers, technicians, and presenters. The only exception is chapter 11, where the author chose to alternate the use of masculine and feminine pronouns.

Introduction

The marketplace for the performing arts in this country is enormous. Indeed, according to the most recent Louis Harris survey, *Americans and the Arts VI,* the number of people who attend arts events (both performances and visual art exhibitions) has remained at an all-time high, despite a serious economic recession. Audiences were attracted to performances sponsored by a variety of performing arts presenters ranging from the independent entrepreneur to colleges and universities, civic auditoriums, arts centers, performing arts companies, alternative spaces, and even service organizations like the YMCA.

The events they saw included opera, ballet, mime, theatre, chamber music, solo instrumentalists, new music, orchestral music, and all varieties of contemporary dance, as well as work which involved collaborations between artists from a variety of media. Some of the productions involved large numbers of people on the stage and behind the scenes and featured elaborate sets and costumes. Other events consisted of a single artist performing on a bare stage. Clearly, there are eager audiences for all types and sizes of performing artists/companies, and somewhere in this country there is a place for every good performer to be seen and heard by the public.

The marketplace for the performing arts comprises a network of buyers and sellers, a continuum of supply and demand. One part of this universe is populated by performing artists/companies, another by presenters and the organizations they serve. Touring artists/companies sell their services—performances, teaching residencies, etc.—to presenters, who present these services to the public or use them within their own organizations (a master class, for example). The interaction of buyers and sellers in a competitive market is one of the principal economic activities of the performing arts industry, and at the center of it is a process known as *booking*.

Regardless of the art form or the geographic area of interest, the booking process necessitates that the artist/company must put together a package of services to offer to presenters, attach a price to these services, and communicate this information to the presenters who are most likely to buy. The desired end of this process is a contract for an engagement to perform, to teach, to create a new work, or any combination thereof which enables you to take your company, or *product,* on the road.

A prevalent myth among many in the performing arts is that in order to book an artist/company successfully you must either already have plenty of solid contacts in the field, or be related to Merlin the Magician. Neither is the case. Booking and the tour administration which follows after you have successfully put together a tour are very hard work, but both can be mastered. The purpose of this book is to help ease you through the entire process by guiding you step-by-step through the key questions you and your colleagues must ask yourselves before deciding to tour, describing all the materials you will need, and outlining in detail the booking process, the management responsibilities during a tour, and the administrative follow-up.

Every art form has unique qualities and requirements, and each individual company will have certain special needs. But the *basic* needs and problems of most touring groups are quite similar. Regardless of your company's size or discipline, there are certain fundamental principles which you will need to observe in order to book and administer a tour effectively.

This book is designed to be used in two ways: (1) as a basic handbook for the people directly involved in touring, including those who may not have been exposed to the subject previously, those individuals or organizations contemplating touring for the first time, and those considering a significant change in the amount or method of their touring; and (2) as a general resource for administrative and financial staff connected with companies that tour who, although not directly responsible for booking or tour administration, wish to acquaint themselves with this component of the company's overall program. The book should also be of interest to board members of touring companies as well as to presenters, whose relationships with the companies they produce will be enhanced by a better understanding of what the performing artist is up against trying to do his best work in unfamiliar surroundings.

This book was originally published in 1986 as *The Road Show*. Most of the planning and procedures for booking and tour management have remained the same, but where that is not the case, the information for this new edition, *Booking and Tour Management for the Performing Arts,* has been changed and updated. The chapters are arranged to follow the basic flow of the booking process and, if read serially, *Booking and Tour Mangagement for the Performing Arts* maps out a coherent plan of action. Each chapter thoroughly and discretely examines a specific component of booking and tour management.

The text has been supplemented with chapters written by three real experts in their respective areas. Susan Farr gives important insights into what the booking and tour management processes look like from the presenter's perspective. Art Becofsky discusses international booking and tour management and how they are both different and similar to what you will find in the U.S. marketplace. And M. Kay Barrell examines the technical end of touring, outlining what companies need to know about a presenter's theatre to give the most professional and technically competent performance possible.

The chapter, "Trends for the Future," is completely new for this edition. It focuses on notable shifts and changes in the evolving marketplace of the 1990s. The trends are surveyed through interviews with working professionals in the field—presenters, managers, and funders. If some of the information in this chapter seems contradictory in places, it is not by accident. The way the marketplace is seen depends very much on the participant's organizational size, geography, and artistic goals, among other factors. The purpose of this chapter is to illuminate the changes so that you can incorporate new market patterns into your strategy for going on tour.

By the time you reach the end of this book, you should be aware of the questions and tasks to be faced, you will have learned many of the answers, and you will know where to look for the others.

CHAPTER 1

Touring: An Overview

T he touring of performing arts presentations makes live cultural attractions available to a vast and disparate audience throughout the United States and abroad. The concept of touring covers a wide range of activities which take place when a company leaves its home base to provide performances or other services to one or more audience groups. While tours are integral to the programs of many different performing arts institutions, "touring" can mean something quite different to a well-established organization from what it means to a small, new company.

Before considering whether a company should tour, the different types of activities that occur under the general label of "touring" should be defined.

Run Out. A run-out, in the classic sense, is an engagement in a nearby town or city which does not entail an overnight stay. However, run-outs have also come to mean an engagement of a couple of days, which may take place quite far from the artist's home city but is unconnected to any other engagement.

One-Night Stand/Single Day Residency. A one-night stand is a single performance for one presenter as part of a tour. This visit can include additional activity(ies) which all take place on the same day (single day residency).

Residency. A residency can best be thought of as a stay in one community for more than a single performance. Activities other than performance are often an important part of a residency. At times a group of presenters within the same community or in adjacent areas share a residency.

Long-Term Residency. A long-term residency is a stay of one or more weeks at one location. Long-term residencies usually involve a considerable amount of performance and nonperformance activity.

Tour. A tour is a series of performances and/or other activities performed by a company in different places on the road without returning to its home city. A tour can be made up of single performances, nonperformance activities, and/or residencies, and can range in length from a few days to several weeks or months.

To Tour or Not to Tour: Who Makes the Decision?

This chapter is designed to help a company ask the tough questions it needs to answer before proceeding into the booking process (See Exhibit 1). In fact, the first few chapters of this book should help you to determine whether your company should tour at all and—if you decide that touring is an option—what you should tour, where, how, and for how long, as well as how much you should charge presenters. The aim is to focus the decisionmakers in your organization on touring in general and, more specifically, what touring would entail for your company.

Decisions of this magnitude should be made in close consultation among senior artistic and management personnel and the board of trustees. (Solo musicians and singers will involve a different group in their deliberations, made up perhaps of the artist, the manager, and the artist's teacher or coach.)

Artistic Staff

The artistic staff is concerned primarily with how touring affects the artistic product (i.e., does the company have specific work it wants to tour, how long will it take to prepare, is there time for rehearsal in terms of other things the company is doing, etc.). If a company decides to tour, then the artistic personnel proposes what work to present and helps to decide how the repertory or production(s) might be modified to be either more cost-efficient or more easily tourable. The administrative staff and board must also be thoroughly acquainted, from the very start of the tour planning process, with the artistic staff's concept of the possibilities for, and limitations on, the activities the company will be able to provide on tour.

EXHIBIT 1

The Planning Process for Touring

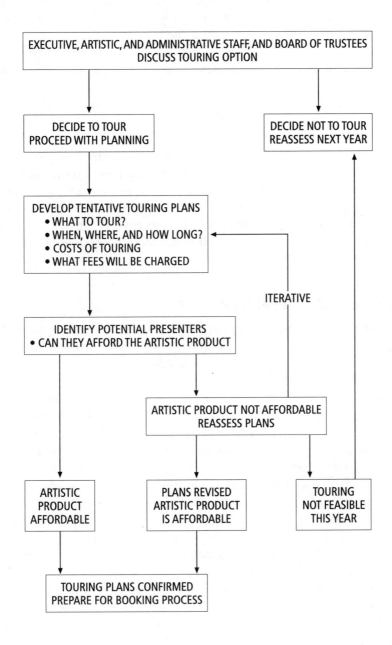

Administrative Staff

The administrative staff concentrates initially on the costs of the proposed tour, the resources necessary to succeed, and the ramifications on other company activities. If the company decides to tour, management must construct a budget for touring the chosen artistic product, and propose where the company will tour and by what method of transportation. Management must also assess the product's salability and the financial and logistical impact of its technical demands because, ultimately, it is responsible for booking and administering the tour properly.

Board of Trustees

The board of trustees is responsible for all fiscal and policy decisions affecting the company, and needs to be an integral part of decisionmaking throughout this process. The trustees not only must agree on such matters as funding any deficit created by a tour, but they also must help to determine whether touring, from a broad perspective, is in the best interests of the company and to assess how it will affect the company's activities in its home city.

Touring Is Not for Everyone

Touring is not for every company, and certainly is never obligatory. No company should ever go out on the road just because it seems to be the thing to do. Rather, you should know in advance exactly why you want to tour and what you hope to gain.

Many organizations choose not to tour at all, or perhaps to tour only briefly every year or so. Several reasons are commonly offered by companies. One obvious reason is that they have too many ongoing commitments to take on new activities such as touring. If a company is a major cultural resource locally, the rehearsal, performance, educational, and outreach activities in its home base area can sometimes leave little or no time to tour. Or, in addition to its regular home base activities, a company sometimes may have a "second home," another community in which it works on a regular basis for a portion of the year. In some organizations, artists have a large amount of regular outside work, and additional work weeks are not a priority.

Some companies can earn more income at home than on tour. As the manager of a ballet company said, "Why should I take the company on the road, with all the headaches and extra expense involved, and bring in $40,000 per week in fees when we can sell $80,000 worth of tickets in the same week at home, do more performances, and my dancers can sleep in their own beds at night?" In addition, all things being equal, a touring program which needs subsidy is less attractive to the company and its board of trustees than staying at home.

Finally, touring is difficult and tiring for artists and the technical and administrative staff who accompany them. The physical and emotional stress involved in performing in a new theatre every day or every couple of days may be more than a company can sustain. In addition, if other company activities take precedence, the administrative staff may not be able to cope with booking and administering a tour.

Some Good Reasons for Going Out on the Road

On the other hand, many companies do choose to tour, for a combination of reasons closely related to the type and size of the company, their sources of income, and their home base activities. The following paragraphs examine some of the primary reasons for going out on the road, in no particular order of importance.

Touring is a matter of survival for many companies. At-home performances and activities are limited by cost, audience size, and repertory. For dance companies especially, there is a limit to the number of works which can be offered during a home season, and there is a very small number of new pieces the audience will not have seen previously. Chamber music ensembles and solo musicians and vocalists must tour to develop national and international reputations.

For some more established organizations, touring enables the company to offer its artists enough work to persuade them to remain under contract. This can be especially important for companies based outside of large metropolitan areas. In many parts of the country, artists cannot easily get another job in their field. To attract and hold competent artists, a company must offer a contract for a substantial portion of the year, including a number of tour weeks in addition to the rehearsal and performance weeks at home.

For some companies, touring is an important means of building a regional image as a company committed not only to its art form, but also to its role as a community resource, developing audiences and providing essential nonperforming services in the region.

Companies also tour to become well-known. Touring generates name recognition among presenting organizations and audiences. It promotes visibility, which can translate into more effective fundraising, higher performance fees, a changed perception by a home audience (which sometimes begins to appreciate a company only when someone else tells them how good it is!), and the ability to attract better artists and gain recognition from regional corporations, national corporations with a presence in the region, national government funding agencies, foundations, and individuals.

Some companies tour simply because they are committed to performing in communities where there is little or no regular access to quality performance, to a particular art form, or to the work of a particular artist.

Artistically, there are two distinct reasons to tour. First, composers, playwrights, and choreographers create work to be heard or seen by audiences. Similarly, people become musicians, dancers, actors, or singers in order to perform. Touring helps both types of artists to gain exposure for their work before the largest possible audience. Second, some argue that the road can provide a good place to hone, develop, or improve a piece of work as it is performed before a variety of audiences.

How to Decide Whether or Not to Tour

There are good reasons, then, both in favor of, or against, going out on the road. Making the decision about whether to tour should be included in your company's overall planning process. The decision will be based on a careful evaluation of your company in several broad areas of concern. Below are some of the factors you will need to consider to reach the right decision for you.

Artistic Compatibility

First and foremost, you must consider whether the work your company produces is compatible with touring. If it requires an extremely complicated technical set-up, a bigger than usual traveling technical staff, extra set-up time, and/or a large group of artists, it may be difficult or impractical to tour. A large company is more difficult to sustain financially, but can usually manage a long tour better than a small company. Large companies have a greater number of people among whom they can divide artistic and technical responsibilities, making them less susceptible to illness, injuries, and burnout.

Is the company relatively inexperienced, or is it used to touring? Experienced companies will know how to pace themselves on tour and will have tricks to ease the strain of being on the road. How does your company add new work or productions? For instance, is the work created from scratch, as is the case with most modern dance companies, or are you working from an existing musical score or script? Almost without exception, a company whose work is originally conceived will require more rehearsal time, hence less time will be available for touring.

Finally, what about obligations at home? For example, the company or its members may be committed to teaching or other special projects and simply not have time to tour. You must sensitively weigh how much touring the company members can manage before their personal lives become disrupted, and they become too physically or emotionally exhausted to work well.

Financial Position

Does the company have ways to produce significant amounts of earned income other than by touring? If it does, then touring may be a less attractive option and the company can more easily decide to tour for shorter periods, or not at all. Does the company make or lose money touring? How much money to underwrite touring can be raised from government, corporations, and foundations that might not be forthcoming for other company programs? If the company tours at a loss, then the funds it can raise from a variety of sources for tour activities may make it possible and palatable to go out on the road.

What financial considerations will the company confront as a result of the artistic considerations just discussed (i.e., length of rehearsal period, length of home season, size of company, repertory, etc.)? Does the company have its artists under a contract for a set number of weeks for which they must be paid?

Can the company anticipate a long enough tour so that it can amortize its start-up costs? Can the company afford to spend the money to book and administer a tour—money for personnel, mailings, telephone bills, promotion, and booking conferences? Keep in mind that even before a tour begins a company may have to lay out at least fifty percent of its costs for booking, promotion, and production. What other major financial obligations does the company expect to take on?

Home Base Involvement

The amount of touring you will be able to do depends upon the demand for your services in your home area, which may be a town, a city, or several counties. Foremost among the factors that determine this demand are the size of the audience, the scope of activities in which you are engaged, and the number of other companies in your home area.

Marketplace Competition

Everyone thinks—or should think—that the company he is associated with is special. But how does it really stack up against other companies in the outside world? Does your company have some exceptional ability or type of activity that presenters will want? If yours is one of a small number of companies which perform something quite unique, or if you have received recent overwhelming national acclaim, potential presenters may be attracted to your company.

Is your company competent and highly professional, and will its artists and technical staff be able to withstand the rigors of touring? Is the company administration ready and able to service the demands and needs of presenters?

A rational, objective analysis of the company will help you to draw the right conclusions. If you have favorably answered these questions, you can feel confident that your company's product can capably compete in the marketplace. On the other hand, booking is a very competitive business, and not all companies will be successful in their pursuit of a tour.

Making the Decision

If the senior artistic staff, administrative personnel, and the board of trustees have honestly reviewed and realistically assessed each of the above considerations, then the company will have a pretty good idea of whether there should be a tour, or if the touring option should be postponed and reconsidered again next year when the company will again focus on its programmatic priorities.

The Ingredients of Planning a Tour

Apart from the artistic product, a tour is shaped by the combination of several distinct ingredients. The decisions your company makes about each of these ingredients will significantly affect the type of tour you book and your potential for success on the road.

What to Tour

Orchestras, chamber music groups, and solo musicians and singers will probably have little difficulty deciding what to tour. Each season, pieces will be added to your repertory. Sometimes special programs are prepared for specific situations. If you contract to perform as a soloist for an orchestra, it will be for a specific piece or pieces of music. Assuming that a string quartet has a well-rounded repertoire, whether it chooses to play Brahms or Beethoven will not have a huge impact on the facilities or logistical considerations of the tour.

Touring opera, theatre, and dance companies are in a completely different position. They need to consider potential programs carefully from two vantage points—technical requirements and salability.

Naturally a company wants to tour its finest artistic product. Yet, from a technical perspective, you must determine the lowest common denominator in terms of the theatre facilities in which the company can play. If the company thinks certain production standards must be upheld on tour, then it must be able to afford to carry lighting equipment on the road. If you plan to present work that requires several drops, you are limited to theatres with fly systems. Is this a realistic expectation? How complicated is your set-up? If your company is usually booked for single performances, and it takes two days to set up (the day prior to performance and performance day) you will be limited to a maximum of two or three performances per week. Will the fees you can charge for those performances come close to meeting touring costs? Can the cost of your fee, along with local presenting costs, be met by the presenters who traditionally book the company?

The choice of what to tour must also be based on an informed consideration of the kind of work in which presenters are interested. You will need to convince the presenter that he wants to produce your work in his theatre, and he, in turn, will have to convince his audience to come see it. You certainly want to encourage touring a company's best work, but if you have two equally excellent productions, one of which won a Pulitzer Prize for best play last year, then obviously that play will be a better candidate for touring.

Work involving nudity, profanity, and blatant sex, as well as work with strong sacrilegious elements, is still controversial in certain parts of the country. What may be absolutely fine in New York, Los Angeles, or other larger cities could be a real problem elsewhere.

It will also be necessary for the artistic staff to set limits on the services that can be provided and the tour schedule that will be permitted. For example, will travel, rehearsal, and performance ever be permitted on the same day? Will one-night stands be permitted? How much rehearsal/set-up time is needed on performance day? Can the company members teach or participate in residency activities on the day of performance? These decisions will affect every detail of the organization's tour budget and schedule. Establishing the parameters of tour activity is one of the most critical contributions that the artistic staff makes to the organization's long-term planning, to the longevity of its artists, and to the viability of the organization over many seasons.

Going Out on the Road: How Long Should You Tour?

The length of a tour is based on many factors. Larger companies can sustain long tours more easily than smaller ones. Similarly, companies whose artists, staff, and technical people are used to touring can tour for longer periods than inexperienced groups. Naturally, how much work a company has in its home community, a "second home," or a long-term residency base is also a factor.

The lifestyle of company members is also important. Long tours are not conducive to stable, rewarding personal relationships.

Review the amount of touring the company did last year, and whether additional work has been promised. How many engagements can be added if management does a really concerted booking campaign?

If your company is just beginning to tour, contemplate a brief tour or series of tours. A company just getting into touring is not likely to attract a large number of presenters.

Mapping Out a Tour

A company can tour nationally, regionally, close to home, or in a combination of the above. On a national tour, a company is usually presented for a brief period of time by presenters with whom it has had no prior relationship and who may or may not present it again. Exceptions to this general rule are very large institutions, such as New York City Opera and the Joffrey Ballet, which repeatedly tour to specific cities that have facilities, audiences, and presenting organizations large enough to support operations of this magnitude.

Some companies tour only within their own regions. In doing so, they try to develop ongoing relationships with regional presenters to build the company's image in the area. Still other companies tour on a regular basis to a region away from their home base. Many companies combine national and regional touring.

The kind of touring a company does depends upon the importance of touring income and activity to the company's survival. For example, modern dance companies which rely on touring as a major source of income tend to tour more widely, more frequently, and for longer periods of time than theatre companies, whose income base is less dependent on this source of revenue. Companies that are able to manage longer home seasons are apt to think they have a greater choice about where and how to tour, and are more likely to keep their tours shorter and closer to home.

Regional Touring. Regional touring has much in its favor. From a purely economic point of view, travel costs by bus, van, or car are always less than airfares. Local telephone calls are much less expensive than long distance. Fees to presenters can be lower than those charged by companies with substantial transportation costs. Thus, a nearby company can be more attractive to regional presenters than a company from another part of the country. (While this generally holds true, in a large region involving many states, like that served by the Western States Arts Foundation, the distances from one end of the region to the other are enormous. One would almost have to bisect the region North/South or East/West to derive these benefits of regional touring.)

Regional touring gives a company an opportunity to develop in several ways. A company can develop relationships with presenters, enhance its reputation among local presenters, and broaden its reputation for regional service with government, corporations, and foundations from throughout the region. And regional touring can help to improve a company's home season by raising its visibility in the regional media. Booking a regional tour can even be done by getting in a car and driving from presenter to presenter.

Regional touring can also be done successfully outside your own region. Some companies have cultivated ongoing relationships with regional presenters in "under-served" areas which allow them to return each year.

National Touring. Other companies want to, and should, tour nationally. If this is what your company's planning group has decided, the road ahead will be rougher and more expensive. With national tours, there is stiff competition for the same presenters. If your company intends to succeed in national booking, you need to be willing to commit a significant amount of money and time to the process. Anticipate that it will take several years before you realize a return on your effort and dollars.

How to Get Around: Selecting Transportation

The mode of transportation your company chooses will depend on the touring company's size, what you are touring, and how far your presenters are from one another. As a rule of thumb, the larger the company the more likely that economics will dictate renting a van or chartering a bus and a truck, as opposed to flying from one presenter to the next. Usually, once you surpass an eight- to ten-person tour, flying becomes quite prohibitive.

On the other hand, look at who your presenters have been and where they are located. If a company, which because of its fees or what it does, can only perform for, say, two presenters in a state, then plane travel becomes a necessity for a tightly booked tour. Otherwise, the company spends all its time traveling and not earning enough income, and you will have to set your fees accordingly.

In evaluating transportation options, the cost of plane fares must always be weighed against how much an extra travel day or days would cost the company (i.e., bus rental, company salaries, per diems, etc.) and how much extra income might be generated through fees if the travel time were shortened.

Another item to consider is the scale of your touring program. If you tour a production or repertory that requires two trailer trucks full of sets, lights, costumes, and drops, driving will be much less expensive than paying air freight and trucking to and from the theatre. Still another option is to send a truck ahead and have the company fly. Public transportation is an option for companies in parts of the country such as the Northeast where good rail service exists. Of course, much will depend upon railroad schedules, the capacity to carry baggage, and the like. Train travel may be feasible for run-outs but is usually impractical for extensive touring.

Public bus companies might also be a possibility, although good service may be difficult to find, and the schedule is inflexible.

Clearing the Calendar

If, out of the planning process, your company has decided to tour, the next step is to determine available touring dates. Take a calendar for the touring year and fill in all existing obligations from your overall plan. Such obligations could include rehearsal periods, home season, and educational activities. With this information in place, available touring time can be determined and then scheduled appropriately.

Some parts of the year are better for touring than others. For most presenters, mid-September through the end of November or early December, and mid-January through mid-May, are considered prime times. Unless you are touring *The Nutcracker, A Christmas Carol,* or a program of holiday music, the Christmas season does not work very well. June, July, and August are also not ordinarily programmed, except by presenters involved in summer festivals of some type. University presenters and towns conform to the school and college schedules, so spring break is a factor to take into consideration. Weather must also be considered. If you plan to tour Montana, Wyoming, and North Dakota, January through March are not optimal months. Nor will you want to be in Florida, Nevada, or southern Texas in July. It is also a good idea to check with regional arts agencies to determine heavy tour times so that you can select a less busy period for touring.

Once you have determined which blocks of time are available for touring, you are ready to launch directly into the process which will make the tour a reality—booking.

Booking: An Overview

B ooking is the process whereby a company booking manager or an independent booking agent sells a company's services to presenting organizations for a period of time, whether for a single performance or for a residency lasting several days or weeks. A series of bookings properly strung together in a cost-effective manner constitutes a tour.

The Booking Process: What It's All About

The booking process can be broken down into a number of steps, as shown in Exhibit 2. As you proceed through these steps, there are junctures at which there are several options from which to choose. The decisions you make will determine how your organization tailors the booking process to its needs and to its artistic product.

Setting Fees

The first area to explore in the booking process is fee-setting—deciding what to charge prospective presenters for your artistic product. Fee-setting can be based on three different financial premises. The first premise assumes that a company at least needs to break even on a tour, the second assumes that it must make money, and the third is based on its willingness to accept a loss. If the company has agreed to lose money on its touring program, you need to be sure there is other earned or contributed income to cover the deficit. If the company is counting on making money or breaking even from a tour, you must carefully assess your financial assumptions. You may find after some analysis that those assumptions have been incorrect and that the company will not be able to bring in as much income as you had figured, or that expenses are higher than you had planned. In either case, there is still time to reassess your plans and recheck your options to see if you can make the tour work financially.

Creating Booking Materials

The next step in the booking process is to assemble your booking materials. How simple or complicated, how economical or expensive these materials should be will be determined by the parameters of the tour. If a company wants to tour for two weeks in its own region and will do only half-week residencies, the required booking materials will be quite different from those needed by a company which does primarily one-night stands and wants to tour nationally for twenty weeks. Not only will the materials be dissimilar, but the complexity of producing them will also differ. What remains the same is the overall intent—to create booking materials that will help you convince a prospective presenter to produce your company in his theatre.

Conducting the Campaign

Regardless of whether your company wants to tour two weeks or twenty, the next part of the process is identical. You must target your prospective presenters and let them know who you are and what you do. Presenters get to know your company from the booking materials which you send through the mail and, afterwards, in follow-up telephone calls in which you make your case personally. Based upon an initial round of calls, prospective presenters are divided into two separate and distinct groups: those who have a possible interest in booking an engagement and those who, for whatever reason, do not. An additional mailing with follow-up materials is then sent to presenters who have indicated some interest.

The next step could be either a face-to-face meeting with a presenter at a booking conference, further telephone calls and correspondence, or both. Several telephone calls and letters will probably be necessary before the presenter comes to a decision.

The Tour Puzzle: Putting It All Together

The next sequence of events is intertwined, often happening simultaneously as a series of tour dates falls into place. This includes routing

EXHIBIT 2

The Booking Process

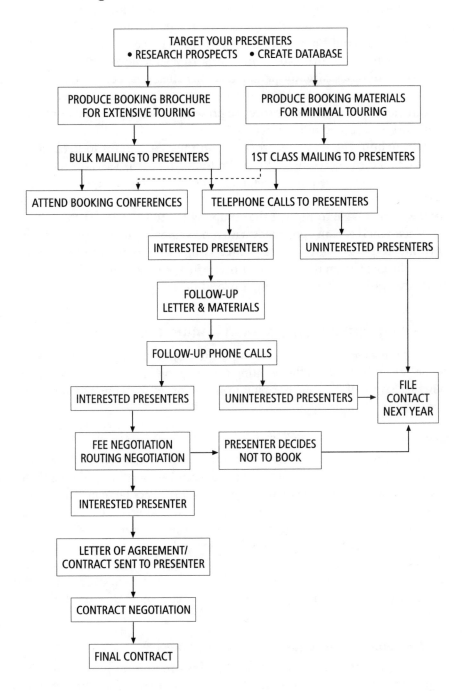

TARGET YOUR PRESENTERS
• RESEARCH PROSPECTS • CREATE DATABASE

PRODUCE BOOKING BROCHURE
FOR EXTENSIVE TOURING

PRODUCE BOOKING MATERIALS
FOR MINIMAL TOURING

BULK MAILING TO PRESENTERS

1ST CLASS MAILING TO PRESENTERS

ATTEND BOOKING CONFERENCES

TELEPHONE CALLS TO PRESENTERS

INTERESTED PRESENTERS

UNINTERESTED PRESENTERS

FOLLOW-UP
LETTER & MATERIALS

FOLLOW-UP PHONE CALLS

INTERESTED PRESENTERS

UNINTERESTED PRESENTERS

FILE
CONTACT
NEXT YEAR

FEE NEGOTIATION
ROUTING NEGOTIATION

PRESENTER DECIDES
NOT TO BOOK

INTERESTED PRESENTER

LETTER OF AGREEMENT/
CONTRACT SENT TO PRESENTER

CONTRACT NEGOTIATION

FINAL CONTRACT

the tour in a manner most advantageous to the company. Ideally, a well-routed tour allows the company to play a reasonable number of connected dates without spending too much time on travel, without dates being too close together, and without doubling back geographically to pick up stray bookings that could not quite fit elsewhere. The company will also be searching for presenting organizations that can book performances between the dates already penciled in for the prospective tour. Concurrently, you will be negotiating types of activities, fees, and technical requirements with various prospective presenters. Some potential bookings will work out successfully; others will not.

Throughout the booking process, you must be careful to keep good notes on all the proceedings. This will remind you of the fees and activities that you have promised to presenters. It will enable you to target presenters better next time and to reactivate those who, although they express real interest, are unable to present the company for this particular tour.

When you reach an agreement with a presenter on all pending matters, it is time to go to contract. Although a company may tend to look upon this as the last part of the booking process, in a sense it is the real beginning of the relationship between company and presenter.

Exploring Options: Who Should Handle Your Booking?

Booking a company can be a complicated and time-consuming process. So before embarking on the booking process, you might want to consider whether you will do your booking in-house or let someone outside your organization handle the job.

Booking In-House

Most companies which tour very little, tour exclusively in their own regions, or are just beginning to tour are often best served by having their booking done by someone on the company's staff. Very large organizations whose touring is extremely complex are also—for different reasons—better off taking this option. (The exceptions to the rule are solo musicians, vocalists, and small music groups which do not have an individual manager all to themselves. These groups or individuals, by the very nature of the music business, typically operate as clients of a management firm which works with anywhere from just a few to sometimes more than one hundred artists.)

Professional Booking Agents: Pros and Cons

If the company has a track record and wants to tour nationally, you might think about employing the services of someone who books professionally. The pros and cons of using a professional booking agent—someone who books several companies, as opposed to having this function carried out in-house by a staff person who works exclusively for your company—have been argued back and forth for a long time. What follows is a compilation of the arguments on both sides.

Arguments in Favor of Professional Booking Agents

1. A professional booking agent is a highly skilled individual who can take a big load off company administration, freeing it to pursue other important functions, such as fundraising and promotion.
2. The professional booking agent devotes all of his time to booking, and therefore has more time to devote to this function on behalf of your company than someone on staff who wears several hats.
3. Professional booking agents have a network of contacts built up over many years in the business. They have special relationships with some presenters and can call upon them on a personal basis. If presenters have been happy with the companies an agent has steered to them previously, they will sometimes book a new, unknown company on the basis of trust.
4. Professional booking agents, in some cases, pay for or advance money for such basic booking costs as mailings, brochures, booking conferences, advertisements, and telephone calls. This can amount to a large sum of money, but arrangements in this area vary.
5. Except for agreed-to expenses and, in some cases, retainers, professional booking agents are not paid until they get a booking for the company.

Arguments Against Using Professional Booking Agents

1. Professional booking agents work with any number of companies. Sometimes the newest, smallest company at the bottom of the booking agent's roster doesn't get the attention it deserves.
2. Professional booking agents take fees, ranging from fifteen to twenty percent of the company fee, plus other expenses depending on arrangements.
3. Professional booking agents do just that—book. You pay your fee for booking, but staff will still be needed to administer the booking once it has been obtained.
4. Some companies claim that there is less personal contact with a professional booking agent than they would like. A company can be booked into places where it would not ordinarily perform or can find itself with tours either too tightly booked or having a large number of days between performances and no geographic coherence.

5. An in-house booking person feels more responsible to the company and is more aware of what a poorly booked tour, or too few bookings, could mean financially to the company.

6. The company can pay its in-house booking person a salary which may be less than the percentage received by a booking agent. The staff person often performs other functions for the company as well.

Quality Booking Representation: Where to Look and What to Look For

If you decide to go the booking management route, there are only a few professional managements relative to the number of artists and companies who wish to tour. Don't take it as a personal affront if a particular management declines to represent you after you approach them. Most managements report numerous calls per week from companies and artists. Booking is a lot of hard work; a management firm must be enthusiastic about what your company does. Your company also must be compatible with the other companies with which the firm deals, in terms of both size of company and type of product. For example, it would be unusual for one management to handle more than a couple of large ballet or theatre companies.

Still, if you have a particular management in mind, do not hesitate to call them. Management professionals have an investment in the arts and are extremely generous with their time and advice. If possible, bring them into your planning discussions early. Their experience can be invaluable. Many will be able to suggest someone else if they cannot handle you.

Where to Look for Professional Management

A prime place to start looking for good management is to ask other companies. It is an excellent testimonial for a management if you can find several companies which are satisfied with the service they receive. If a booking professional is doing his job, the client companies should be working—assuming they wish to do so—quite consistently. Naturally, this will be relative to who the company is and what it does. You could not, for example, expect a booking agent to produce a ten-week tour for an unknown, untested company. However, if you can find a management which appears to be generally successful in booking the companies it handles, pursue it.

If you are involved in music, *Musical America International Directory of the Performing Arts* examines the programming of a number of presenting organizations across the country. *Dance Magazine* has a monthly "On Tour" calendar. *American Theatre,* the magazine of Theatre Communications Group, the national service organization for theatre, publishes a list of tours by its constituent theatres. Dance/USA publishes for sale its annual Member Profiles, which contains a directory of membership and performance calendar. In addition, regional organizations make public a list of the presenters funded through their touring programs and the companies involved in these performances. By reviewing these listings, you can see which companies are touring and where. Also, the management ads in *Musical America, Sterns Performing Arts Directory, Inside Arts,* and *Chamber Music* will tell you which managements book which companies and artists. Putting these sources side-by-side will give you a sense of how managements perform for their clients.

In-House Booking: Defining the Job

If you have considered the management alternative and have decided instead to go the in-house route, you will need to hire or assign someone to book the company and perhaps perform other administrative duties related to touring. You should have a good idea of what your company expects of such a person and of the kind of person you want to fill the position. The job description for a booking person should include such duties as these:

1. Meeting with the artistic director, the general manager, and the board of trustees to ascertain touring priorities and budget;
2. Overseeing the production of marketing materials;
3. Procuring mailing lists and overseeing mailings;
4. Making telephone calls to presenters;
5. Sending follow-up letters and materials;
6. Attending booking conferences;
7. Negotiating fees and services, and constructing tour routing;
8. Negotiating the tour contract; and
9. Keeping an updated file system of presenter contacts and maintaining correspondence.

Characteristics of the Ideal Booking Person

No matter whether in-house or independent, the ideal person to market (i.e., book) a company for touring, is someone who is:

1. Enthusiastic and has a real understanding of the company's work;
2. Intelligent, responsible, and articulate;
3. Persistent, persuasive, and not easily discouraged, who is able to call and relate to strangers with ease, on the phone and in person;
4. Confident enough to handle the reality that the company will not be booked by most of the presenters solicited;
5. Sensitive to the needs and concerns of the company, and able to relate to you well; and
6. Able to make a commitment to the position for a minimum of two

years (because booking is a process that typically takes place over a several-year period).

Remember that there is a valid place for both the individual working for one company and the management which works for a number of companies. Much depends upon where a company stands in its development, and where and how much it wants to tour. A company may decide to use either an in-house person or engage a booking agent, and then, as its touring activities evolve over several years, switch to the other. Ultimately, the question should be reviewed annually during the planning process.

Preparing a Budget for Touring

A fter deciding what, where, and how long the company would like to tour, the next task is to figure out how much the company will charge presenters for its services. To determine these fees, the company needs to prepare a budget for the year during which the prospective bookings will take place—usually twelve to twenty-four months in the future. Clearly, this kind of budgeting involves some solid advance planning.

Failure to consider the company's future plans and direction can produce a budget with income figures which do not coincide even remotely with expenses. With a proper expense budget in hand, you can determine how much income the company must have to cover its costs of operation for the period. This will enable you to figure out how much the company must charge a presenter for a residency or performance.

Where the company wants and expects to be in the future artistically will directly bear on the company's budget. For instance, do you plan to add artistic or production personnel for the productions contemplated? Do you intend to add new works or productions which will require extraordinary rehearsal time or large amounts of money for costumes or sets? Does the company project adding new music to its repertory that is unfamiliar, therefore necessitating additional rehearsal? Are there other plans which will involve an extraordinary expense? These artistic questions create specific cost considerations that must be discussed and resolved before anything else is done.

Once artistic goals and programs are set, the company must construct an expense budget which allows for various business imponderables (e.g., how high can gasoline prices be expected to rise, what about increases in plane fares, mailing rates, insurance, artists' salaries, per diems). In this process, each line item in the budget must be analyzed in light of how it will be affected by both internal and external happenings twelve to twenty-four months in the future. Comparing last year's projected budget with the actual expenditures recorded in the company's books can be an enlightening way to determine how successful your company has been with past financial forecasts.

Program Budgeting

The easiest way to put together a company budget is by program. *Primary programs* are those for the sake of which the organization exists. *Support programs* are those without which the primary programs could not succeed, such as fundraising, administration, and public relations.

For example, a company's programs might include home-season performance, rehearsal, tour, and school. Organizations might divide their rehearsal time into "creative" rehearsal, during which new material is worked on or created, and "tour" rehearsal, during which the existing repertory is prepared to tour. Within each program—primary and support—costs should be itemized for all the various expenses, from artists' salaries to administrative costs. (Some organizations prefer to make administration a separate support program.)

Program budgeting enables you to see what each facet of company activity costs and how much income each produces. Some programs will pay for themselves, others will not and, if important to the company, must be subsidized by outside sources or by other programs.

Do not be concerned if some expenses are not easily classified. Deal with them as best you can. For example, how should production costs be allocated for a work to be produced for a company's home season and then toured? Obviously, if all costs are attributed to the home season, your program budget will look different from one where costs are divided in some way between home season and touring. If it is easier to raise money for home season production, then you might want to reflect the majority of costs there. This is an opportunity for the company's administration to do some creative budgeting.

Constructing the Touring Program Budget

To construct a budget for your touring program, review all your budget categories which are directly attributable to touring, using the format shown in Exhibit 3. In this model, expenses have been divided into several categories—salaries, per diems, travel, publicity materials, booking management, tour management, insurance, royalties, and certain non-amortizable performance expenses. Depending upon your company, you may have some additions to the format, or there may be items you will want to delete.

Production costs have been omitted from this format, but feel free to allocate a portion of these costs, along with rehearsal or other program costs, to your tour expenses. If your company primarily tours and does little production at home, then the bulk of the production costs, as well as the administrative costs, belong in this category. Production costs are often amortized over the life of a production. It is also possible to amortize such promotional materials as posters, production of TV spots, and the like over a period of more than one year. Ask your accountant how all this should be handled.

Estimating Touring Expenses

Try first to anticipate costs listed for all expense categories which will be more or less fixed for the type of tour you have planned. Salary, per diem, and travel will vary according to the final plans for touring and will be contingent upon such things as the number of weeks and the geography involved.

You will need to do some tough research to determine as closely as possible what your expenses will be. For example, look at the booking management expense category. Begin by analyzing the booking process and itemizing each area of expense. What mailing lists will you use, if any? How much will they cost to purchase? Call your mailing house to determine how much it will cost to prepare the mailing, i.e., affixing labels, sorting by zip code. If you plan to put together your own mailing list, will it be typed on labels, or put into a computer for future use? How much will this process cost in terms of salaries, computer service, purchase of labels? How many organizations will be on your mailing list?

Discuss with a printer the cost of production and printing for the size, shape, and quantity of booking brochures that you plan to use. Are the brochures to be black and white or full color? What kind of paper will they be printed on? If your organization is new or has never printed brochures before, take another company's brochure that you admire, and ask for a price quotation.

EXHIBIT 3

Tour Budget Model

SALARIES/WAGES/FRINGES

_____ Artistic personnel × $_____ per wk(s/w) × _____ tour weeks = $_____
_____ Technical personnel × $_____ per wk(s/w) × _____tour/work wks = $_____
_____ Tour mgt. personnel × $_____ per wk(s/w) × _____tour/work wks = $_____
_____ Booking personnel × $_____ per wk(s/w) × _____work wks = $_____
Fringes on above personnel @ _____ % × total $_____ s/w = $_____
TOUR SALARIES/WAGES/FRINGES $_____

PER DIEMS

_____ Artistic personnel × $_____ per wk × _____ tour wks = $_____
_____ Technical personnel × $_____ per wk × _____ tour wks = $_____
_____ Tour mgt. personnel × $_____ per wk × _____ tour wks = $_____
TOTAL PER DIEMS $_____

TRAVEL

AIR TRANSPORTATION:
Air Fares: _____ personnel × _____ trips × $_____ fare = $_____
Air Freight: _____ lbs. freight × _____ flights @ $_____ per lb. = $_____
Ground transportation for freight: _____ hrs. × $_____ per hr. = $_____
or _____ miles × $_____ per mile = $_____

GROUND TRANSPORTATION:
Car/Van/Truck/Bus:
_____ vehicle(s) × $_____ wk/daily rental × _____ wks/days = $_____
Gasoline/oil:
Total tour miles: _____ est. miles per gal. _____ × $_____ per gal. = $_____
Mileage Cost:
Total Tour Mileage _____ × $_____ per mile = $_____
Driver Fee:
Total Tour Mileage _____ × $_____ per mile = $_____
or Daily rate _____ + Per Diem _____ × _____ tour weeks = $_____
Permit for trucks if applicable = $_____
TOTAL TRAVEL $_____

PERFORMANCE EXPENSES

Non-amortizable costume expenses for tour year:
Costume Cleaning $_____   Shoes $_____   Tights $_____   Misc. Notions $_____

Non-amortizable set/prop/hardware:
Tape $_____   Gel $_____   Other $_____   Paint $_____   Fabric $_____

Road Boxes:
Total cost of boxes used this tour = $_____
TOTAL PERFORMANCE COSTS $_____

PRESENTER RELATED PUBLICITY MATERIALS

Fees to copywriter/graphic designer $ _____

Fee to photographer _____

Printing, reproduction of posters, flyers, pictures, press kits _____

Mailing and postage _____

Imprinting _____

Production video tapes, slides _____

Other _____

TOTAL PUBLICITY MATERIALS $ _____

BOOKING MANAGEMENT

Telephone $ _____

Mailing house/labels _____

Fees to copywriter/graphic designer for brochure _____

Printing brochure and related materials _____

Postage _____

Convention attendance (hotel, food, transportation, fees, display) _____

TOTAL BOOKING $ _____

TOUR MANAGEMENT

Telephone $_____ Postage $_____ Travel $_____

TOTAL TOUR MANAGEMENT $ _____

INSURANCE

_____ weeks × $_____ premium per week = $ _____

TOTAL INSURANCE $ _____

ROYALTIES (Choreographer, composer, playwright, etc.)

_____ performances work × $_____ per performance = $ _____

TOTAL ROYALTIES $ _____

TOTAL BUDGET $ _____

Salaries and wages need to reflect weeks of preparation as well as tour weeks for personnel whose wages for pre-tour work are not picked up by other company programs.

Call the post office. How much does it presently cost to mail bulk rate? How much should you budget for potential increases?

Follow this procedure for each budget category, identifying each item of expense and researching the costs to be incurred. Explain to everyone you speak with during this process that you are budgeting for one to two years ahead and want estimates of expenses that will be realistic over this period of time. If you are new to all this, call another company in your area and ask how much they budget for a particular item.

Projecting Travel Costs

Travel costs are difficult to approximate without knowing where within a particular area you will be touring or what distances will be between stops. The worksheet developed by the Mid-America Arts Alliance, shown in Exhibit 4, is designed to ease this task and help you to project reliable travel costs.

Transportation. Budgeting for transportation can be particularly tricky. Ground transportation by chartered bus is the easiest option to deal with. Bus companies usually quote a flat weekly fee which includes bus rental, driver's salary, gas, oil, and maintenance. To figure your costs, simply call several companies and get their rates. Budgeting for rental of a van, truck, or several cars is more difficult because it means factoring in not only the rental fee, but mileage and gas. Compare rates among rental companies and budget for the best and worst of all possible worlds. A figure somewhere in the middle will probably be on target.

If you anticipate situations where the company will have to fly between engagements, use your travel agent to help you research plane fares. For example, a company based in California which has decided to tour on the east coast needs to build in plane travel for at least one cross-country trip, unless it can realistically anticipate a string of bookings that will take it coast-to-coast and back. In budgeting for transportation, be especially pessimistic rather than optimistic about your costs.

Per Diems. In calculating per diems you have two options. You can decide that the company will pay individuals on tour a flat sum to cover both hotel and food costs, or the company will pay for hotel rooms and give company members meal money only. In either case, investigate hotel rates and restaurant costs in the geographic area where you plan to tour (most companies assume people will double up in rooms). Travel guides (such as those available from the American Automobile Association and Mobil) and your travel agent can be helpful in doing this research.

If yours is a union company, per diem amounts will be mandated by contract. In any case, make sure that your company members will be able

EXHIBIT 4

Worksheet for Projecting Realistic Travel Costs

Deciding on a touring fee has its pitfalls, especially when you are contemplating a tour over a large, multi-state region. Whether you are a large ballet company or a solo artist, salaries, gasoline, food and a roof over your heads need to be accounted for—not to mention special, unavoidable costs related to the production itself.

This worksheet is designed to help you project realistic travel costs. After feasible travel costs are established, *other costs need to be figured into the budget.* However, completing these steps can provide a starting place for beginning to establish a touring fee—based on touring costs.

Directions:

Step 1 Route a "disaster tour" that takes in five performances in seven days. Plan on extreme travel distances between dates, with travel costs that boost your costs up, up, up. Record total costs in the chart under #1.

Step 2 Route a "dream tour" that takes in five performances in seven days. Plan on reasonable routing, with performances within easy traveling distances that keep your costs low, low, low. Record total costs in chart under #2.

Step 3 Subtract the "dream tour" costs from the "disaster tour" costs. Record in chart under #3.

Step 4 Find what amount equals 40% of the difference determined in Step 3. Record in chart under #4.

Step 5 Add the 40% to your "dream tour" costs. Record in chart under #5.

No. 1: "Disaster Tour" Costs $ _____
No. 2: "Dream Tour" Costs $ _____
No. 3: (Subtract) $ _____
No. 4: 40% of Line #3 = $ _____
No. 5: Add Line #4 to Line #2 = $ _____

The final figure should give you a close estimation of travel costs incurred in the type of tour that will most likely be booked. After adding your other touring costs to this travel sum, you may realize that the logical fee that is derived from your budget needs adjustment to work within the marketplace. However, at least you have a starting point that is not way out in left (or right) field.

to get along comfortably with their per diems. In some situations, the company should plan to supplement the per diem at specific stops. For example, if your company plans to make stops in several major cities, tour members will need higher per diems for those dates to afford the more expensive room and restaurant costs encountered in major metropolitan areas.

How to Use Your Budget

The purpose of the budgeting process is to analyze all aspects of your operation that pertain to touring in order to determine the cost for each. Do not be concerned, for instance, if the brochure you eventually come up with is a different size or a different type of paper than had been budgeted.

Similarly, the budget is a guide to your total costs for the tour. Certain expenses will be unchangeable, while other costs will be flexible, enabling you to make shifts within sub-categories or within major budget categories. For example, if you have budgeted the total cost of your tour at $100,000, you may later decide to shift certain expenses, opting to spend $2,000 less on booking brochure materials in order to produce better quality posters and flyers. Using a budget in this fashion enables you to set parameters for your total costs, yet affords you the flexibility to adapt to changing conditions.

Budgeting Options

The company's touring program can be viewed in one of three ways. It can be thought of as a program which must produce income at least equal to its expenses. It can be planned to generate income over and above tour costs to subsidize other company programs. Or, if the company considers it important enough, a touring program can be consciously budgeted to lose money, with the excess expenses subsidized by other programs or by outside sources of income. The determination of the tour fee depends upon which of these three situations is applicable to a particular company.

Budgeting to Break Even

If the company's touring income must simply meet its own program expenses, then arriving at a touring fee is a simple matter.

1. Make a firm decision about how much touring the company wants and can reasonably expect to do for the year. Consider questions such as these: How much touring did the company have last year? Has it been promised additional work? If management does a really

concerted booking campaign, how much can the work be increased? Be pessimistic rather than optimistic or you will throw off your projections. Figure all expenses for the amount of time you determine the company can reasonably expect to tour.

2. Total all touring expenses for this program.
3. Divide total touring expenses by the number of weeks of touring anticipated. The result is the weekly touring fee which you must charge to balance the touring portion of the company's budget—in other words, to achieve a break-even tour:

$$\frac{\text{TOTAL TOURING EXPENSES}}{\text{NUMBER OF EXPECTED TOURING WEEKS}} = \text{WEEKLY TOURING FEE}$$

Budgeting for Other Than Break-Even Tours

If income from touring must help to pay for other company programs, or if the income from other programs (or unearned or contributed income) will subsidize touring expenses, the determination of a final touring fee must await the completion of the budget for other company programs. In either of these cases, to arrive at an appropriate weekly touring fee:

1. Total all touring costs, as discussed earlier.
2. Complete budgets for all company programs in addition to the touring program.
3. Add the expenses for all company programs, both touring and nontouring.
4. Total the income from all programs other than touring. Add to this the contributed and earned income the company can anticipate receiving from such sources as: private foundation and corporate grants; federal, state, and local arts agency grants; individual contributions and memberships; endowment income; and benefit and concession income.
5. The difference between total expenses for all programs, including touring, and total income from all programs except touring is the amount of income which must be earned through touring (unless the company has made a conscious decision to accept a deficit within its overall budget). Divide this amount by the number of anticipated tour weeks. Your answer, the dollars per week the company has to earn from touring fees, must now be analyzed in light of a number of different factors.

Testing the Tour Fee: Is It Realistic?

To determine if the weekly touring fee derived from the above process is one you can live with, the company needs to assess itself, its competition, and its presenters. A company should consider several factors to determine whether its weekly fee, as defined by income and expenses, is realistic within the marketplace. The first step is to assess objectively your own company.

Assess Your Company

Perhaps you have decided that the company needs to gross $15,000 per week from touring. Is this too much? Can you realistically count on presenters to book the company at $15,000 per week, or whatever this breaks down to per performance? Does the company offer something that will sufficiently stand out in the marketplace? How is your company perceived? What are its strengths and weaknesses from a presenter's viewpoint? What is exceptional about the company? Determine what you can do to accentuate your strengths and to improve areas that are problematic to presenters. Would these improvements be cost effective? For example, if the company presently has a reputation for poor publicity materials, would producing topnotch materials enhance the company's attractiveness and make a difference to presenters? If so, producing materials at that level must be reflected in your budget.

Consider the Competition

Now consider the competition—companies which offer a similar product and price, and which sell their services to the same segment of the marketplace. Is your company's price structure similar, less expensive, or more expensive than theirs? If a similar company is charging much more than you, perhaps you should raise your fees, or maybe you have forgotten an item in the expense budget. If your fees, based on accurately calculated expenses, are much higher than a competitor's, his expenses may not be realistic (or he may have substantial income from other sources to cover the expenses of touring). Still, you may have to cut expenses if you think the other company is real competition.

Study Your Presenters

Now examine the fees that you are contemplating from the perspective of your potential presenters. Often, presenters depend upon box office proceeds to cover the costs of a performance. While some presenters receive grants to aid in their presentations (at colleges and universities, student fees or other education dollars sometimes underwrite a portion of cultural programming), the majority of the monies to support your company's engagement will come from ticket sales. Consequently, price will be of great concern. With this in mind, it is a good idea to try to determine if your "average presenter" can afford your proposed weekly fee.

First, examine booking patterns. Do presenters generally book the company for a single performance, a residency of one-half week, or a week of six to seven performances?

For example, consider a presenter who primarily books single performances in its 500-seat theatre, with an average ticket price of twelve dollars. A sellout would produce $6,000. At eighty percent of capacity, a performance will yield $4,800 in ticket revenues. How large are the houses your company draws compared to this one?

In addition to the performance fee, the presenter will have expenses related to production and publicity (salaries for stage crew, ushers and box office staff, ads in the local media, etc.)—say costs of $2,000, which leaves $2,800 to pay the company fee.

But what if your company fee is $7,000, not $2,800? If, in addition to earned income, the presenter can raise the balance of the total cost for presenting his season from grants, student fees, memberships, contributions, and the like, then the presenter can afford a fee in the $7,000 range without losing any money on your performance. (In our example, $7,000 fee plus $2,000 other costs equal $9,000 total costs; $4,800 ticket revenues leaves $4,200 to be raised, or 46.7 percent of total costs.)

If the company can do a two-and-one-half day residency which includes three performances, and you can afford to charge the presenter only $6,000 for each of the three guaranteed performances, the presenter's total expenses would be $18,000 plus $6,000 other costs to equal $24,000; with earned income of $14,400, this leaves $9,600 to be raised, or now only 40 percent of the total budget. (Note that the presenter's technical and promotional costs are likely to be less than three times the single performance costs, requiring even less to be raised from outside sources, or giving the presenter a "cushion" against not being able to sell 80 percent of each of three performances.)

In planning your fees, bear in mind that most master classes, lecture demonstrations, and other educational activities which complement residency performances do not often bring in much additional money to the presenter, even though they are time-consuming for the company.

If you conclude that your fee is too high, rethink your options. Consider re-budgeting for a smaller, less expensive production or traveling with fewer people. Or, you might extend the length of the tour to amortize production and rehearsal expenses over a longer period of time (and more presenters). You could investigate additional subsidies to underwrite presenter costs. Or, you may need to rethink who your presenters are and aim for those with larger facilities.

Pricing Your Services

Based on the above analysis, the company should now have a weekly price that is both competitive in the marketplace and sufficient to cover expenses to the extent needed. Call this number the weekly break-even. You must then determine how to translate your weekly break-even fee into half-week and single performance fees.

Meeting the Weekly Break-Even

If a company has decided that it needs to charge $25,000 to meet its weekly break-even, does it charge $12,500 for a half-week and $5,000 for a single performance? Absolutely not! Travel is one of any touring company's biggest expenses; it is also grueling for the performers and crew. This being the case, give a price advantage to presenters who book the company for an extended stay.

So, while the company's fee for spending a week with one presenter is $25,000, a half-week residency might be $14,000, and a single performance $9,000. If your company does mainly single performances (one-night stands) and can usually do three performances in a week, then the single performance fee should be $8,500. By setting the fees in this manner, the company can meet its $25,000 weekly break-even even if it ends up doing four single performances, or a half-week residency and one single during a week. Thus, when setting fees, also look at the *way* your company tours.

Negotiating Fees

This type of fee-setting also puts the company in a good position to negotiate its fees. For example, you might charge a presenter only $22,000 for an entire week but more than make up the difference the following week with two singles at $8,000 each and a half-week residency at $13,000. In negotiating, constantly keep an eye on your weekly break-even figure. The total income from all engagements, divided by the number of weeks in the tour, should equal your weekly average break-even number.

Many companies like to set their fees ten percent or more higher than the weekly break-even to allow for fee negotiations and situations where the weekly break-even will not be met. Thus, a single performance might be priced at $7,200 instead of $6,500. This gives the company an opportunity to negotiate the fee significantly, enabling it to offer a special break to a consortium of presenters or to a presenter who can take an enroute booking. Occasionally, this approach can backfire, especially if a prospective presenter sees a fee that puts the company out of his price range and is unaware that it is negotiable. More about negotiating fees in Chapter 6.

Government and Corporate Support for Touring

In addition to presenters' fees, various opportunities exist for companies of all sizes and types to receive support for their touring activities from a variety of funding sources. Decisions to underwrite tours or specific engagements are usually based on a company's artistic quality, ability to tour, geographic need, and a variety of other considerations as perceived by the funding source.

The National Endowment for the Arts

In the past, one of the most visible sources of support for touring was the National Endowment for the Arts (NEA). The NEA, a federal agency, supported in one form or another the touring and presenting of dance, opera, and theatre companies, soloists, chamber groups, and orchestras. The NEA's budget has been recently cut substantially. How or whether the Endowment will continue to underwrite touring remains to be seen. For up-to-date information contact the National Endowment for the Arts, 1100 Pennsylvania Avenue, NW, Washington, D.C. 20506.

Regional Touring Programs

Regional arts agencies are independent consortia formed by groups of state arts agencies. They evolved to tackle problems that are better addressed regionally than by individual states. In most cases, the states involved are contiguous and share similar problems in fostering and presenting the performing arts.

Regional arts agencies have been crucial to the development of touring over the past fifteen to twenty years. In areas where there has not been a history of presentation, the regional arts agencies have served as catalysts. They have organized presenters in their regions into groups able to book several days or weeks of a company's tour, thus making touring into their areas attractive.

The goal of many regional agencies in the area of touring has been twofold: first, to make quality groups available to presenters in the region and, second, to develop a strong presenter network.

Touring programs sponsored by regional arts agencies vary widely. Some limit their support to companies based within the region; others encourage companies from outside the area to participate. In most, the presenting organization applies to the regional agency for a percentage of the fee charged by the company they wish to present. Deadlines and regulations also vary widely from region to region, and from year to year. For up-to-date information, contact the applicable regional arts agency.

State Arts Agencies

Many states have touring programs in addition to the regional and national programs. Generally, companies must be based in a state to receive support for tours within that state's boundaries. Some states offer support directly to the company, while others support the presenting organization. In cases where program monies go directly to the presenter, he is sometimes able to book a company based either within or outside the state.

Again, deadlines and guidelines vary, so check for specifics with the state arts agency in your home state, or the state in which your company wishes to tour.

Corporate Support

There continue to be a few large corporations underwriting national tours by major performing arts institutions: American Express has underwritten recent tours of the Dance Theatre of Harlem, AT&T's Dance on Tour supports the touring of several companies each year, and Philip Morris has regularly supported the touring of the Joffrey Ballet.

Most corporate support for tours is based on marketing decisions and tied into the need to sell a product to a particular segment of a market. For example, Movado Watch Company underwrote a tour of American Ballet Theatre several years ago. In that case Movado may have been trying to reach the well-heeled audience they perceive attends ABT in major cities across the country.

There are several levels of corporate support, and a company might be successful in getting corporate underwriting for a tour in a particular state or region if the company can make a case for its ability to bring out an audience the corporation is particularly trying to reach.

Although tours by major institutions have received the bulk of past corporate underwriting, this area of support should not be overlooked by smaller or less well-known companies. And while marketing is the focus of most touring support, corporations sometimes support performing arts companies which they believe contribute significantly to the quality of life in cities and towns where they are headquartered or have operations. Companies which can successfully argue that they are willing and able to take an excellent product into corporate communities may find this a useful avenue to pursue.

Nongovernment Touring Programs

There are also several independent, nongovernmental touring programs presently in operation. Their approaches are diverse: some work with individual artists, others with companies. The programs mentioned here do not constitute a complete list of programs run by nongovernmental organizations, but describe a number of the more established programs currently in operation.

The Lila Wallace-Reader's Digest Arts Partners Program. Association of Performing Arts Presenters, 1112 16th Street, NW, Washington, D.C. 20036, 202/833-2787, FAX 202/833-1543.

Arts Partners is a residency program and not a touring program, but it definitely deserves mention. The program is administered by the Association of Performing Arts Presenters (APAP) and is intended to help presenting organizations and their communities develop adult audiences for the performing arts. Presenters apply through a two-step process—first a planning grant and then a project grant. Projects involve a residency planned and developed cooperatively by a performing artist or company, a presenting organization, and other organizations in its community. Residency structures vary according to the specific project; some have included the commissioning of new work, and all involve extensive work in the community, with activities dependent on the needs of the participants.

The National Performance Network. Dance Theatre Workshop, 219 West 19th Street, New York, N.Y. 10011, 212/645-6200, FAX 212/645-6317.

National Performance Network was initiated by Dance Theatre Workshop (DTW) to support the touring of contemporary artists in dance, theatre, music, performance art, and puppetry. NPN makes it possible for artists and companies to have one- to two-week residencies at 51 primary sponsor sites based in 26 cities. Residencies usually include both performance and extensive teaching and outreach activities in diverse settings in the community. Presenters are free to choose the artists. Fees to artists/companies are set by a formula depending on the number of people travelling with the company. The primary sponsor sites receive funding for 40–50 percent of the formula fee. The Network also has monies available for underwriting new work, projects involving intense interaction among culturally diverse groups, travel to see new work, and other projects.

Meet the Composer. 2112 Broadway, Suite 505, New York, N.Y. 10023, 212/787-3601.

Meet the Composer awards grants to presenting organizations that perform, present, or commission original work. The grant enables the presenter to bring a composer who can interact with their community through performance, conducting, lectures, teaching, or other activities. The grants are administered through the regional arts organizations. Deadlines and procedures vary from region to region.

Lila Wallace-Reader's Digest National Jazz Network. New England Foundation for the Arts, 330 Congress Street, Sixth Floor, Boston, MA, 02210-1216, 617/951-0010, FAX 617/951-0016; National Jazz Service Organization, P.O. Box 50152, Washington, D.C. 20091, 202/347-2604, FAX 202/638-3460.

The Lila Wallace-Reader's Digest National Jazz Network is a nationwide network of 20 presenting organizations and six regional organizations. Administered through the national Jazz Service Organization, the program offers fee support to 20 presenting organizations for performance and community opportunities for jazz artists. Organizations are free to book artists of their choice. The six regional organizations help to support satellite tours that are booked around network members in their areas. The regional organizations also have funds for artist showcases, educational programs, and regional radio networks. The activities of the regional organizations are administered through the New England Foundation for the Arts.

Chamber Music America—Presenter-Community Residency Program. Chamber Music America, 545 Eighth Avenue, New York, N.Y. 10018, 212/244-2772, FAX 212/244-2776.

Chamber Music America, the national service organization for the chamber music community, runs a Presenter-Community Residency Program which supports presenting organizations for short-term residencies by chamber music ensembles. The program's goal is to increase audiences for chamber music, to encourage chamber music presenters to build partnerships with other community institutions, and to promote appreciation for diversity in chamber music programming. Residencies range in length from three to seven days. Presenters match grants on a two-to-one basis and are free to apply for groups of their choice.

The Bottom Line: Does Your Tour Make Financial Sense?

While many opportunities for tour underwriting exist, you cannot depend upon underwriters to provide a major portion of the company's tour budget.

Any commitment to undertake touring that does not pay for itself must be carefully considered by the artistic director, the administration, and especially, the board of trustees. The decision to tour should only be made in conjunction with a rational plan for eventually absorbing any planned deficits.

At times, the company's projected cash flow (for the year for which the budget is being prepared) will be insufficient to allow the company to operate successfully. In such a situation, it may be decided to raise the necessary cash by obtaining long-term obligations of some kind.

Many companies will still face a deficit in their touring program, even after anticipating all possible sources of income, including funds from outside sources (e.g., grants, memberships, etc.). There will be expenses that the company will be unable to meet during the fiscal year. In such cases, it is essential that the deficit not come as a surprise. Only with a thorough, carefully prepared budget can this be avoided.

The Booking Brochure

Assume that you are the director of public events for a Midwestern university which presents events in music, theatre, and dance. You enter your office at 9 A.M. and, as always, there is a stack of twenty to thirty pieces of mail. Most of it has come from groups of all types which want to perform at the university. Although sympathetic to the groups and eager to present the best in each field, you are a busy person who also administers many ongoing programs. You open your mail and go through it.

What will you look at in that pile of mail? What will you take out and put aside to consider later? What will you simply file with the other recently received materials? Unless you have previously heard of a particular company or are interested in a specific group, your attention has no doubt focused on the best-designed materials, those which immediately command your attention with their graphics, compelling you to read them. This is precisely what a well-prepared booking brochure can accomplish for you.

Creating a Unique Image

Competition in booking is intense. To book successfully, a company needs a booking brochure as unique as the company it represents. Booking materials can be designed in many ways and can cost a lot or a little (expensive does not necessarily mean it is effective), but there are some important general rules to consider when shaping the brochure.

A booking brochure should be based on a unique and clearly focused concept. Ask yourself several questions. What is unique or exciting about the company or production? What does it do that nobody else does? Put yourself in the presenter's place. What can your brochure convey to him about the company to make it stand out among 150 other companies which also send materials?

The brochure should be as complete and explicit as possible. It is the most permanent, tangible source of information a presenter will have on your company. Most likely, the presenter (and the selection committee) will refer to this piece after you have spoken by phone and/or met at a booking convention. Although the reviews and other materials you send as follow-up are considered, the booking brochure is the centerpiece of all your printed materials.

How to Tell Your Story

Although you are intimately acquainted with your company, you must assume that presenters and the people on their committees are not. The booking brochure enables you to present distinctly and convincingly what the company can do and how your artistic product can benefit the presenter. This does not mean, however, that the text in your brochure should be endless. Rather, use the space to say what is important as clearly and concisely as possible.

Booking materials are only part of the story, of course. *Do not expect bookings just because of a well-designed brochure. It takes much more than that.* But the brochure is important: It prepares the presenter for your telephone follow-up. To be effective, a good booking brochure should include (in no particular order of priority):

1. *Brief Highlights of the Company's History.* This should include how long it has been in existence, the kind of work it was founded to do, the background of the artistic director, and any major awards received by the artistic director or the artists.
2. *Touring History.* If the company has toured frequently in this country or abroad, or under regional or state touring programs, mention it. This kind of information assures presenters that you know what touring is all about. They know that a company which has only performed at home will find many surprises on the road, and they prefer that this not happen in their theatres.

3. *Repertory or Production.* List the productions, repertory, or type of repertory that the company will be touring.

4. *Technical Information.* If your company has specific technical requirements, such as minimum stage size or special equipment, it is best to warn the presenter in the booking brochure. (Does your performance of *Aida* require a live elephant?) On the other hand, if your needs are not so unusual or critical, save the details for a technical information sheet and include it with materials sent later in the booking process.

5. *Activities in Addition to Performance.* If you offer activities in addition to performance, mention what you do or simply list them under a heading "the following residency activities are available...." The more important these activities are to your company, the more prominently they should be discussed.

6. *Excerpts from Reviews.* Include excerpts from excellent reviews along with the name of the newspaper and the critic, if he is prominent. These reviews should be definitive statements on the artistic product, not just "'Terrific!' —*New York Post.*"

7. *Presenter Testimonials.* Testimonials give your prospective presenter an opportunity to see what others, perhaps someone they know, thought about the company. (See Chapter 10 on post-performance follow-up for suggestions on how to obtain testimonials.) The best presenter testimonials talk about specific advantages of presenting your company, such as how easy the company was to work with, the excellence of your promotional materials or technical staff, how much the students enjoyed the master class, and how pleased the presenter was with the full house. Leave praise of the artistic product to the newspaper critics.

Design Guidelines

1. The amount of space allotted for each piece of information included in the brochure is determined by its degree of importance. If properly conceived in this manner, the brochure will tell your story convincingly and satisfy the presenter's need for information in a clear, concise manner.

2. Try to incorporate all the information you intend the presenter to have into one mailing piece. The more separate pieces in your mailing, the more likely that key information could be lost. Either include excerpts of reviews in the text of the brochure or (as will be explained in Chapter 6) send the reviews later, in their entirety. Five

loose pieces of paper in an envelope can be lost in the shuffle on somebody's desk or during a campus committee meeting at which artists and companies are represented by a pile of brochures heaped on a table.

3. Fees are important to presenters—they want to know not only how good you are, but how much you cost. However, the wisdom on including fees within the booking brochure is definitely divided. Some companies choose not to include fees in their initial brochure. By not printing the fees you have an opportunity to order extra copies and use what is probably an expensive brochure for more than one year. A printed fee can also run you the risk of losing a presenter who might otherwise be interested but considers your printed fee too high for his budget. On the other hand, your company's fees may be listed in a regional touring program guide anyway, so it's public knowledge. It's a matter of personal choice and what works best for you.

   If you decide to include fees and will use the brochure for more than one year, you have several options. A brochure with last year's fees crossed out looks bad. Instead, before you go into production, decide where the fee should go and leave a blank space on the brochure. Before mailing you can either stamp the fee schedule on the piece or attach a printed adhesive strip. An adhesive strip may also be used to cover last year's fee, if it appears on the brochure. Another alternative would be to use a separate fee sheet. This should be the same size as the brochure and clearly marked "XYZ Company Fees." The type style should match the one used in the brochure.

   If you choose not to include your fees in the brochure, be sure they are clearly stated in your follow-up letter to an interested presenter.

4. Use photographs in the brochure that are sharp and clear and represent the company well. Grainy or fuzzy pictures (obviously supposed to be otherwise) work against the company.

5. The brochure should be produced so that it can be mailed at the nonprofit bulk rate. It can either be a self-mailer (a self-contained piece, with the company's name, address, and not-for-profit indicia on the front), or it may be designed to mail in an envelope (with your return address and not-for-profit stamp printed on it). Be sure to check with the post office about size and weight regulations before the brochure goes into production. Postal regulations change, and you do not want to be caught with brochures that cannot be mailed.

One example of how all these elements can be put together to create an effective booking brochure is shown in Exhibit 5.

EXHIBIT 5

Sample Booking Brochure

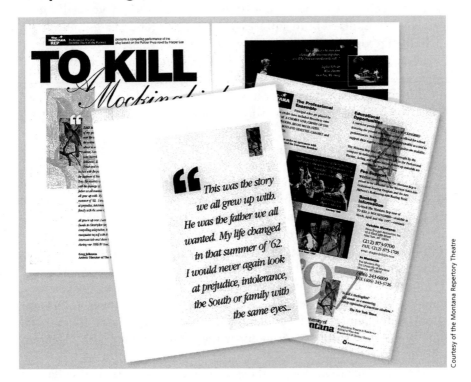

Courtesy of the Montana Repertory Theatre

Return Postcards

A return postcard is a highly recommended feature. This may simply be a perforated portion of your brochure, or it may be an insert. Most copy shops can print postcards. The cards should be preaddressed to your company. There should be a message that reads "I would like further information about the XYZ Company," and space should be provided for the presenter's name, address, organization, phone number, etc. The postcards may require the interested presenter to affix stamps, or you can arrange for prepaid, business reply postcards, whereby the post office charges you for postage only when a card is returned to you through the mail.

The cards that are returned will give you further clues about which prospective presenters already have an interest in the company and should be contacted first. However, you should not anticipate a lot of responses, and failure to receive a return postcard should not discourage you from contacting a particular presenter.

Producing the Brochure

A booking brochure should be produced by professionals with snap, style, and coherent copy. Do not try to put it together by yourself unless you have the skills of both a professional copywriter and a graphic artist.

Many factors affect the way a brochure is considered by its recipient. For instance, the way a brochure is folded can determine whether it is even opened. The positioning of the text and the style of typography may make the difference between whether it is read or discarded. Only professionals know the ins and outs of this sort of thing. Let them take care of it for you.

Professional services may cost less than you anticipate. Start out by approaching an advertising agency in your area. Many will donate the labor for copywriting and graphic art to nonprofit organizations if you give them credit in the brochure (or elsewhere in a list of corporate donors) for their in-kind contribution. Some agencies will volunteer to do the work after hours. Most likely, you will still have to pay for typesetting, paper, printing, and other production expenses, although printing and typesetting firms sometimes donate their services as well.

Sit down with the advertising experts and work out a concept for a booking brochure that sells the company in the same manner as business clients sell themselves to consumers. Tell the experts your financial limitations and problems. Sometimes they can come up with ingenious solutions.

Another place to go for good design work is a university or college in your area which has a graphic arts or advertising department. Some companies have had their booking brochures done as class projects. Under such an arrangement, the class assumes the role of ad agency and the company acts as its client.

Desktop publishing software is another option that allows companies to produce a professional-looking booking brochure or materials.

When Not to Use a Booking Brochure

The above material has been directed primarily at companies that have a kind of work that enables them to tour extensively, companies choosing to highlight a particular production or new direction, and artists introducing themselves to presenters early in their careers. There are many companies, however, which should not make a booking brochure a priority. For instance, very well-known companies of national repute do not need to spend money telling presenters what they do and how well they do it. And you could not recommend a costly booking brochure to companies which tour very little, which appeal to a very limited audience, or which have so little money that producing the brochure will seriously compromise their artistic priorities.

For example, if a theatre company wants to tour its mainstage production regionally for two or three weeks, it would be difficult to justify spending more than a minimal amount on booking materials, since the company only needs to convince a maximum of 12–15 presenters. A group that specializes in performing contemporary music might have a good idea in advance about which specific presenters have a particular history of presenting contemporary work and are potential presenters for their type of product.

Over the last several years more companies have found that a packet of booking materials serves them better than a brochure, can be changed or added to during the course of the season, and is perhaps less expensive. Packets of materials are usually sent after direct contact is made with a presenter, either at a booking conference or over the phone. You couldn't afford to send a packet of materials to a large number of presenters; mailing costs are often in excess of a dollar per piece.

The packet should include a letter introducing the company or production. Use a computer to personalize the letter. Send with the letter a description of the company, the productions or repertory being offered, the fee for the performance/residency, the available dates, a selection of good reviews, and a few pictures of the company in performance. The elements which make up the packet can be assembled inexpensively from existing materials and placed in a neatly prepared folder of some kind with the company's name on it.

While this sort of approach is much less expensive than a full-fledged brochure, each piece of material in the packet *must* be of excellent quality: well written, clear, and precise. The reviews should be reproduced clearly (photo offsetting is an excellent process) and the pictures should be clear and sharp.

Often, a company's professionalism and the quality of its work are judged by the company's salesmanship, rather than by the artistic product itself. For this reason, no matter how you decide to proceed, the image you present in your booking materials (and at booking conventions, as you will see in Chapter 7) will be very important to your success in the marketplace.

CHAPTER 5

Targeting the Presenter

A presenter is an organization (often with not-for-profit status) which produces performing arts events and special activities for a local audience. In addition to paying the company a fee, the presenter typically provides a performance facility, handles publicity, sells tickets, and provides various other services associated with performing arts presentations.

Understanding the Presenter

A touring company faced with the complex challenges of preparing, booking, and managing a tour tends to see the presenter's job as a comparatively simple one. In truth, however, a presenter's responsibilities are equally complex. Not only must presenters be knowledgeable in the general areas of ticket-selling, contract negotiations, advertising, and budgeting, but they must also have a thorough understanding of their own resources and limitations, including the performance space, available stagehands, the local media, the board of trustees, and the sensibilities of their audiences. Further, they must keep informed about what is happening around the country in each of the performing arts they present so that they, and the people who work with them, can program companies appropriate to the interests of their audiences.

The best presenters go another step: they are a cultural force in their communities. They feel it their mission to help lead their communities to a broader awareness of the various performing arts disciplines—and to raise the critical standards of local audiences. They do not limit themselves to programming only what their ticket buyers or subscribers are accustomed to getting for their money; they are also willing to stretch local audiences, to give them the opportunity to see a play or listen to a piece of music that is in an unfamiliar vein.

Although certain adversarial elements exist in the relationship between presenter and company, touring groups must remember that presenters are human beings with an important job to do and a necessary point of view. Only if a company takes the time to understand the specific needs and unique personalities of its various presenters can a harmonious business relationship and successful artistic presentation take place. Without presenters, the performing arts companies which need and want to tour will find themselves "all dressed up with no place to go."

What follows is a brief rundown of the various types of presenting organizations which you are most likely to encounter during the booking process, along with discussions of the special opportunities offered by each.

The Presenting Universe Described

Colleges and Universities. Presenters based on college and university campuses are one of the largest groups of presenters in this country. Typically, there are two types of campus groups that present the performing arts: an office responsible for booking performing companies for the institution as a whole (arts and lectures series, artists series, cultural events office, etc.) and individual departments involved with the specific performing disciplines (the theatre and music departments, for example). Often, the cultural events office is concerned primarily with performance, while academic departments may be interested in a wider range of services. At times, a faculty member from a specific discipline sits on the college or university's overall cultural events committee. And in some instances, the cultural events office and the academic department will work together to present a company of joint interest. Student union activities boards also present events on a campus, often those of a more popular nature.

Presenting-Focused Organizations. Some organizations have as their primary mission the presentation of performing companies to their communities. They range from major institutions with several performance spaces to smaller groups with more limited seating capacities and budgets and an interest in the work of experimental or emerging groups. Usually, both large and small organizations of this type are interested primarily in performance. The Houston Performing Arts Society, the Washington Performing Arts Society, and the Brooklyn Academy of Music are examples of large-scale presenting-focused organizations. Smaller organizations include The Kitchen in New York City and On the Boards in Seattle.

Arts Councils. The community arts council movement has grown in importance. In fact, in some rural areas, arts councils are the only means to bring the performing arts into the community. Frequently, they work with other groups, such as local school districts, and some have gone so far as to form consortia which block book performing companies, jointly publicize their performances, and route them efficiently from one community to the next.

Festivals. Festivals represent another important source of presenters, and some have become major tourist attractions in their regions. A number have developed prestigious training programs to complement their performing operation, such as the summer festival in Aspen, Colorado.

Presenters Outside the Arts. Several different types of organizations, which primarily function outside of the arts, present touring groups—regularly or occasionally—to serve a specific interest, such as fundraising, entertainment, or promotion, or to take advantage of a special connection (for example, programming a nationally known touring company with which someone from the community now performs). Presenters in this general category include service organizations such as Kiwanis and Rotary Clubs, Y's, churches, synagogues, public libraries, hospitals, and special interest groups. On one end of the spectrum might be a YMCA with a reputation for presenting emerging companies, and on the other might be a hospital planning to present a benefit performance to help finance the building of a new wing.

Public Agencies. Over the last ten years, city governments across the country have built major performing arts centers and are now involved, at least tangentially, in the business of presenting performances. California has been one of the most active areas, with facilities built and run by the cities of Escondido, Visalia, San Francisco, and Cerritos, among others. In addition public school districts, parks and recreation departments continue to act as presenting organizations, often with an interest in outreach activities.

Corporations. Finally, there are corporate presenters. Their sponsorships range from engaging a string quartet to play a special performance for employees and their families, to lunchtime performances in downtown malls. Funds may come from either promotional budgets or corporate contributions departments. Businesses are particularly receptive to performances or events which generate good will among their employees or within the local community.

Clearly, the range of presenting organizations available to touring companies spans a wide variety of types, sizes, and interests. Some presenters will be better suited to a particular type of company than others, and it is important to devise a rational method for deciding which of the many potential presenters your particular company should contact.

Building Profiles of Prospective Presenters

The size of your prospective presenters list will depend upon the nature of your company, your fee and technical needs, and the type and amount of touring you plan to do. For example, a large theatre company with complex technical requirements and a relatively high fee would be unlikely to find as many presenters in a single geographic area able to accommodate its fee and technical requirements as would a chamber music quartet. Conversely, the smaller group—with its lower fee, availability for single performances, and less stringent technical requirements—would be able to target a far larger universe of possible presenters in the same area.

At this point, you need to create profiles of all presenters in the area in which you want to tour. Each profile should tell you:

1. The type (or types) of performing company booked in previous seasons (i.e., the particular art form(s) the presenter has shown an interest in presenting);
2. The names of companies booked previously;
3. The presenter's overall budget for artists' fees;
4. The seating capacity of the auditorium(s) or performing facility(ies);
5. The type of performing facility (proscenium theatre with fly space, multi-purpose room, etc.);
6. The number of events presented per year or season;
7. The highest fee paid for a single event; and
8. The times of year and days of the week during which they usually present events.

Using Profiles to Target Presenters

Once assembled, these profiles will help you to determine which presenters are most likely to be interested in your company. This will enable you to know who to contact first. For example a ballet company with a single-performance fee of $15,000 will be able to tell which presenting organizations have a theatre large enough to earn sufficient ticket revenues to make a booking feasible. A presenter's budget for artists' fees might indicate that a single performance by a company of such scope and price would wipe out half a season's budget for performing arts events.

Similarly, it would not be a high priority for a contemporary dance company with a single-performance fee of $5,000 to contact an arts center with a seating capacity of 250 and an annual budget of $20,000 to cover the artistic fees for eight events per year. Unless the company has a substantial subsidy to offer the presenter, the fee (25 percent of the arts center's total budget) would be prohibitive. Even a sold-out house, at ten dollars apiece for 250 seats, would cover only half of the fee—and artistic fees are only a portion of the total presentation costs. (Presenters do not always rely on ticket sales exclusively and sometimes subsidize performances with unearned income.)

As another example, a presenter with a 2,000-seat auditorium and a million dollar budget is not a good prospect for a relatively unknown company or artist. In all probability, such a presenter is looking for groups with more established reputations whose drawing power will give the organization a chance to fill the large theatre. (While this method of targeting presenters is not always absolutely accurate, it has proven true to form in many cases.)

Where to Find Presenter Information

There are several sources of information from which you can put together accurate profiles of presenting organizations. Several regional arts collect and disseminate this valuable information to performing companies in a variety of forms: computer printouts, booklets, and printed or mimeographed lists. Each listing usually includes the art forms a presenter produces, the type of performing space, or spaces, available (proscenium stage with fly loft, arena, gymnasium with stage, etc.), and the number of seats. Also listed are the presenter's budget for artistic fees, the number of events presented each year, and, sometimes, the highest fee paid for an event. Other useful information may also be included. (An example of a typical page in a presenters' directory is shown in Exhibit 6.) Most printouts and booklets must be purchased, but they are well worth the cost if your company is planning to tour a particular region. Although some state and regional lists are free, you will receive just that—names, addresses, and phone numbers. Contact the regional and state arts agencies to find out what is available and at what cost.

Often, the personnel at regional and state arts agencies can be immensely helpful in pinpointing presenters whom you should contact. They know their presenting organizations well and should be able to tell you quite easily who will likely have an interest in the work you do and who can or cannot afford the fee. Because these people are often busy, obtain the agency's list before calling them so that you can simply check off the presenters they suggest.

Association of Performing Arts Presenters (APAP) (1112 16th Street, NW, Suite 400, Washington, D.C. 20036, 202/833-2787, FAX 202/833-1543) is a national organization of presenters whose members range from organizations with presenting budgets of several million dollars and 4,000-seat facilities, to those with yearly presenting budgets of $25,000 or less and 250-seat theatres. The organization has a computer data base that can be accessed by both members and non-members. The data base can be queried on any number of specifics, from what kind of work a presenter has on its series to number of performances and months when it presents.

Western Alliance of Arts Administrators (WAAA) (44 Page Street, Suite 604B, San Francisco, CA 94102, 415/621-4400, FAX 415/621-2533), a group of presenters based in the western part of the country, produces a book of profiles of its membership.

Arts Northwest (P.O. Box 55877, Seattle, WA 98155, 206/365-4143, FAX 206/365-8618) is a consortium of presenters in the northwestern part of the United States which prepares profiles of its members, similar to those offered by Western Alliance of Arts Administrators and the regional and state arts agencies. Only members are listed. Performing companies can obtain the list by joining for a nominal yearly fee.

National Association of Campus Activities (NACA) (13 Harbison Way, Columbia, SC 29212-3401, 800/845-2338) is an organization of student activities organizations at colleges and universities across the country. NACA has a reference guide that lists names, addresses, and phone numbers of 1200 members. The individuals on this list will for the most part be different from members of Arts Presenters (APAP).

There are also several additional sources of information which can be helpful in targeting prospective presenters:

Sterns Performing Arts Directory (33 West 60th Street, New York, NY 10023, 212/245-8937, FAX 212/956-6487) is an invaluable tool for organizations which want to tour. Published each fall, the directory contains an extensive list of concert series, festivals, and theatres which have an interest in presenting dance and music.

Musical America (International Directory of the Performing Arts, 10 Lake Drive, Highstown, NJ 08520, 800/221-5488, 609/371-7879) is the "bible" for those involved in booking any kind of musical event. Published annually, it lists all musical organizations (orchestras, opera companies, etc.) which book artists and companies, as well as foreign and U.S. festivals, performing arts series, music schools and departments, and musical competitions. It also carries a list of selected presenters and their presentations for the previous season.

EXHIBIT 6

Page from a Presenter Directory

CA

Venue Type: Proscenium with fly
Owner Status: Exclusive Tenant or Renter

Venue: Schoenberg Hall
Capacity: 528
Venue Type: Proscenium with fly
Owner Status: Occasional Tenant or Renter

Season: OCTOBER->JUNE
No. of Annual Contracts: 49
Artist Fees Budget: $800,000

Disciplines Presented: Mod/Contemporary Dance, Jazz/Tap Dance, Chamber Music, Choral Music, Contempory/New Music, Folk/Traditional Music, Jazz Music, Pop/Country Music, Instrumental Recital, Vocal Recital, One-Person Shows, Theatre for Young Audiences, Interdisciplinary/Performance Art, Films

Sample of Artists Presented: The King's Singer, Griot New York - Garth Fagan Dance & Wynton Marsalis Septet, Miami City Ballet, Yo-Yo Ma, The Cleveland Quartet, Ensemble Project Ars Nova, Chanticleer, Festival of Korea Series, Toshiko Akiyoshi Jazz Orchestra, and Iso & the Bobs

UNIVERSITY OF CALIFORNIA, RIVERSIDE
Desiree Mallory, Director
Cultural Events
133 Commons Complex
Riverside, CA 92521-0406
Phone: 909-787-4629 Fax: 909-787-2221

Legal Status: Public College/University
Type of Organization: College/University - Public

Venue: University Theatre
Capacity: 488
Venue Type: Proscenium with fly
Owner Status: Occasional Tenant or Renter

Venue: University Of California - Riverside Gym
Capacity: 1200
Venue Type: Gymnatorium
Owner Status: Occasional Tenant or Renter

Season: OCTOBER->JULY
No. of Annual Contracts: 17
Artist Fees Budget: $100,000

Disciplines Presented: Folk/Traditional Dance, Mod/Contemporary Dance, Jazz/Tap Dance, Chamber Music, Contempory/New Music, Folk/Traditional Music, Jazz Music, Classical Theatre, Theatre for Young Audiences

Sample of Artists Presented: "A Slice of Rice" - Great Leap, El Teatro Campesino, Hugh Masakela, Jai Uttal, Donald Byrd/The Group, Lewitzky Dance Company, Limon Dance Com-

pany, Ying Quatet, Quartet Sine Nomine, Stanford String Quartet, Nels, American Indian Dance Theatre and Pablo Rodarte and Dance Espana

UNIVERSITY OF CALIFORNIA, SAN DIEGO
Lynne Peterson, Director
Univ Events & Student Activities 0078
9500 Gilman Drive
La Jolla, CA 92093
Phone: 619-534-4090 Fax: 619-534-1505
E-Mail: LPETERSON@UCSD

Floyd Gaffney
Dept of Theatre Arts
9500 Gilman Drive
San Diego, CA 92093
Phone: 619-534-2062

Legal Status: Public College/University
Type of Organization: College/University - Public

Venue: Mandeville Auditorium
Capacity: 788
Venue Type: Proscenium, no fly
Owner Status: Occasional Tenant or Renter

Venue: Price Center Theatre
Capacity: 494
Venue Type: Lecture hall w/ stage
Owner Status: Occasional Tenant or Renter

Venue: Price Center Ballroom
Capacity: 1500
Venue Type: Other
Owner Status: Occasional Tenant or Renter

Venue: Main Gym
Capacity: 2200
Venue Type: Gymnatorium
Owner Status: Occasional Tenant or Renter

Season: OCTOBER->MAY
No. of Annual Contracts: 17
Artist Fees Budget: $200,000

Disciplines Presented: Folk/Traditional Dance, Mod/Contemporary Dance, Chamber Music, Folk/Traditional Music, Other Musical Theatre, One-Person Shows

Sample of Artists Presented: Les Ballets Africains, Parsons Dance Company, Chitresh Das, Kronos Quartet, Christopher Parkening, Tokyo String Quartet, New Vic Theatre, Peter Dennis, Eric Bogosian, Inti-Illimani, San Jose Taiko, Throat Singers of Tura, Tish Hinojosa and Diamanda Galas

Dance Theatre Workshop (219 West 19th Street, New York, NY 10011, 212/691-6500). Dance Theatre Workshop's mailing list, gleaned from a variety of national lists, includes approximately five thousand organizations which present dance. It is available on labels that can be affixed manually or by machine, and can be obtained in zip code order, which makes it possible to send materials only to certain areas of the country. The purchase price is based on how much of the list you buy, but there is also a sliding scale which lowers the cost for companies with smaller budgets. This list contains most, if not all, of the potential dance presenters included in the other lists mentioned above, but does not include any of the information necessary for developing presenter profiles. However, it can serve as the basis for developing your own mailing list and is excellent for mass mailings until your list is complete.

Theatre Communications Group (355 Lexington Avenue, New York, NY 10017, 212/697-5230, FAX 212/983-4847) is the national service organization for nonprofit professional theatre. One of its publications, *Theatre Profiles,* lists the names, addresses, and other information on the activities of each of its constituent theatre companies. It also publishes *American Theatre,* a monthly magazine which includes up-to-date listings on plays and other events in production at theatres around the country.

Chamber Music America (545 Eighth Avenue, New York, NY 10018, 212/244-2772), the national service organization for chamber music, maintains a mailing list of its presenter members, also available on labels, all of whom have an especially strong interest in chamber music. Many of these presenters are chamber music societies based in cities and towns across the country.

Performing Arts Yearbook for Europe (Arts Publishing International Ltd, 4 Assam Street, London E1 7QS England, 441/71/247-0066, FAX 441/71/247-0066). This annual directory gives comprehensive information on European venues including festivals, promoters, and governmental organizations who work in support of touring. The venue information lists the types of work presented and the size of the theatre(s). It could be a valuable initial resource to an organization considering touring in Europe.

The same organization publishes a similar book for North America, *Music, Opera and Dance in Canada and the United States of America.*

Other Ideas. A great place to learn more about presenters is through their season ticket brochures. There is often a table with presenters' brochures at each of the booking conferences, or you could call an organization and ask to receive their information. A brief perusal can help you determine which organizations might have a special interest in the type of work you do.

Additional Sources of Information

In addition to using the various listings described above, you should carefully examine the presenters for which your company has performed during the past several years: Are they a special group? Are they unique in some way? What do they have in common?

It can also be helpful to find out where companies comparable to your own have recently been booked. You might even check the tour dates of groups whose work—although in a different art form—relate to your company's work in tone, point of view, or level of experimentation. If your group performs contemporary music, for example, you might be of interest to organizations which have presented an experimental theatre company or post-modern dance.

And don't forget that the colleges and universities at which members of your company trained are often interested in presenting events which feature alumni performers. In fact, college and university departments can be the best source of bookings for emerging groups. Faculty members tend to keep up with what is happening artistically in their fields, and they may be more likely to know that your company is producing interesting new work which deserves to be seen than the people who run the more mainstream-oriented arts and lectures performance programming. Finally, do not overlook family and personal contacts: Does Aunt Mary work in a school district with a performing arts program that hires companies for in-school performances?

Presenter Consortia

One of the significant trends in the field is the development of presenter consortia or networks, groups of presenters located close to each other—within the same state, for example, or encompassing parts of several contiguous states. Consortia may serve a variety of purposes, holding workshops to better educate presenters, commissioning new work, running booking conferences, as well as serving the more traditional block booking role.

An example of an extraordinary consortium is the State of Wisconsin Presenters Network. Each year presenters in the state have gotten together to choose one dance company to be in the state for a five- to six-week period. The company does extensive performance and outreach activities in large and small communities across the state. On two recent tours the presenters have commissioned a work which premiered at the start of the tour. The presenters have hired a consortium staff person who coordinates the residency and raises money for the project. Presenters end up paying significantly lower fees for the performances. Not only have they been able to take advantage of block booking fees, but also as a group they have been successfully able to convince corporate sponsors to put their names on a highly visible tour. They have also been able to leverage government grants for their tours.

The Wisconsin example is fairly unique, however. Many other networks exist primarily for block booking purposes. A consortium may offer a company or companies a number of easily accessible additional bookings when the company tours near the area. Joint booking may even make a special trip into the area attractive in cases where a single booking would not be feasible.

The advantages for both presenters and touring companies are significant. A group of presenters that wants to bring in a larger, more expensive company may find the consortium especially useful, as many established companies are loath to travel off the beaten track to accommodate a single presenter. And as members of a consortium, individual presenters can usually pay a lower fee per engagement than would be required if they had only their own bookings to offer. Through the process of researching and choosing a company for a block book tour, presenters can learn more about a variety of artists.

There can be a disadvantage for companies if the fees for a block are too much lower than what they would normally charge. But because the presenters are generally no more than a few hours apart, touring groups can save a substantial amount of money on transportation. Decreased revenue on individual engagements can be made up in overall volume and continuity (the company may have booked a solid week of its tour, for example, rather than a single date), and with less travel time, wear and tear on the performers is significantly reduced.

A distinct problem with blocks is that consortium members sometimes end up booking work that is not appropriate to their community, simply because a company or artist is touring to nearby presenters. When presenters have different needs, block booking can lead to a choice of the lowest common denominator and preclude some members of the consortium from researching and developing relationships with artists and companies on their own.

Among the presenter consortia operating in recent years are those in Ohio, Colorado, West Virginia, Montana, Indiana, Hawaii, California, Florida, Pennsylvania and the New England, Green Mountain, and Rocky Mountain areas. From year to year, participants change, new consortia are formed, and others become inactive. The state and regional arts agencies will be able to tell you if there are consortia currently active in their respective states/regions and who to contact for information.

❦

CHAPTER 6

The Nitty Gritty of Booking

The booking process comprises all the tasks that must be systematically carried out to set up a tour for your company. Anyone who undertakes the responsibilities of this process must be patient and capable of hard work, have a high tolerance for frustration, and possess a large measure of what used to be called "stick-to-itiveness."

Obviously, the process has a number of variations, and will need to be expanded or scaled down depending upon whether you are working on behalf of companies which are small or large, new or established, and whether you are arranging a regional or a national tour. Like most successful booking people who employ the techniques described below, you must also be prepared to adapt to any special circumstances you may encounter and to add your own embellishments as you see fit.

It is important to think through the entire process before you begin. You must know ahead of time what you will do and why, for each step of the process. Too often, new managers fail to do this and are unprepared to respond when a presenter does express interest. Keeping communication between you and the presenter moving forward is critical to making the sale. With this in mind, if you follow persistently the basic procedures outlined in this chapter, your efforts should be successful.

The Mailing

If you have done your homework and have prepared a smashing booking brochure, flyer, or other type of written presentation, and compiled a mailing list of prospective presenters, the next step is to undertake a major mailing to them.

The booking process seems to begin earlier and earlier each season. Generally, your initial mailing should be sent late in the summer or early in the fall, preferably in September, since this is when presenters return from summer vacation. (See Exhibit 7 for a basic schedule of booking activities.) Smaller presenters often book later; if this is your market, the timetable can be adjusted accordingly. On the other hand, the largest presenters begin booking in the preceding spring, and some presenters actually use the December booking conferences to begin exploration for two seasons hence.

Your mailing list, whether it is one of the standard lists mentioned earlier or a combination of many lists, should be copied for future use. Additional copies of mailing labels may be used as headings on index cards (or other filing materials) on which you can keep records of presenters' responses to your mailings and phone calls if you are not using a computer.

Mailing Options

You should send your materials not-for-profit bulk mail, unless you are dealing with a small number of prospective presenters (less than two hundred), in which case you must mail first class. Bulk mail is considerably less expensive, but there is a catch: you must allow two to four weeks for delivery. Also, postal regulations require that bulk mail be bundled by zip code. Pay a visit to your local post office and pick up a copy of the complete regulations; then decide how best to proceed.

If you do not have not-for-profit status, look for an arts service organization or other umbrella group in your community that might allow you to use its permit and indicia. It is also possible, but more expensive, to mail at commercial bulk rates.

Targeted Personal Letters

In addition to the general bulk mailing, you may want to send personal letters to presenters whom you have targeted specifically. This is especially effective for soliciting presenters in whom the company has a particular interest, either because they tend to book your type of company or because they happen to be located in a part of the country in which the company especially wants to tour.

Because of the extra time and effort involved, however, you will likely be able to prepare only a limited number of personal letters (to be sent

EXHIBIT 7

A Booking Calendar

JANUARY	FEBRUARY	MARCH	APRIL
Begin reappraisal for tour to begin in September of the following year.	Tour plans, budget, fees submitted to artistic staff and Board of Trustees.	Meet with graphic designer and copywriter to discuss concept for booking brochure.	Have photos taken for brochure if necessary. Follow up presenters interested at previous fall/winter conferences. Begin work on project-oriented residencies.
MAY	**JUNE**	**JULY**	**AUGUST**
Revise contract. Finalize brochure format and get necessary approvals.		Brochure to printer. Notify mailing house per presenter list revision.	Phone presenters who said previously interested in booking.
SEPTEMBER	**OCTOBER**	**NOVEMBER**	**DECEMBER**
Mail brochure. Western Alliance, Southern Arts, Midwest, Northeast booking conferences Follow-up mail to conference attendees. Begin phone calls. ----	Follow-up mail to interested presenters. ----	----------------------	ISPA and Arts Presenters National Conferences
JANUARY	**FEBRUARY**	**MARCH**	**APRIL**
Follow-up ISPA, Arts Presenters. Phone calls. ---- Follow-up mail. ---- Begin sending out contracts. ----		Begin follow-up for fill-in dates.	
MAY	**JUNE**	**JULY**	**AUGUST**
---- ---- ----	Finalize all contracts.		
SEPTEMBER	**OCTOBER**	**NOVEMBER**	**DECEMBER**
Tour begins.			

first-class mail with your brochure enclosed). This is one of the areas in the booking process in which computers (especially word processing software) can dramatically simplify your work. In fact, personal computers can simplify your work throughout the booking process.

The Heart of the Booking Process: The Telephone Campaign

Your brochure may be the most beautifully and shrewdly designed piece possible, *but it won't make your phone ring.* Consequently, begin your follow-up phone calls as soon as you determine that the presenters within a certain area or state should have received your booking brochure. (Your presenter profiles can be very helpful in determining whom to call first, but in all probability there will be lots of prospective presenters for whom no profile information is available.)

Planning the Campaign

Before beginning to make calls, study a map of the area, state, or states through which you plan to tour and work out an ideal route, noting approximately where you will be at any given time. In the end, your actual route will undoubtedly look much different, but a careful plan will enable you to give prospective presenters a good idea of when the company will be near their facility.

Make your first calls to presenters who, from their profiles, appear most likely to book your company; those who send back your return postcards should be your highest priority. Your next group of calls in the same area should be made to presenters who seem less likely prospects, followed by those about whom you have no information. The prospects whom you have identified as least likely should be contacted last—but they should be contacted.

Do not avoid making contact simply because you have classified a prospect as "unlikely," especially if the classification is based on your perception of the presenter and his facility as a distant aspiration—the kind of presenter for whom you hope to perform someday. Booking is not a one-year process; it is ongoing for your company, whether or not you, personally, continue to do it. Cultivating the interest of unlikely but desirable prospects can take time, and some presenters may hear about your company and observe your progress without commitment for several years before considering a booking. But it is up to you to make sure the prospect has heard of your company, and to keep up the contact. Even if a presenter said last year that he really had no interest in what your company had to offer, call him again this year. Things may have changed.

Once you have targeted the prospects to call, set up a file mechanism to keep track of the process with each presenting organization. The file mechanism can be as simple as index cards or a fairly complex computer data base system. If you are using a computer, you will want to be sure to maintain a "hard" back-up for each presenter record. Your computer can be programmed to generate mailing labels as well. Each record should contain a presenter's name, organization, address, phone and fax number, along with important additional information culled from presenter profiles—budget, previous companies booked, house size, etc. A sample presenter record is shown in Exhibit 8.

EXHIBIT 8

A Presenter Record

```
eeeeeeeeeëëëëëëëëëëëëëëëëëëëëëëëëëëëëëëëëëëëëëëüeeeeeeeeëëëëëëëëëëeeeeeeeeeeeeeeeeeeeeeeeeı
¤  The Presenting Organization            ¤                        Page 1      ¤
äëëëëëëëëëëëëëëëëëëëëëëëëëëëëëëëëëëëëëëëëëëëëë¥                                   ¤
¤  Name:   Ms.   Sally              Stoner                                     ¤
¤  Dept.:  Director                 Address:  1234 Main Street                 ¤
¤  City:   Any City          St.:   MA    Zip Code: 62546                      ¤
¤  Country:                                                                    ¤
¤  Office Ph: 410-777-1387      Ext          Home Ph: 410-777-1390f            ¤
¤  L. Date:                          Tic. Date:                                ¤
¤  Sal.: Sally                                                                 ¤
¤  Prog. Bdgt:        100,000    HC A: 775     B: 250        C:                 ¤
¤  Num Events:        12         Fee Range   Min:     3    Max:        12       ¤
¤  Disciplines 1: theater     2: contemp     3: ballet      4: wld.musi        ¤
¤              5: recital     6: chamber     7:             8:                  ¤
¤              9:            10:            11:                                 ¤
¤  History:                                                                    ¤
¤                                                                              ¤
¤  RSA_Booked:                                                                 ¤
¤  When_Present: Oct - May  Days_Present:T  - Th   When_Book: Dec - Mar        ¤
¤  Clients 1: AR  2: MR  3: SM  4: BH  Cont_Date:                              ¤
¤  Person: 1 ,   How:        Followup:       Lst_Tel:                          ¤
¤  Misc.:                                                                      ¤
äëëëëëëëëëëëëëëëëëëëëëëëëëëëëëëëëëëëëëëëëëëëëëëëëëëëëëëëëëëëëëëëëëëëëëëëëëëëëëëëëëëëëëëëëë¥


eeeeeeeeeeeeeeeeeeeeeeeeeeeeeeeeeeeeeeeeeeeeeueeeeeeeeeeeeeeeeeeeeeeeeeeeeeeeeeeeeeeeeeeı
¤  The Presenting Organization          ¤   REC #   1 FOR THIS INSTITUTION     ¤
äëëëëëëëëëëëëëëëëëëëëëëëëëëëëëëëëëëëëëëëëëëë¥                                    ¤
¤                                                                             ¤
¤                           PRESENT CONTACTS                                  ¤
¤                                                                             ¤
¤                                                                             ¤
¤ Present: 8/17 Too early to talk but are changing series somewhat 9/20 Spoke ¤
¤                                                                             ¤
¤ Sally, new auditorium, switching to series Tues, Wed, Thurs eves and        ¤
¤                                                                             ¤
¤ expanding program to be more eclectic, send info.  11/6 Package sent        ¤
¤                                                                             ¤
¤ 12/5 Left name and number 1/15 She called back, committee still meeting,    ¤
¤                                                                             ¤
¤ reminded regional deadline, call back early Feb. 2/3 Interested but date    ¤
¤                                                                             ¤
¤ no good, definite interest for next season.                                 ¤
¤                                                                             ¤
¤                                                                             ¤
¤                                                                             ¤
¤                                                                             ¤
äëëëëëëëëëëëëëëëëëëëëëëëëëëëëëëëëëëëëëëëëëëëëëëëëëëëëëëëëëëëëëëëëëëëëëëëëëëëëëëëëëëëëëëëëë¥
```

Making the Calls: What to Say and How to Listen

The telephone call is the heart of the booking process. It is the crucial, direct contact between company and presenter. Remember, presenters are busy people. Not only do they receive calls from numerous booking people representing all the art forms, they also produce their own series. Work out a basic telephone presentation before you start to make calls. Practice with a tape recorder to hear what you sound like, and then tailor the presentation to each individual you call.

Telephone contacts are not just sales calls. Each call should be approached as an attempt to understand the presenter's particular needs, and an opportunity to demonstrate how your company can meet them. This means that you must not only talk but listen hard during these calls, and ask questions if you can. The more your booking call becomes a two-way conversation, the more effective your efforts will be. Understanding what the presenter needs in a company will enable you to make a strong presentation about your group's ability to meet those needs.

The first time you call, identify yourself as a representative of the company and remind the presenter that he should have recently received your materials. Try to talk about your company's unique qualities, what it does that is special. If your artistic fee is particularly attractive, emphasize that. Most importantly, focus on how your company can meet the presenter's needs. If possible, discuss specific dates, or at least a time frame. For example, "We could be in your area during the last week in October." The point is to give the presenter convincing reasons for booking your company.

Make no attempt to negotiate the fee during this initial call. It is best simply to state the figure and mention that it is somewhat negotiable, depending upon a variety of factors, such as travel distance, number of performances, etc. It is also important to mention whether you have any state, regional, or private support for your tour and how much this will decrease the presenter's fee. If the presenter says the price sounds high, you might talk about combining a number of organizations in the community to present your company jointly. A presenting organization and a school district might pool their resources to present a theatre company. Perhaps the actors could offer special performances for children, in addition to performances for the general public, to make the engagement financially viable.

If you are not familiar with the presenting organization, try to use the first call to ascertain how the presenter makes decisions and how long the process takes. Find out whether an individual or committee makes the decisions. Most often on campuses there is a committee made up of student and faculty representatives along with the presenter. In community groups, there may be selection committees made up of board members or others active in the group.

Keep things moving. Do not give the presenter the opportunity to say "no." A suggestion from the presenter—or from you—that additional information (reviews, for example) would be helpful gives you an opportunity for future contact, and the printed matter will provide another visual impression of the company. You might also suggest that he check your company's references with presenters in his area with whom you have already worked successfully.

Finally, it is a good idea to remind presenters that they might be eligible for state or regional arts agency funds to subsidize local presentations of touring groups. You might also suggest that the presenter solicit local corporations and foundations which might want to support performance activity of this kind in their community.

Keeping Records

As you make your calls, note the dates and the response of each presenter on the index cards or whatever you have set up. Jotting down a brief summary of the prospect's response will give you an idea of when to call next and what to say. Note if the presenter seems interested, wants additional information or has special interests, what companies the presenter has booked for this year's series, and anything else which seems pertinent. If the presenter is not interested in your company, indicate why.

Put away the records/cards for the presenters who tell you right away they are not interested. These records can be used again next year. All of the others are worth a follow-up call later on in the process.

Reinforcing Your Calls: Follow-Up Letters

If he shows any interest, the presenter should be sent a personal follow-up letter restating the uniqueness of the company's offering, any special logistical information discussed in the phone call, the time frame, fees, special services the company can provide, and so forth. Again, the computer can be enormously helpful in following through on this kind of personal communication. A word processing program can be integrated with your data base to generate letters.

Exhibit 9 shows a computer-generated follow-up letter with the personalized portion circled. The remainder is standard and was developed by the booking person before the initial round of calls was begun.

Along with your follow-up letter, send recent company press clips in full. Other possible enclosures include a company history, a description of residency activities, a technical-requirements sheet, a list of previous presenters, perhaps a program from a past performance, and a list of the

EXHIBIT 9

A Follow-Up Letter

RENA SHAGAN ASSOCIATES, INC.
180 Riverside Drive, New York, N.Y. 10024
212-873-9700 Fax 212-873-1708

October 1,

Ms. Janet Smith
Director
The Presenting Organization
1234 Main Street
Any City, Any State

Dear Janet:

This note is to follow-up on our phone conversation about SUSAN
MARSHALL & COMPANY performing on your series next season.

What people seem to find most appealing about Susan Marshall's
work is that is it not abstract at all, but about people in real
relationships. That's something audiences relate to. Said one
critic, " her dances combine wit, compassion, satire, sexuality
and a pleasing 'non dancey' approach to movement. When you watch
this company, you are not so much conscious of watching dancers
as you are of seeing real people expressing honest--albeit
exaggerated--emotions through dance."

Within the last year Susan Marshall has won several major awards,
including a Guggenheim Fellowship and the American Choreography
Award from the National Corporate Fund for Dance. In addition to
domestic touring, she and her company frequently perform abroad,
including a 5 week USIA sponsored tour of Eastern and Southern
Europe.

For the 1994-'95 season the company will tour a Repertory Program
including KISS, COMPANION PIECES and UNTITLED (DETAIL) along with
other work. A second program will include the two works the
company will premiere at the BAM NEXT WAVE FESTIVAL; VICTORY with
music by Philip Glass, and SPECTATORS AT AN EVENT, music by
Henryk Gorecki, which draws its inspiration from the photographs
of WeeGee. The WeeGee work will use 20-30 people from the
presenters community.

The residency activities we discussed could certainly be done in
the three day period. The company will be in your area during
the first two weeks in March, with a residency in Greendale on
the 2nd-4th, and could come to your community just before or
after those dates. The fee is usually   , but would be
negotiable if you could work into the timeframe.

The materials you requested are enclosed. I look forward to
talking with you again soon.

Sincerely,

Rena Shagan
Rena Shagan Associates, Inc.
Booking Management for Susan Marshall & Company

works in your touring repertoire, if this does not appear in your booking brochure (you might even enclose an additional copy of the latter).

Follow-Up Phone Calls: Cultivating Presenter Interest

If possible, presenters should receive follow-up calls four to six weeks after the first call (unless you agreed during your initial conversation to call them at some other time). At that point, they will have received the material you sent after your first call and will have had time to digest it and pass it on to their committees.

You might begin a follow-up call by asking the presenter if the material has arrived and if he has any questions about your company. This is a good, nonthreatening opener, much less pressured than if you call and immediately ask whether the committee is interested. It opens the door for you to talk further about the company, and to indicate if other dates in the area have fallen into place, whether any fee reductions might be possible, and so forth. Try to get an idea of the timing involved in the organization's decisionmaking process so that you can contact the presenter again before a final decision has been reached. And be diligent about sending requested follow-up materials.

If you have a video/audio tape of the company, suggest sending it for viewing/listening by the decisionmakers. Be sure, however, before making this offer that the tape is technically excellent and shows the company to its best advantage.

As people respond, winnow down your active records. Remember, you must be persistent, patient, and resist frustration. Over several months, it may take a number of follow-up calls to a presenter before you find out what he has finally decided to book, and his choices may very well not include your company. The key is not to let the process get you down. Each call is another opportunity to emphasize your company's special qualities and why you would like to perform at the presenter's location.

Many times presenters are not in or cannot be reached. Sometimes you can spend an entire morning on the phone and not reach anyone. Do not get discouraged. Most people booking extensive, multi-week tours are on the phone many hours every day, at least five to six months of the year.

If a presenter is not in, leave your name, the name of the company, and your phone number. That way, even if your phone call is not returned (and many are not), the presenter will be aware that you called.

Persistence Pays Off

A conscientious booking person repeats this procedure hundreds of times each season. At the same time that you are giving the presenter information on the company, you are eliciting information on the presenter's facility and special needs, the kinds of programs he usually presents, and what has succeeded with his audiences in the past.

You must realize that the chances of getting anyone to book the company on a first telephone call are very slim. Don't expect it. Among the responses you can expect—even from presenters who show some interest—are:

"I'm sorry, but we've already booked another company of your type."

"Our committee just began to meet."

"We have no money this year."

"It's too early."

"The theatre is booked during the period you'll be in the area."

"We're considering your company along with ten others."

Do not let these kinds of responses get you down. The presenter is interested, and you now have an opportunity to convince him to book the company on the second telephone call—or the fifth. Persistence *will* pay off.

Another Approach to Booking

Another way to pursue prospects which has worked well for companies who want to tour in their own region is the direct, personal approach. The person doing the booking loads video equipment and booking materials into a car and drives from presenter to presenter, talking to each in person. If you have the time and the money, the face-to-face approach can be a very effective way to get bookings. Most often, this approach works best for booking in a small geographic area.

Negotiation

Perhaps there is a presenter who has a genuine interest in booking your company, but for a variety of reasons, you cannot reach an agreement. In such a situation, when both parties have concluded that the booking meets their needs but that they cannot agree to a contract without some modification of terms on both sides, you will have to negotiate. Among the instances in which negotiation may occur are cases in which:

1. A presenter can get a better price for presenting a company for several performances rather than for a "single";

2. A company has a few extra days between engagements, and rather than having its members sit idle and incur all the running expenses of a tour, it will negotiate a substantially lower fee with a presenter whose facility is en route between two existing bookings;

3. A company wants to appear in a particular facility or city because

it could significantly boost the company's image locally or nationally, in which case the company will accept a lesser fee to ensure the exposure (similarly, a company may choose to appear at a lesser fee in a particular city to be reviewed by a nationally recognized critic, or to be seen by foundations and corporations which could make a meaningful contribution to unearned income in the long or short run);

4. The company needs the work and exposure and cannot seem to get presenters to pay the fee it originally set; and

5. The company fits the presenter's needs, and the presenter really wants to book the company, but the box office and other monies available for presentation will not cover the cost.

Companies routinely negotiate two elements with presenters: the amount of compensation—monetary or otherwise—and the number and types of services the company is to provide. Often, both are negotiated simultaneously.

Negotiating Compensation

Fees. The most common compensation negotiation concerns the fee. Companies routinely reduce fees for a variety of reasons as outlined above. However, in some cases the company may need to agree with the presenter to split the box office and expenses for their performance. Some types of performers, such as jazz and popular music artists, do this on a regular basis. However, it is the exception rather than the rule in the performing arts. But arranging a split of the box office could be a viable option if there is a hole in a tour, and a presenter on the way to the next date will work with you on this basis.

Arrangements vary, but often presenters will guarantee a set fee and then agree to a split of the box office after their costs have been covered. The split of the box office can be set on various ratios: 40-60, 50-50, etc. Be sure the presenter specifically sets out what the expenses will be (rent, publicity, crew, and so forth), so you are not caught with your income substantially reduced by hidden or unforeseen presenting costs. Before agreeing to split box office receipts, you must:

1. Know how many seats in the theatre can be sold for your performances (seats with partially obstructed views of the stage, acceptable perhaps for a chamber music group, may not be saleable for a dance or theatre performance, or may have to be sold at a discount);

2. Know how the seats are priced, and the potential gross from ticket sales at 100 percent of seating capacity;

3. Know the number of seats sold for comparable companies over the

past several seasons (which will give you some idea of the percentage of the seating capacity upon which your earnings will be based);

4. Reach an agreement with the presenter on when the percentage will be paid, and when the company will receive a box office statement;
5. Find out how well the presenter has promoted his presentations in the past (with nothing but a percentage of the box office, your company risks playing the date for free if the presenter does not have an excellent track record).

Housing and Food. These are both forms of compensation which companies and presenters can negotiate. For the company, the best option is to have a local hotel agree to contribute rooms to the presenting organization. Alternatively, college/university presenters may be able to offer a company free meals and housing in dormitories. The company saves on its per diem costs, and the presenter's out-of-pocket expenses for such compensation are often minimal. However, beware of:

1. Institutional food and noisy dorms without private bathrooms (try to opt for guest or faculty housing);
2. Company members spread out all over a campus or community with no means to communicate schedule changes;
3. Lack of convenient transportation to and from rehearsals and performances.

Arrangements of this type can be hard on the artists, staff, and crew. Try to avoid making too many of them. Companies operating under union contracts will not have this option at all, as most agreements require payment of per diems regardless of what arrangements the company might make.

You will also want to avoid situations where a presenter and his committee put artists up in their homes, unless you are in a very small community and there is no hotel/motel in the vicinity. No artist should be subject to the personal vicissitudes of someone else's family, no matter how well-intentioned.

Travel. Companies whose touring primarily consists of single performances or residencies to which they must fly can also negotiate travel. In bookings of this kind (sometimes incorrectly known as run-outs), the company may at times negotiate a fee plus air transportation for company members, staff, etc., and freight costs. The number of company personnel involved is specified in the contract.

In such an arrangement, the transportation and freight costs charged to the presenter will be based on the airline fares to the particular city current at the time of the run-out. With today's constantly changing air fares, keep this option in mind if your company frequently accepts bookings of this type.

The Negotiation of Services

A presenter may want to negotiate for services beyond what the company normally offers. These can include an extra lecture demonstration, additional classes, a television taping, or performance of a particular work.

Extra performances may be important to the presenter as well. For instance, a company may be negotiating a half-week residency which usually involves only two performances, but the presenter is hesitant about the fee. The company's willingness to play an extra children's matinee (travel and other factors permitting) might persuade the presenter that, with extra box office income, the company is a good deal. Such a gesture also demonstrates the company's responsiveness to the presenter's needs and concerns.

Throughout the negotiation process, you must always keep in mind the minimum average weekly fee which the company can afford to accept. Never strike an agreement that is not cost-efficient in terms of the economics of the entire tour or that does not, in at least some way, make sense for your company.

Turning a Booking into a Tour

A tour is a string of several engagements connected as closely as possible through careful routing. The geographic proximity of one engagement to the next sometimes benefits presenters located in the same, or nearby, states or regions. It is always important to the company, in terms of convenience and lowered expenses.

If you have carried out the booking process to this point, perhaps your company has a booking or two. How do you turn them into a tour?

Ideally, you want to construct a tour which will begin in your home area, take the company to its various booking dates along a logical route, then direct it home via another logical path. The best, most cost-effective routes move a company in a circle, in a loop, or in a figure-eight formation around home base. Conversely, doubling back along your route is wastefully expensive and should be avoided unless absolutely necessary. Good routing is critically important to successful touring.

Suppose you have succeeded in obtaining two weeks of engagements in Texas. From an economic point of view, which would be most effective: (1) Travel to Houston for a week, return home, then a month later play a week in Dallas, or (2) Go directly from the week in Houston to the Dallas booking and return home with both engagements completed?

Usually the second alternative would substantially cut down transportation costs and reduce wear-and-tear on company personnel. All other things being equal, this is the preferable option. It should be noted, however, that all things may not be as "equal" as they seem. For instance, for those companies travelling by air, inexpensive airline fares which require a Saturday night stayover could result in a lower fare for two run-outs than a connected full week tour, assuming the company could pay its artists for less than one week of salary, or has other income-producing work to fill out the week at their home base. The function of good routing, then, is to provide the company with the most cost-effective (and energy-efficient) means of achieving its touring goals.

Touring expenses fit into three general categories: (1) salaries and per diems while on the road; (2) travel-related costs; and (3) all other tour-related production expenses which a company runs up over the year (see Chapter 3 on budgeting).

For most companies, salaries and per diems will not change regardless of the way the tour is routed; this category can be thought of as fixed or stationary. The remainder of the weekly touring fee must be enough to cover all transportation costs and all other tour-related expenses. Thus, the only way to increase the money available for tour-related expenses other than travel is to reduce the transportation costs which will result from the particular logistics of the tour.

Routing Strategies

The way to make this happen is through careful routing and proper selection among transportation options. For example, booking several engagements in a single area means that the company can travel in a bus or van instead of by plane. Travel for three performances in southern California will cost less than one in Los Angeles, another in Sacramento, and a third in Arcata.

You hold an ace when you have even one definite booking! You can call presenters in adjacent areas and say, "The ABC company will be appearing at Slippery Rock State on February 15. Would you be interested in an engagement just before or just after those dates?" You would be surprised at the impact it has on a presenter to know that a compatriot nearby is presenting your company.

Begin to look for additional presenters in both en route and adjacent areas. For example, if your New York City–based company has a booking in Knoxville and you have not previously sought additional presenters in Tennessee, you should do so now. Send your material (first class) even to the Tennessee presenters you have already contacted, this time enclosing a note informing them of your Knoxville engagement. Follow up with phone calls. At the same time, contact prospects en route—moving south from New York, then west to Knoxville—as well as those in the states beyond Tennessee (Ohio to the north, Georgia to the south).

Wherever you tour, you must have a good atlas, showing the entire country as a whole and each state individually. There are several computer programs available to supplement your atlas in helping to calculate mileage. Early on, study your map closely and pinpoint a route that makes sense geographically and in terms of the presenters who fit into your marketing strategy. Things probably will not work out exactly as you plan, but it is helpful to have an ideal at which to aim.

Putting the Pieces of the Tour Puzzle into Place

As a tour falls into place, it begins to look like a big jigsaw puzzle. A presenter can take a date and leave you several days to fill before the next engagement. Do not make absolute commitments to specific dates until the tour begins to shape up. Otherwise, you may find yourself locked into dates which, as booked, take you several hundred miles out of your way, yet two weeks later would work perfectly. However, when the routing does begin to shape up, you will want to negotiate fees and activities and go to contract quickly.

As discussed previously, additional services, such as children's matinees and master classes, can help to clinch a booking. And flexibility with your fee is particularly important during this final, accelerated phase of the booking process. You may need to reduce your fee slightly to obtain an especially desirable booking; if so, you will probably want to try to negotiate a somewhat larger fee than usual with the next presenter to offset the loss incurred in the previous engagement.

Be sure to leave the company plenty of time to travel between engagements, and allow for one full day off each week. Companies touring under union contracts have travel time and the number of days off specified, and you will have to work within these parameters. Do not be afraid to ask a presenter to change a date if it will help you out. Explain your problem. Most presenters will try to be helpful. Ask the presenter if he knows anybody in the area who might pick up part of your time.

Often, arrangements are being made simultaneously for more than one tour: while you are booking a Southern tour for the fall, you may be booking a tour of the West Coast for the spring. Be sure to keep your basic budget constantly in mind to make sure that the costs of the tour will be covered by the money you will be receiving from week to week.

Travel Economics of Booking the Tour

It makes no sense for a company to fly across the country for only one week of touring. By the time plane fares and salaries are paid, there would be nothing left for all your other expenses. But it does make sense for a West Coast company to come east if it can arrange to work its way across the country—or if it can find several weeks of bookings in the southeastern or northeastern part of the country.

Although car and bus tours are cheaper than touring by plane, take into account that your artists and staff will be far more tired after driving eight hours than if they had flown for one hour. Also, if the drive involves an extra day of transportation (or several extra days), during which salaries and per diems must be paid while no earnings are coming in, flying may be a bargain. This would be especially true of cross-country engagements, any long-distance bookings, or at the beginning or end of a tour.

The most uneconomical engagements are the one-shot performances or residencies which do not take place near your home base. Very little, if anything, is gained from these. However, a few presenters around the country are so prestigious that it can be really important for a company to appear as part of their series, even if the only dates available do not fit into the company's optimum tour schedule.

You can even lose money from bookings with those special presenters; just be certain that you have consciously chosen to do so. There cannot be more than ten to fifteen presenters in the entire nation who are worth a financial loss. If you accept such a booking, try to cut your losses by contacting nearby prospects.

Some companies, especially those just beginning, will perform anywhere, regardless of cost, regardless of the fact that they have no way of making up the loss. This can work for a while, but if a company continues to tour this way, it will eventually spell trouble.

Sometimes it is just not possible to make routing work satisfactorily every week. You may find that you can get many engagements within a state or in adjacent states but no en routes, or lots of en routes but not much in any one area or on the way back. This is fine as long as it fits into the budget.

Professionalism in Booking

As you work your way through the booking process, you will hear many, many more presenters say "no" than "yes." In order to get a booking, you may be tempted, at times, to promise something to a presenter that your company may be unable to deliver. To help you work through these rough spots, there are several points which you must always remember.

Handling Rejection

Never, never take personally a presenter's rejection of your company. Whether he decides to book or not to book will be determined by a variety of considerations, including balance of programming, total artist fees, and box office potential. For example, if yours is a ballet company and the presenter featured ballet last season, he might prefer to vary his programming with a modern dance company. Is someone in the dance department particularly anxious to have a certain company? This may mean that your company, perhaps the preference of the presentations committee, nevertheless might not be chosen. How has dance in general been doing at the box office for this presenter? Does another company have additional regional underwriting that makes them especially attractive?

Keep your pride—and your sanity. If the presenter does not book your company, look on it as your initial opportunity to convey the company's special abilities, a necessary first step which may lead, in two or three years, to a new booking.

Honesty and Ethics

Deal with presenters honestly and ethically. Most, if not all, of those who are interested in your company will want to know certain specifics, such as what kinds of things the company does best, and the kind of performing space you require. Lack of honesty can lead to problems on both sides.

If yours is primarily a performing theatre company with little interest or skill in teaching, and the presenter wants company members to spend most of a residency working with children in an instructional situation, be honest—and complete—in what you report to the presenter. If there are ten dancers in your troupe and the presenter has a very small stage, it is perhaps best not to pursue the engagement. You might even suggest a company that you know to be a viable alternative. If your ten dancers should get to the theatre and find only a fifteen-by-twenty-foot stage, they will be very unhappy, and so will the presenter when he finds your actors less than enthusiastic about their obligation to teach a group of fifty elementary school children.

Be honest and firm. If you cannot or do not want to do something, say so, but be sure to have ready an exciting, imaginative alternative.

CHAPTER 7

Booking Meetings

A number of organizations conduct booking conferences to which both presenters and touring companies are invited. In certain circles, these events have developed a bad name among companies and managements (some call them "Meat Markets" and feel their companies are somehow degraded by the impersonal, bazaar-like atmosphere). However, although some may grumble, managers who regularly attend booking conferences over a period of years find that they provide an extremely valuable opportunity to relate to a presenter's season and his needs in a very personal way.

Talking with a presenter across a table provides an opportunity to relate to him as an individual and not as a faceless voice over the telephone. The rewards from this exchange of information may not always be tangible for next year or even the year after, but they are extremely important for your company over the long haul. Of course, the presenter also uses the booking conference to get to know you and your organization. After talking to a presenter, you may indeed find that your company meets his needs, and a booking or several bookings can result.

Booking conferences are organized by service organizations such as the Association of Performing Arts Presenters, regional organizations such as Arts Midwest, or presenter consortia such as New England Presenters. The organizer rents space in a large hotel or conference center and, for a set fee, allows performing companies and managements representing a number of companies or artists to attend. Each is provided with a table on which to display materials, posters, videotapes, etc. In what is usually called the resource room presenters will find row upon row of booths where they can pick up materials and, if they wish, stop and talk (see Exhibit 10 for a floor plan of the New York APAP Conference).

Most booking conferences now include showcases or showings. These provide an opportunity for presenters to see and perhaps become interested in artists with whom they are not familiar. Some conferences include them as a formal part of the activities. For example, the conference organizers may rent a theatre, hire the technical staff and take applications for showcase performances; each group is usually given 10–20 minutes. In other instances, there are showcases and informal showings of work going on as ancillary activities, not officially connected to the conference. Companies rent their own venues and can therefore choose to present a fully mounted production or a studio showing. Local companies often issue invitations to conference participants to view productions running simultaneously with the conference. With showcases/showings, as with everything else in the booking process, if you can't be sure that the company will be seen in a way that will enhance what it does, it is probably better to opt out of the process.

Another important part of most booking conferences is the educational sessions that are run for both managers and presenters. Session titles can range from "Creating Community Audiences through Residencies" to "How to Use Volunteers in Your Organization" to sessions on specific art forms. These sessions are not only valuable as a place to learn and ask questions, they are also an excellent place to meet presenters on common ground. While educational or social functions are not a good place to walk up to a presenter and start talking business, having sat next to the presenter at a session earlier in the day can go a long way toward stimulating a discussion of mutual interest.

If you go to a booking meeting, try not to feel as if you are on trial— the company is not dead if you do not get any concrete presenter interest. At your first conference, most likely you will not know anyone there— either presenters or other companies. By the second meeting you will be a veteran, and perhaps some of the presenters you met last time will now be able to say to the others, "We had the ABC company in our community this year and they were great."

EXHIBIT 10

Booking Conference Floor Plan

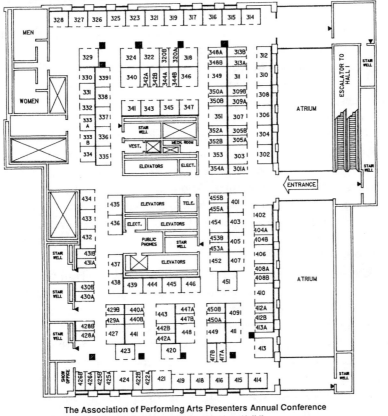

The Association of Performing Arts Presenters Annual Conference
The New York Hilton Americas Hall II

Courtesy of the Association of Performing Arts Presenters

Cultivating Interest in Your Company

A good way to insure activity at your table is to make contact in advance of the booking conference with presenters in whom you are particularly interested. If you think a certain college or community where you have not previously appeared is a likely prospect, contact the presenter and find out if he plans to attend the conference. If so, make an appointment. You should also contact several presenters who have previously sponsored your company and are likely to attend the meeting, and ask if they will serve as references. It is particularly valuable to have a satisfied presenter vouch for the company to others so that, at the end of a chat with a prospect, you are in a position to say, "John Jones presented the company last season and thought it was excellent. He's here at the conference. Why don't you ask him about it?"

What to Bring to a Booking Conference

If you plan to attend a booking conference, you will need to bring:

1. Thirty-five booking brochures (you would need more materials for a large meeting like the national APAP conference);
2. Fifteen packets containing recent reviews, production information, technical specifications, company history, photos;
3. Your touring schedule for the current year;
4. A calendar or schedule for the upcoming booking year;
5. Videotapes, slides, and audio cassettes; and
6. Your display.

A videocassette player and monitor, a slide projector and screen, or a tape recorder can be brought from home or rented at the conference. In each case, be sure to have earphones—a requirement at all conferences.

Always carry extra brochures and other materials in your carry-on luggage. Airlines have been known to lose checked-in boxes, and a booking conference can be quite frustrating if you arrive empty-handed.

The Table Display

An attractive, well-organized table display is extremely important, since there may be more than a hundred performing organizations and managements competing for the attention of prospective presenters. Artfully designed and executed signs and displays convey an image of professionalism and competence. Videotapes, slides, and sound tapes are excellent tools for demonstrating the nature and quality of your company's work.

The display should be lightweight and does not have to be expensive. It might be as simple as a good photo of the company or a production shot, enlarged to three feet by four feet, mounted on styrofoam board, and placed on a table-top easel.

Initiating Contact with Presenters

As presenters approach your table, be pleasant and solicitous, but avoid the hard sell. Think of how you would feel in their place: presenters attend booking conferences to browse, chat informally, and pick up materials from the companies that interest them. They do not enjoy being accosted by over-eager managers. There is nothing wrong with taking the initiative with the presenters who pause to look at your display, but the line between aggressiveness and obnoxiousness can be a thin one. It is never to your advantage to cross it.

When a presenter comes to your table, take the opportunity to point out your company's outstanding qualities and the special repertory, productions, events, or features which you feel will meet the presenter's needs. The presenter will want to know when the company will be in his area, and the fee. Have your answers prepared in advance for these types of questions. Invite the presenter to sit down and watch your videotape or slide presentation, or listen to your audio tape.

Following Up Leads

Seldom do booking meetings result in any firm presenter commitments; in most cases, the best you can hope for is an "indication of interest," an opening for talking further in the future. After chatting with a prospective presenter at your table, mark his name on the list of conference attendees and briefly summarize your discussion. After the conference, send the presenter a friendly note thanking him for stopping by and answering any questions which you were unable to deal with on the spot. Enclose any requested follow-up materials, along with a full set of the company's basic booking materials—even if the presenter took a set away from your initial meeting. Two or three weeks after the conference, follow up the note with a phone call.

When to Attend Booking Meetings

Early in a company's existence, attendance at national or regional booking conferences far away from home base is not mandatory or even necessarily wise, considering the expense. For example, it could cost a New York–based company more than $2,000 to send a representative to the Western Alliance of Arts Administrators' conference. This would include expenses for membership in the organization sponsoring the meeting, a fee for a table, creating a table display, transportation, hotel, and food. In this case attendance would only be a sound investment if the New York company projects that its product will be of major potential interest to a group of West Coast presenters. The same rule holds for any company considering attendance at a distant conference.

Companies that tour primarily in one region or that are just getting started might be well advised not to tackle the national meetings too soon. National presenters—those with larger-than-average auditoriums and budgets—are probably looking for companies with an established artistic track record. In addition, they tend to expect not only a high level of product excellence, but top-notch management expertise as well. Without both these elements, a young company—if it manages to obtain such a booking—runs the risk of acquiring a less than stellar reputation on the national scene before it can get its feet wet.

National touring can be expensive if you are unable to route really tightly—a more difficult task for young, relatively unknown groups. If your company is among the latter, you might be better served financially and artistically by limiting your attendance to meetings in your own region or surrounding regions and postponing attendance at national meetings until you have acquired a major reputation.

Still, if you can afford them and if you think the presenters who attend are viable prospects for your company, booking meetings can be rewarding.

Major Presenters of National and Regional Booking Meetings

The following organizations should be contacted individually for the dates, times, costs, and locations of particular meetings:

Association of Performing Arts Presenters (APAP), 1112 16th Street, NW, Suite 400, Washington, D.C. 20036, 202/833-2787, FAX 202/833-1543. APAP holds a national meeting in New York in December. Membership includes presenters of many college and university concert series as well as community arts series presenters.

National Association for Campus Activities (NACA), 13 Harbison Way, Columbia, SC 29212-3401, 803/732-6222, 800/845-2338, FAX 803/749-1047. NACA holds its annual national conference in February. The location varies from year to year, but the Arts and Lectures Conference is a regular feature. Attendees are primarily students accompanied by campus activities advisors. The presenting organizations at these meetings have smaller budgets than presenters at the other booking conferences, and many new companies with low fees have done well here. Some NACA members book only a term ahead, so this might be a good place to pick up a fill-in date. In addition to the national meeting, NACA also sponsors a series of regional meetings around the country in the fall.

Western Alliance of Arts Administrators (WAAA), 44 Page Street, Suite 604B, San Francisco, CA 94102, 415/621-4400, FAX 415/621-2533. The Western Alliance holds a regional meeting of APAP-type presenters in the western states, usually during September. Many WAAA presenters do not come east for the national APAP meeting in December.

International Society for the Performing Arts (ISPA), 2920 Fuller Avenue NE, Suite 205, Grand Rapids, MI 49505-3458, 616/364-3000, FAX 616/364-9010. The presenters in this group tend to be uniformly larger and include an international membership from Canada, Europe, and Asia. It is usually the largest companies or managements that attend this conference. They meet in New York in December just prior to the APAP conference, and many remain for the other meeting. Only one day of the conference is devoted to resource room activity. The remainder of the time is spent in exchanging ideas at a variety of sessions. ISPA also sponsors an international meeting held in a different country each June. Some sites have included Paris, Vienna, and Sydney.

Southern Arts Exchange (SAE), Southern Arts Federation, 181 14th Street NE, Suite 400, Atlanta, GA 30309, 404/874-7244, FAX 404/873-2148. The Southern Arts Federation is the regional organization for the states of North Carolina, South Carolina, Georgia, Florida, Tennessee, Kentucky, Mississippi, Alabama, and Louisiana. Attendees have primarily been mid- and small-size presenters from these states. The fall meeting traditionally alternates between Atlanta and another southern city.

New England Presenters (NEP), 2 Curry Hicks, University of Massachusetts, Amherst, MA 01003, 413/545-0190. NEP, in conjunction with the Mid-Atlantic Arts Foundation, runs a regional booking conference in the fall that encompasses presenting organizations from Maine down through West Virginia. The meeting site switches yearly between a New England site and a site in the Mid-Atlantic region.

Arts Midwest, 528 Hennepin Avenue, Suite 310, Minneapolis, MN 55403, 612/341-0755, FAX 612/341-0902. The Midwest conference is held in September of each year and is run by Arts Midwest and the Mid-America Arts Alliance. The site switches yearly between the regions. Arts Midwest includes the states of Iowa, Minnesota, North Dakota, South Dakota, Wisconsin, Illinois, Indiana, Michigan, and Ohio. Mid-America covers Arkansas, Kansas, Oklahoma, Missouri, Nebraska, and Texas.

Attendees at the regional meetings tend to be medium- to larger-size presenters. However, there is usually a contingent of smaller organizations from the general vicinity of the conference location.

Arts Northwest, P.O. Box 55877, Seattle, WA 98155, 206/365-4143, FAX 206/365-8618. Arts Northwest sponsors a yearly conference at a site that rotates among the states of Oregon, Washington, and Idaho. Attendees tend to be smaller presenting organizations and regionally based companies/artists.

American Symphony Orchestra League (ASOL), 1156 15th Street NW, Suite 800, Washington, D.C. 20005, 202/776-0212, FAX 202-776-0224. The American Symphony Orchestra League holds its national conference each year in June. The site is alternated among various cities in the U.S. and Canada. Attendees include musical directors, conductors, managers, board members, and others working in the field. There are separate conference sessions devoted to a variety of topics, and a room is set up where managements and artists can meet with those people who hire soloists, music groups, dance companies, etc., to perform with orchestras. This is a very important booking meeting for any musical solo artist or group.

CHAPTER 8

Contracts

O nce you have a booking, the presenter will ask you to send a contract. What do you send? To arrive at a sound and reasonable contract, you will need expert legal advice. In many cities you can find low-cost expertise through nearby Volunteer Lawyers for the Arts groups.

A session with an attorney will be a good investment. Bring this book along and have your lawyer review this chapter and the sample contracts supplied. Two sample contracts are included in Appendix A, one with a separate technical rider and one where the company's technical requirements are an integral part of the contract. Although each is used by a performing company, neither will be exactly right for you. Your company's contractual needs will derive from your own unique profile.

Inform the attorney of your particular goals, needs, and problems as you have defined them and then let him draft an appropriate document. Review the draft contract carefully and raise questions about it; the attorney may have missed something you wanted, or you may have forgotten to raise a particular point during your initial consultation.

Your contract should spell out exactly what the company will do for the presenter (performances and other activities) and exactly what you expect in return. If your company has special requirements (artistic or practical), they must be specified in the written agreement.

You should hesitate before accepting a situation in which you are signing a contract written by the presenter. You want to insure that the interests of your group are primary; and the presenter's contract will certainly not be drafted with your interests in mind. Consequently, the company should send out its own contract. Some university systems require that their contract be used. If this is the case, insist that your own contract also be signed by the presenter and made part of the presenter's contract. Although the result may be a crazy-quilt of sometimes contradictory terms, it is better than having a completely one-sided, pro-presenter agreement.

Elements of the Contract

Regardless of the type or size of performing company, there are a number of standard elements that all contracts should contain:

1. The date of the agreement;
2. The company name, address, phone number, and primary contact person;
3. The presenter name, address, phone number, and primary contact person;
4. A list with dates and times of the performances and other residency activities the company has agreed to provide;
5. The location of the theatre and other spaces in which performances and other residency activities will take place;
6. The company's fee; the time and manner of payment(s); and a guarantee that there will be no taxes, union charges, or other surprise deductions from the fee when it is paid;
7. A clause setting out the program and/or publicity material the company will provide, and describing the presenter's obligations concerning both (e.g., the presenter will pay for printing of programs, but guarantees that the text will read exactly as it appears in the company's program copy);
8. A clause indicating that the presenter will supply—at its expense—theatre, performance, and other residency spaces that are properly insured, lit, cleaned, heated or cooled as required by the circumstances, with floors suitable for the company's needs, and suitable dressing and storage rooms for company personnel and its costumes and equipment, and an adequate "front of house" staff (e.g., ushers, ticket sellers, and ticket takers);
9. A requirement that the theatre and other residency areas be clear and ready for the company to set up and that no other activity interfere with residency activities;

10. A clause setting out whatever crew, equipment, and other facilities the presenter is required to provide, at its expense, to supplement that with which the company travels, including a careful statement of what must be set up and ready when the company arrives;

11. An "Act of God" clause which releases the company from liability for failure to perform if such failure is caused by an event beyond its control; and

12. A detailed description of all technical requirements and a commitment by the presenter to meet them without any charge to the company. This may be an integral part of the contract or may be attached through a section at the end of the contract—but still a part of it—called a *technical rider*. If a separate technical rider is attached, both the contract and technical rider must be signed.

Some presenters request that the contract contain a contingency clause. Such clauses specify that the contract is contingent upon receipt by the presenter of funding to underwrite the company's performance/residency from specific private touring programs or their regional, state, or local arts agency. Unless the presenter receives the specified funding, the contract is not valid or is negotiated. Each company must decide during negotiations whether it will agree to include a presenter's request for a contingency clause.

Contract Negotiations

Normally, the company mails to the presenter two or more unsigned copies of the contract. The presenter reviews the contract, makes any changes necessary from his viewpoint (by initialing and dating the deletions or additions on each copy), signs all copies in the space provided, and returns them to the company.

Do not be surprised if your contract comes back with clauses crossed out or new ones added. You will routinely find yourself negotiating everything from acceptable stage size to the mode of payment (i.e., certified check, cash, etc.). Decide which elements of your contract must stand as drafted and which areas can be modified.

The most troublesome (and potentially expensive) areas of misunderstanding often are those concerning the number of on-stage technical and rehearsal hours to be paid for by the presenter. Be realistic about your needs and, if the final contract requires you to pay for crew overtime or some other extra charge, take care not to incur it.

If you really need the booking, you will have to be more tolerant of contract changes than if the date is of marginal importance to you. Telephone the presenter to discuss any deletions or changes he has indicated. Stand up for those items the company truly needs, but do not be unreasonable. Where changes are acceptable, initial and date them, sign the contracts, retain one original, and send one original to the presenter.

As your company gains experience in touring, you will continue to confront new situations which will suggest ways to tighten your contract, and new clauses should then be added or existing clauses modified. For now, a careful review of the sample contracts included in this book and of the various clauses they contain will give you an idea of the types of problems others have experienced and which you should anticipate.

Look upon the contract as the place for your organization and the presenter to exchange information on mutual needs. While the fee promised by a presenter and other matters you have negotiated are no doubt very important to your organization, it is unlikely that you will want to litigate if the presenter were to cancel your date or renege on some terms and conditions. The same is true from the presenter's side.

Letters of Agreement

When you agree to send the presenter a contract, ask him how long it will take to process and return. If it is going to take more than four weeks, you should issue a letter of agreement along with the contract.

A letter of agreement is used when one or both parties is unable to sign a contract immediately. A letter of agreement, usually a letter from the company to the presenter, is just as binding as a contract, but typically covers only the main points of the agreement. It states that the company will perform certain services at a place, time, date and for a fee which are specified. A sample letter of agreement appears in Appendix A.

A presenter should be able to sign a letter of agreement and return it to the company in ten days to two weeks maximum. Once in hand, a letter of agreement gives a company written assurance that the presenter has agreed to the engagement, even though it may be quite some time before the contract is signed.

Nailing Down the Contract: Getting Agreements Signed

Most often, delays occur when a presenting organization has a cumbersome bureaucracy through which the contract must travel. In some university systems, for example, the contract for an engagement may need approval from the state attorney general's office, a process taking several months. Sometimes, even when there has not been a long delay, there can nevertheless be a rush to meet a regional or state arts agency touring program deadline which requires a signed agreement between the parties to be funded. Be firm about your need to receive a signed letter of agreement and/or contract from the presenter in a reasonable time. Be wary of any presenter who says he will not sign a letter of agreement and cannot return your contract shortly. You may be running the risk of a cancellation in the middle of your tour several months down the road.

Call your presenters on a regular basis until you receive signed contracts. Some companies go so far as to insert a clause into their contract which states that it is valid only for a limited period of time and, if not signed and returned within that time, becomes void. But that is probably extreme. Instead, the company should work closely with the presenter to monitor the process and be sure the letter of agreement and/or the contract are dealt with in a timely manner.

CHAPTER 9

Promotion

Since presenters must cover most of their presentation costs at the box office, one of their major concerns is selling tickets. Generally, a sold-out house means a happy presenter. When the house does not sell well, the beleaguered presenter tends to blame the company. And success or failure at the box office quickly becomes part of the company's "word of mouth."

Of course, an experimental music group cannot rightfully be expected to draw the same kind of house as Itzhak Perlman, and there are presenters who—often within the context of a well-rounded season—are willing to support new or controversial work of outstanding artistic merit fully aware that box office returns may be modest. Still, a responsible presenter must attempt to get the best possible return from each company he has chosen to present. Only companies willing to share this responsibility can expect the presenter to recommend them to his colleagues and, perhaps, invite them back.

Promotion encompasses the various efforts of the presenter and the company to generate public interest in the company's engagement and thereby to stimulate ticket sales. In most cases, the presenter is in charge of these efforts in his own area, but the company must supply him with the necessary tools. Attractive posters, fliers, and newspaper ads, high-quality photographs, and interesting press stories are extremely important.

Also effective are personal appearances by company members on local television and radio talk shows, intriguing radio commercials and, if the company can afford them, well-produced television spots.

The Marketing Plan

Whatever tools are used, they cumulatively must help to establish a unique, coherent public identity for the company. This can be achieved only through a carefully conceived and executed marketing plan.

Long before promotional materials are expected to arrive at a presenter's office, a company's promotion process begins with the development of an overall marketing plan for the season—which includes performances both at home and on tour. In constructing a marketing plan, a company defines who its market is, the message that needs to be communicated, and the media which will best carry the message. The plan typically centers on a common theme or concept which is reflected in all the materials used to sell the company during a one-year period.

An opera or theatre company may derive its unifying theme from a particular production or series of productions. A dance company would probably emphasize the type of dance in which it specializes. The central focus for an orchestra might be its well-known musical director. Other themes might tie into a notable achievement or event, such as a milestone anniversary or a new facility. By using a common theme, a company creates and reinforces a unique image in the eyes of the public.

A concept that works well graphically makes a concise, positive statement about the art the company produces every time the graphic appears. This continually reinforces the public's image of the company. For example, the first visual impression made on a prospective audience member by a television p.s.a. may be fleeting. However, each successive impression—through newspaper ads, posters, and fliers using the same logo, type style, and overall visual treatment—reinforces the company image and, if exciting or interesting enough, will convince people to purchase tickets.

Advance planning also saves money. Because the company's stationery, press release paper, souvenir books, programs, and booking brochure will all be based on the same basic visual elements (type style, photographs and artwork, logo, etc.), these items can easily be ordered at the same time, which results in considerable savings in typesetting and printing costs. With only a few changes, the same posters and fliers used for a home season can frequently be used on tour. The same is true of ad mats, and radio and TV spots.

Creating the Promotional Materials

To create a unified set of promotional materials, your company might approach an ad agency in your home city. The agency may even take your company on as a "pro-bono" client. Understandably, however, if the firm is not being paid, your work is unlikely to receive top priority. Consequently, you should begin to conceive and produce your materials well in advance of need. Deadlines must be reasonable and mutually acceptable with the agency, and the overall timetable should insure that the company's expectations are met without agency personnel feeling that you are taking advantage of them. (See Chapter 4 for other ideas about where materials could be produced.)

Company pictures—which the ad agency needs to do its work—should be taken by a professional photographer with previous experience in photographing your art form. Five to ten good pictures will suffice for a small to mid-size touring company, and will probably be useful for a year or more in newspapers, posters, fliers, and the booking brochure. As many of the pictures as possible should relate directly to the productions you are presenting; others (rehearsal shots, home season productions, etc.) can be used in newspaper features to provide a context for the tour performances.

In general, the pictures should have high contrast. Figures in dark costumes photographed against a light background, or vice versa, reproduce sharply. Avoid taking group shots which include more than four people; newspapers usually do not use them. Newspapers have greatly increased their use of color photographs, so you should also supply a variety of 35mm color slides with high contrast.

A photographer will be able to do his best work if you invite him to rehearsal and performance prior to the photo session. Forethought should be given to the particular scenes or portion of a work which can be captured most effectively by the camera. For instance, with a well-known play, opera, or story ballet, you would probably feature those artists who play leading characters.

Performance photos are usually best shot in a special dress rehearsal called for this purpose, where the photographer can have the stage lighting set in a way that produces the best pictures. This will enable him to avoid the often difficult task of trying to take good pictures using the lighting designed for the production. Studio sessions allow considerable control over the subject, and work well for theatre, opera, and music. However, for a movement oriented art form like dance, posed studio pictures can look stilted.

The press releases, bios, company history, and feature stories included in the company's press kit should be written by a professional—or at least by someone who writes well. If your company does not have a public relations person on staff, you may need to hire a free-lancer. Pulling together all the facts he will need to do the work will make his job easier and faster—and thereby save you money.

Radio spots are relatively inexpensive to produce, and you may be able to obtain free use of recording and duplicating facilities from a local station. A staff deejay may even be willing to serve as your announcer. Producing television spots is more involved, but again, a local broadcaster may be willing to help, particularly if you already have some video footage of your company. Four or five slides with a script can also be used to put together a public service announcement.

What the Presenter Needs: Basic Promotional Materials

A company should be able to supply a presenter with a press kit containing the following basic materials for publicizing a performance:

1. Five to ten different black and white 8" × 10" glossies, five 35mm color slides;
2. A one-page bio on each of the major artistic figures in the company (i.e., the artistic director, the general director, etc.);
3. Brief bios of other artists associated with the company;
4. A description of the company and a company history describing major artistic events, awards, and tours of special note (this material should be kept to one or two pages);
5. Sample press releases, feature stories, and a script for radio commercials;
6. 35mm color transparencies of the company's name and logo, superimposed over an excellent production shot, for television public service announcements.

In addition to the press kit, you should supply the presenter with posters. Be sure to leave several inches of white space at the bottom of your standard poster or flier so that the presenter can insert information such as the name of the theatre at which the company is appearing, performance dates, ticket prices, etc.

Extra materials which are useful but not essential for a presenter to have include:

1. Fliers;
2. Thirty-second tape cassettes for radio p.s.a.'s with time allowed for the presenter to overdub performance and ticket information;
3. Thirty- or sixty-second videocassettes of television spots for p.s.a.'s or paid ads; and
4. Ad mats in various standard sizes, with room left for the presenter to insert performance information.

Be sure to send the presenter a plan for how and when to use all the above materials. The more material the company gives to presenters, the more control it has over its own image. For this reason, some companies even print their own programs.

Press Releases: Stimulating Interest in Your Company

Press releases should be written so that they can be used at key points during the presenter's promotion of the company. The first release announces the upcoming engagement. This might be used during the previous season to announce the next season's subscription campaign, or if the presenter sells only single tickets, as late as twelve weeks before performance. The second release might announce the opening of the box office. Another release would be designed for use during the week of performance. The information in the releases can also be used by a creative presenter drafting his own releases tailored to his particular needs.

Each release is designed to reiterate the who, what, when, where, and how of your event. Who is the company? What does it do? When will the performance happen? Where will it happen? And how can you buy tickets? The release should begin with a headline and lead paragraph which attracts the reader's attention and stimulates his interest. This should be followed by the information about who the company is and what it does.

The feature stories supplied by the company will form the basis of articles that appear just prior to performance, perhaps in an entertainment column or the Sunday arts or leisure section. The type of features you create will depend on the nature of your company and what you have chosen to offer on tour. To be effective, try to present story ideas with an especially exciting human interest element—perhaps your company uses some sort of unusual technology or technique, plays out-of-the-ordinary instruments, or performs the work of a new playwright. Features on a string quartet might include one story on the members of the group and how they work and rehearse with one another; another might discuss the special all-Beethoven program they will perform. The presenter will need several feature stories, a different one (with appropriate photographs) for each publication in his area.

Establishing Limits on What You Provide to the Presenter

Many companies specify contractually the types of promotional materials they will supply to the presenter and in what quantities. If a presenter wants more of a particular item, he is charged an additional fee equal to the cost of its production. Other companies, under the assumption that a presenter will ask only for what is needed, supply whatever quantity of material is requested. If your company chooses to limit the quantity of materials supplied without charge, it is important that every presenter be assured a "reasonable" number of each item. For most presenters 100 posters and 500 fliers are adequate. You should charge extra only if a presenter's request for materials is unusual.

Some companies absorb the postage costs for sending their materials. Others specify in the contract that posters, fliers, and other items shipped in quantity be sent to the presenter's facility collect. Each company sets its own policy on these matters, but finances are usually a major influence. Newer, less well-financed companies often opt for the "collect-on-delivery" option.

Timing

Presenters must receive promotional materials in a timely manner. It is crucial to your success. Many presenters need an initial press kit early in the spring of the performance year preceding the year in which the company is to perform (for example, in March for a performance that takes place between September and the following June). This lead time is necessary because your company's performances will frequently be packaged as part of a series of events and sold initially by subscription in the spring.

The first materials you send out should include pictures, a press packet (releases, features, camera-ready logo, bios, company description and history), and reviews. If you cannot supply specific information on the touring program you will be offering during the following season, the presenter must at least be supplied with some type of graphic representation of your work, along with favorable reviews of previous productions. For example, an excellent representational drawing of the two leading characters in *Madame Butterfly* could substitute for a production shot.

Posters, fliers, ad mats, and radio and television spots should be received by the presenting organization no less than twelve weeks prior to the company's arrival. This timetable normally allows the presenter plenty of time to place your materials in the local media. Be sure to check with the presenter to see if these materials are needed even earlier.

Although late receipt of promotional materials is one of the most frequent gripes among presenters, it is not enough for you to send out your materials and assume that your job is over. You need to try to make certain that the presenter makes adequate use of them. One hundred fabulous posters, if tucked away in the mailroom or in the corner of someone's office, will not help sell your performance.

Presenters vary widely in their promotional abilities. Some are conscientious and well organized; others need to be prodded. Some lack experience and are too timid to ask for help, while others are eager for suggestions and pointers. Remember, to a certain extent, the company will be blamed if its performances do not sell, so it is your responsibility to see that your engagement is properly promoted.

Send the presenter a set of week-by-week promotional recommendations broken down by task (mailings, poster and flier distribution, etc.). This will give the presenting organization a tangible plan to follow. Your schedule will probably be discarded by more experienced presenters but could be especially valuable for organizations which are just beginning to present and have not yet evolved a marketing strategy and schedule of their own. Even with established presenters, however, it helps to make your expectations clear and explicit. Plans differ from one company to the next, and most presenters will adapt your suggested schedule to fit their own marketing methods. Each situation should be appraised early so that you can reasonably estimate what the presenter's schedule will be and how you can best work with it.

Following Up with the Presenter Before You Arrive

After sending your materials and suggested timetable, check with the presenter to make certain they have arrived and to find out if additional materials are needed. Although you will talk with the presenter frequently as your performance time approaches, begin to make contact regarding promotion early—about twelve weeks before the engagement. Check with the presenter at least every three weeks or so just to see how things are going. By establishing and maintaining a close relationship with the presenting organization, you will be demonstrating your eagerness to help make the performance a success. This will enable you to earn the presenter's cooperation, putting you in a good position to discreetly find out if they have run into any problems and need your help.

These inquiries should always be handled tactfully as part of your regular discussions with the presenter regarding final plans, logistics, and programming. There is also no harm in calling and asking, for example, whether anyone in the general public has commented on the posters ("We have had a lot of positive response in other cities.").

This gives the presenter an opportunity to tell you that "the posters are not up yet," or that "ten people saw them downtown and said they were great," or whatever. If the posters have not yet been put up, you can (diplomatically) reiterate how important it is to use them and to adhere to the media schedule, again referring to past successes in other cities. If things are not going well, listen to the presenter's problems, offer encouragement, and make suggestions based on previous experiences.

A few companies have room in their budgets for an advance person, whom they send to each tour location prior to the company's arrival. The advance person not only looks over the facility but also meets with the presenter to check on the progress of the promotional efforts. Sometimes he can do interviews on television or radio talk shows to stimulate public interest in the company's performance.

Media Activities: Planning for Your Arrival

Make certain that at least some of your company members will be available for media appearances as soon as you arrive in a city or town. Arrange in advance with the presenter to have someone on the early morning TV and radio news and talk shows. Know which members of your group enjoy and are most effective in this kind of situation, and, if possible, rotate the individuals who appear on various shows. Brief your artists in advance about what will be expected of them in each appearance. They may be asked to perform a piece of music, an aria, or a scene as part of an interview. They should have some idea of how long the interview will take and whether they need to wear something special. It is also helpful to know who the interviewer or host will be.

If possible, have a video segment of a particularly exciting performance or specially-shot studio piece that can be shown as part of a TV interview. Telephone interviews taped in advance for use in radio broadcasts or as the basis for newspaper features are easy to arrange and should be encouraged. In most cases, the local media will be eager for material of this kind.

Residency activities, if your company does them, provide a useful focus for local media involvement prior to a performance. For instance, if you have scheduled a lecture-demonstration at a high school the morning of a performance day, the presenter should be able to persuade local television crews to attend and tape a segment for broadcast during the evening news, just a few hours prior to the performance. Media events of this kind are very important in selling tickets, and the longer a company stays in one place, the more of this kind of coverage can be obtained. But they must be arranged by the presenter well in advance of the company's arrival, as part of the overall schedule.

Quality and Cooperation Breed Success

Promotional materials are a precious resource and one of a company's most important investments. The manner in which they are designed, produced, and distributed will have a significant impact upon your success on the road. Of course, no amount of promotional expertise can disguise a mediocre artistic product once the curtain goes up. But if your company is to have the chance to demonstrate its excellence, it is essential that there be good materials, a meticulous plan, and a cooperative spirit between company and presenter.

CHAPTER 10

Tour Management

All tours are subject to Murphy's Law: anything that can go wrong will. Consequently, the company must make every effort to anticipate any problems which might arise and iron out the rough spots before leaving home base. The same degree of vigilance must be maintained throughout the tour, for no matter how conscientious and thorough your preventive efforts, there are bound to be problems which you cannot foresee.

To be sure that a tour is as trouble-free as possible requires meticulous attention to detail. Every arrangement—for travel, accommodations, and production—must be checked and rechecked by the tour manager. A healthy, compulsive personality will stand him in good stead. The tour manager's job is to create an atmosphere in which the performer is free to focus all his energies on the stage without having to worry about whether he will be able to find a diner open after the performance or to cash his check so he can send the rent home on time.

Fulfilling the Functions of a Tour Manager

Throughout this chapter—to simplify the presentation of material—the person responsible for the company's tour preparations and for overseeing tour administration on the road is referred to as the *tour manager*. In your organization the title may be different (*company manager* is a frequent variation), or the responsibilities may be divided among two or more individuals. Perhaps one person is in charge of tour preparations at home, and another travels with the performers. In some companies, only the preparatory work completed prior to departure is handled by management, with the artists handling their own daily dealings with presenters and tour logistics. Most solo instrumentalists, singers, and chamber music groups operate this way, for example, while dance, theatre, and opera companies generally have a nonperformer available to assume some of these responsibilities, even if it is simply the stage manager.

Sometimes, particularly in smaller companies, a tour may be booked and managed by a single individual. But even when different people are in charge of each area—which is most frequently the case—everyone must work closely together. Ultimately, whatever arrangements the booking person makes will fall on the tour manager's shoulders to administer. Ideally, both should be in constant communication. Each has a definite stake in how the other does his job.

Always, the exigencies are the same: everything must be minutely planned; every conceivable crisis must be anticipated; and if an inconceivable crisis arises (it will!), it must be averted as swiftly and smoothly as possible.

Mutual Cooperation and Consideration

Two parties are represented in the booking contract: the company and the presenter. Their respective goals may be parallel, but they are not always the same—sometimes they conflict. The tour manager, even though he works for the company, must keep both parties happy. A happy company means good, energetic performances. A happy presenter means good word of mouth—and future bookings.

To keep people happy you must understand them—their similarities and their differences. In managing a tour, you must understand that presenter and artist are identical in one major area: both want a successful engagement. However, the contrasting ways in which each may view success, the different pressures experienced in striving for it, and the unique expectations and needs which each brings to the enterprise are much more numerous.

The Stress of Being on Tour

For company members, the pressures of touring are both professional and personal. Working and living together in extremely close proximity for days, weeks, even months on end can create tensions among even the most easygoing and mutually respectful performers. Long hours of traveling between engagements and irregular eating and sleeping schedules can be enormously taxing. And constant exposure to new audiences, new places, and new stages, although perhaps invigorating at first, can rapidly lose its novelty. Frequently, artists are called upon to give their best performance under less than ideal conditions. With all of these pressures already built in, a light plot not hung when the company arrives for the evening performance or no means of transportation to get to the only restaurant in town open after ten can be more than a little unsettling.

The Pressures of Presenting

Presenters have problems of their own, many of them having to do with money. Whether he represents a college or an independent community arts organization, the presenter will have invested a large chunk of his organization's budget in your appearance. Usually he must not only pay the company a set fee regardless of how many (or how few) people come to the event they have scheduled, but he must also pay for advertising in local newspapers, radio, and television. He supplies the facility in which the company performs, hires the crew, the ushers, and the ticket-takers, prints the programs, and on and on. In the end, he will examine the box office figures with great interest; whatever altruistic motives he may have had for presenting your company's work in his community, his colleagues—and his superiors—will, in most cases, judge his success or failure by the numbers.

The Need for Diplomacy

Any tour manager who has ever produced his own company's home season will know already the hassles and expenses involved in this sort of enterprise. Where such experience is lacking, the manager must work hard to understand the presenter's point of view. But however it is accomplished, cooperation is essential: everybody benefits from its presence; everybody suffers from its absence.

This is not to say that you should not stand up for the things the company needs and wants, as enumerated in the contract. But in most cases, a request tempered by tact and empathy will be much more effective than an angry, contract-waving outburst. The tour manager is the company ambassador and liaison, not the secretary of defense.

Hopefully, of course, the presenter and his staff will return the favor and make an equal effort to understand the company's needs and pressures, treating their guests with as much consideration as they receive. Potentially difficult situations on the road have often been transformed into rewarding experiences for everyone by the unflagging efforts of conscientious presenters to make performers and crews feel welcome and appreciated. Certainly, presenters who extend themselves to this degree have a right to expect the company's eager reciprocation. But a company must never take a presenter's willingness—-or ability—to empathize as a given. And the tour manager must be willing to shoulder full responsibility for keeping the channels open.

The Presenter's Liason

A company usually works primarily with two people at the presenting organization: the technical director of the performance facility and the presenter-administrator, the person responsible for administering the details of the performance/residency on the presenting organization's behalf. In some organizations there may be more than two contacts—-for example, the presenter may have a separate staff member handling public relations or supervising the teaching part of a residency. As with the term *tour manager, technical director* is not always the precise designation given to the person in charge of a theatre's technical facilities, and *presenter-administrator* is seldom anyone's actual title, but has been used here as a descriptive term.

Constant contact with both the technical director and the presenter-administrator is crucial to the success of a touring performance. Normally, the tour manager works closely with the presenter-administrator, and the stage manager (or the company's own technical director) works closely with the theatre's technical director. To be successful, however, all four must be in constant communication with each other.

The Performance/Residency Checklist

The exchange of information among tour manager, presenter-administrator, stage manager, and technical director will include details of the arrangements for all the components of a performance/residency. One effective way to keep track of these details is through a performance/residency checklist like the one shown in Appendix B.

The checklist should be attached to the file that you create to hold all pertinent material for each booking—correspondence, the signed contract, technical data, questionnaires, etc. This will enable you to note carefully each step of the company-presenter communications process—sending and receiving materials, post-contract negotiations on certain matters, scheduling, accommodations, etc. In this way, the progress of your planning is easily visible at a glance. (A wall chart encompassing an entire tour can supplement the checklist and provide you with needed data without referring to the file.)

The first page of the checklist should contain the phone numbers and addresses of the presenter and his technical director, followed by a list of all the major materials and communications to be sent to both. The list should be ordered according to the approximate chronology in which the materials should be sent. Provide space to the right of each item to note the date it was mailed (or the phone call placed) and by whom (initials), the confirmation or return date, comments, and who was sent a copy, on what date.

Provide space on additional pages to summarize various arrangements as they are confirmed. These include hotel and travel information, scheduling, and repertory and casting. By reviewing each item on the checklist, it is easy to see how each component of the performance/residency is administered.

The Technical Questionnaire

Many of the difficulties between presenter and company arise because of technical problems: what equipment a presenter can or cannot provide, the condition of the stage, the masking, the dressing rooms, and the like. One way to forestall these problems, or to keep them to a minimum, is to send each presenter a technical questionnaire that solicits specific information about the theatre or space in which the company will perform. The technical questionnaire shown in Appendix C includes most of the questions you will need to ask about a space.

Finding out early on that a presenter has a splintery stage will enable a dance company not carrying its own dance floor to negotiate with a presenter to provide one. And learning that the entire lighting inventory consists of one follow spot and ten fresnels will enable a theatre company to negotiate with the presenter to rent or borrow the equipment necessary to present the production properly as specified in the contract. On the other hand, if this knowledge is not obtained in time, surprises can lead to hostilities.

While the person who has booked the company's tour will have tried to ascertain, before agreeing to go to contract, such basics as stage dimensions, a question to a presenter about the lighting equipment is sometimes met with a response like, "Well it's o.k." Obviously, what is "o.k." for the presenter—even if it has worked for another touring group—may not be adequate for your company. Groups to whom a theatre's technical specifications and equipment are truly critical to its ability to perform should check out the facility carefully prior to signing the contract. In fact, as suggested later in Chapter 12, they should insist on receiving a completed technical questionnaire from the presenter before signing a contract. Another option is to have someone from the company's staff (preferably the stage manager) call and get basic technical information directly over the phone from the presenter's technical director. There are many companies, however, which decide to perform with whatever equipment and in whatever physical situation is involved.

In some cases, you may have to arrange to bring some of the equipment yourself—-supplementary lights and an extra dimmer board if important effects are otherwise unattainable, or in the case of a dance company, portable flooring, if a consistent, smooth surface is essential. The larger the company—-and the more well-heeled—the more feasible this option becomes.

Except as noted above, the technical questionnaire is usually sent to the presenter with the contract or shortly after it is signed, or in the late spring (see Tour Manager's Timetable in Exhibit 11) for bookings during the following season. The technical questionnaire should be sent directly to the technical director, after you have informed the presenter-administrator that you plan to do so. A company usually needs to have a completed technical questionnaire in its hands at least sixteen weeks (preferably longer) before a performance. The tour manager and stage manager should discuss each questionnaire as it is returned from the presenter to spot any potential problems and to communicate these as soon as possible to both the technical director and the presenter-administrator.

Performance/Residency Information Packet

Concurrent with sending out the technical questionnaire, the presenter-administrator should be sent a performance/residency information packet. As shown in Appendix B, the packet consists of three items: an activities information sheet, a presenter's questionnaire, and a residency calendar, if a residency is involved.

The Activities Information Sheet

The activities information sheet is designed to help the presenter get the most out of your visit to his community without overtaxing the company's energies and resources. It describes the various activities the company offers and notes the amount of time needed to prepare for and conduct each of them, any special technical requirements (such as a microphone for lecture demonstrations), and the number of activities the company can handle during engagements of various lengths.

Most experienced presenters will know exactly what activities they would like in addition to performance; others will look to the company for guidance. Review the activities list with the uncertain presenter. Let

EXHIBIT 11

Tour Manager's Timetable

JANUARY	FEBRUARY	MARCH	APRIL
	Contract sent to presenter. Tech Questionnaire to Technical Director. Basic P.R. kit and glossies to presenter.	Communication with Presenter-Administrator and Tech Director.	Contract returned and countersigned. Send P.R. Request Form, Presenter Questionnaire, Performance/Res. Memo, and calendar.
MAY	**JUNE**	**JULY**	**AUGUST**
Follow up request for all materials before summer vacation.		All requested information from presenter received. Send requested P.R. materials. Begin making air/ ground trans. and hotel reservations.	Meet with Artistic staff and Stage Manager to determine program, O.K. residency activities. Program copy.
SEPTEMBER	**OCTOBER**	**NOVEMBER**	**DECEMBER**
Final schedule activities and travel. Payroll arrangements. Send light plot, crew letter. Confirmation letter.	Reconfirm all air/ ground trans. Reconfirm local trans., hotel, banking. Final schedule to company. Engagement!	Follow-up phone call. How did performance/ residency go?	
JANUARY	**FEBRUARY**	**MARCH**	**APRIL**
MAY	**JUNE**	**JULY**	**AUGUST**

him know what has worked in similar situations, but be sure to offer alternatives. From the presenter's responses to your suggestions, you will begin to develop a better understanding of the interests and expectations of his particular constituents.

Still, in your eagerness to please, you must avoid making promises you cannot keep. Whatever package of activities you agree to, the company must be able to do them—and do them well—within the time allotted and without undue stress and strain on performers and technicians. Be prepared to explain to a first-time presenter why the number of residency activities the company can manage in a single day is limited or why, in some cases, performers will not be available at all on performance days. Often, inexperienced presenters have no idea how much energy and concentration a two-hour performance requires of an artist ("After all, most folks work a full eight-hour day.").

Any necessary special arrangements—such as a late meal after the performance, when all the restaurants in town may be closed—should be requested during these discussions. If you take the time to explain the company's needs well in advance of the engagement, and if you are honest about what the artists can and cannot do, there will be fewer last-minute surprises for everyone.

The Presenter's Questionnaire

The questionnaire portion of the performance/residency information packet asks the presenter-administrator for the following:
1. The names, addresses, and phone numbers of everyone in the presenting organization who will have anything to do with any component of the performance/residency (including home numbers for last-minute emergencies!);
2. Information on hotels and motels convenient to the performance space;
3. A list of restaurants that are open late, laundromats, local physicians, and banks;
4. A map of the city or town and the surrounding area.

The Residency Calendar

The final item in the packet is a blank calendar on which the presenter indicates the activities selected, where each will take place, and at what time (Exhibit 12). The schedule suggested by the presenter should be reviewed by the tour manager, the stage manager, and the artistic director, after which any changes should be discussed with the presenter. Once a final agreement has been reached, note the scheduled activities on the

EXHIBIT 12

The Residency Calendar

DATE/DAY	ACTIVITY	TIME BEGIN/END	PLACE BLDG./ROOM	STUDENTS/AUDIENCE NUMBER/AGE/LEVEL
DAY 1 Thursay, Nov. 17	Lec Dem	10–11 a.m.	Auditorium Jansen Elem. School	500, grades 3–6
	Mini-Concert Seniors Q&A Session	2–2:30 p.m.	Multi-purpose room	150 seniors
	Master Class	7–8:30 p.m.	Dance Studio, Phys. Ed. Bldg.	30 community dancers
DAY 2	Lec Dem	10–11 a.m.	Auditorium Swanson Elem. School	400, grades 4–6
	Workshop	1–2 p.m.	JS Black Sr. Center	15 seniors
	Workshop	1–2 p.m.	State School Physically Disadvantaged	6 students
	2 Workshops	2–3 p.m.	Swanson	30- students, grade 6 30 students, grade 5
DAY 3	Open rehearsal	2–4 p.m.	BSU Auditorium	Dance and theatre students
	Pre-performance talk	7 p.m.		General Audience HC: 1200
	Performance	8 p.m.		
	Meet the Artist Reception	10:30 p.m.		
DAY 4				
DAY 5				

checklist, along with information about hotels, restaurants, and local services received from the presenter on the questionnaire.

Of course, a presenter may be interested only in performances, in which case the portions of the performance/residency packet having to do with special activities are obviously unnecessary. But the other information on the questionnaire is always essential to preparations for the tour.

Promotional Materials

A request-for-promotional-materials form (Appendix B) not only reminds the presenter of his promotional responsibilities, it also makes it convenient for him to let you know the range and quantity of materials he will need to fulfill them. Chapter 9 discusses all the materials you will need to prepare, but perhaps the most important point to be made is that the presenter must receive the materials in time for his staff to make proper use of them. Consequently, the request form should accompany the performance/residency information packet to enable you to respond to the presenter's needs. Along with this should go a selection of glossies and basic information on the company. These materials are frequently needed at a very early date, as many presenting organizations prepare brochures for the following season in the spring, shortly after engagements are contracted. A full complement of the remaining materials offered in the request form can be sent later.

Promotion, by the way, is only one kind of activity among a whole range of concerns embraced by the broader term public relations. It is important to remember that the company's public includes both audiences and presenters. When your stage manager arrives at the theatre and pronounces it "a dump" within earshot of the presenter and his tech crew, it is definitely "bad p.r." When company members make it clear that they cannot wait to get out of "this provincial hellhole," or when one of your artistic staff has a shouting match with the presenter's personal assistant, your company's image will not be enhanced. Enough said.

Transportation and Accommodations

Travel arrangements include transportation to and from a booking, local transportation, and accommodations and meals (on the road and during the performance/residency). As these items are confirmed, you should note the dates and summarize specific arrangements on the checklist.

Transportation

Inter-Performance Transportation. Companies travel between bookings either in motor vehicles (car, van, or bus, depending on the size of the company and the amount of equipment) or in planes. In general, a regional tour is best handled through ground transportation, while a coast-to-coast, national tour with large distances between bookings will probably involve some air travel.

The choice also depends upon the size of the company and the amount of equipment it carries. Solo instrumentalists and singers, chamber music groups, and small dance companies with few members, no technical equipment, and little in the way of costumes and the like, are most likely to travel by air. Larger companies—particularly those whose casts and equipment are so extensive that they can perform only in the opera houses of major cities—will have to transport equipment separately, perhaps by truck (or trucks), with artists traveling by plane or by bus.

Like all tour arrangements, plane reservations should be checked frequently, even after the tour is in motion. Flights are often rescheduled or cancelled, and an artist may find himself stranded en route to his next performance unless someone routinely rechecks the reservations. Arrangements for special meals, for seats in a specific part of the airplane, and for carrying on musical instruments must all be made in advance—and periodically reconfirmed.

From a logistical standpoint, the bus-and-truck (or plane-and-truck) approach can be very efficient. The crew can strike the set and equipment immediately after a performance, drive on to the next destination, and be ready to start setting up early the next morning; the artists can get a full night's sleep and do their traveling the next day. In a tightly booked series of one-night stands, performers do not have to arrive until the afternoon preceding an evening performance. (Although this kind of scheduling is sometimes the most cost-efficient, it can very quickly burn out both the tech crew and the artists.)

In arranging tours that involve extensive bus or van travel, try to plan for extra seats so that company members can stretch out. If you plan to transport equipment, costumes, etc. in the bus, find out exactly how much room it will take up. Make certain there is enough luggage space left to accommodate everyone's personal belongings. If there is not, personal luggage may have to be more severely limited or an extra vehicle hired to carry the excess. There are bus companies in most cities that specialize in rentals for tours.

Plan for rest stops; some union contracts mandate them. Decide in advance where you will stop for lunch and at what restaurant. If there are more than ten people in your group, make reservations. With a sizable group, a company roster can be helpful, too, as a means of quickly making sure all company members are on board before resuming your journey.

Local Transportation. Transportation within the presenter's community—whether from airport to theatre to hotel, or from residency activities to promotional appearances to performances—is an important component of any tour's logistics. It can be handled in several ways:

1. A company traveling in its own vehicles assumes complete responsibility for its own local transportation;
2. A company arriving by plane does the same by arranging to pick up rented vehicles at the airport;
3. The company requests that the presenting organization provide transportation (if so, this must be specified in the contract); or
4. A combination of the above arrangements is devised.

Obviously, handling your own local transportation will give the company the most flexibility. The ability to go out in the evening, to try new restaurants, to just get away from it all, can spell the difference between a happy company and one suffering from an advanced case of cabin fever—especially during a residency of several days. However, company morale—like everything else—must be weighed against costs, and local rentals may not fit into your budget. Most companies which travel to performances in their own vehicles use them for local transportation.

If your company chooses option number three, you must work out a pick-up schedule with the presenting organization well in advance of your arrival to ensure that you are met by the necessary number of vehicles and personnel in time to get to your activities. Make sure there is a restaurant in or near your hotel, since presenters usually will not be responsible for ferrying people to meals.

Sometimes a combination of these options will be possible at different stops on a longer tour. The company may opt to rent vehicles for longer residencies, while depending on the presenter for shorter stays. Or, a company using a bus will ask the presenter to be responsible for transportation to activities when the company is split up—a master class, for example. Under this type of arrangement, the bus is usually then used for some other activity in which a majority of company members is involved.

Accommodations

Hotels. In choosing lodgings, the tour manager must keep a number of considerations in mind, some more or less important depending on the artistic discipline. Most companies prefer to stay as close as possible to the theatre in which they will be working. This allows artists and crew to come and go according to their specific needs and minimizes local transportation requirements. A restaurant in the hotel or within easy walking distance is a must for some companies, in which case serving hours should be checked out in advance. Dancers routinely require bathtubs as well as showers in their rooms, so that they can soak sore muscles after performances.

Finances and logistics permitting, certain extras along the way can help keep the company's spirits up. Access to a heated pool may be worth a few extra dollars during a residency of several days. On long tours, occasional accommodations that are a bit special—a historic inn in New England, for example—can offer a refreshing change from the plastic atmosphere of most of the accommodations encountered on the road.

There are a number of travel guides which contain a wealth of information useful in choosing hotels. There are entries on the features and services available at various establishments, the costs, the credit cards accepted, and some give overall quality ratings. Some excellent sources include the regional *Mobil Tour Guide* and the numerous guides available from the American Automobile Association. The presenter questionnaire is an excellent source of advice on the relative merits of local hotels and motels.

The company can make its own hotel reservations, or this can be done through a travel agent (discussed later). In either case, the reservations must be guaranteed, which may necessitate partial or full prepayment. Depending on the number of rooms and the length of your stay, you may be able to negotiate a discount. In addition, a very large group may be able to get a certain number of complimentary rooms, especially if it is staying for an extended time. Occasionally, the local presenter may be in a position to obtain a special rate from a local hotel owner. If your hotel reservations are made through the presenter, be sure to confirm and prepay them well in advance of your arrival.

For tour groups with more than ten to fifteen members, each hotel should be sent a company list indicating who will be sharing rooms and who should have individual accommodations. The hotel can then translate the tour manager's request for eight doubles and five singles into specific room assignments, which means that the company is preregistered.

Find out the hotel's standard checkout time when you make the reservations so that, if necessary, you can request a delay. Also confirm how the final bill is to be paid—by cash, check, or credit card.

Some companies prefer that the tour manager take care of everyone's basic hotel bill. Others provide a per diem allowance to cover not only food costs but accommodations as well, and have each member pay the hotel individually. The former method makes hotel checkout simpler, especially with a large group. In either case, each individual is responsible for such additional charges as room service and telephone calls.

Meals. It is standard practice to provide all company members with meal money or per diem allowances for food so that everyone can eat when and where he wants. The amount should be based on food costs at moderately-priced restaurants. This may vary somewhat from place to place, and in some parts of the country, particularly larger cities, the allowance may need to be increased. In companies with union contracts, however, the meal allowance is set and must be observed.

In certain situations, meals become a tour manager's responsibility. For example, if the company is performing in a town where all the restaurants are closed by 8 P.M. and your artists prefer to have their evening meal after performances, you will have to make special arrangements. (These arrangements should be detailed on your checklist.) Explain your needs to the presenter. He may be able to persuade a local restaurant to remain open for a group, or one of his board members might be willing to provide a home-cooked meal. Make it clear that neither a hamburger, fries, and a shake at the local "golden arches" nor punch and cookies at an after-performance reception will be sufficient.

Travel Agents

A good travel agent can be a tour manager's best friend. In fact, some agencies now specialize in the touring of performing arts companies. They have great experience and expertise which can be especially valuable in moving large groups of people around.

Whether you have one of these specialists available to you or simply use a regular travel agency in your area, a travel agent can arrange for hotels to hold rooms after six, for the company to pick up plane tickets away from their home city in case of problems, and for prepayment of van and car rentals. He can also make and prepay plane and hotel reservations so that the company's financial outlay before leaving on a tour is nil. A specified number of days later, when reimbursement is due, the amount can usually be covered by funds the company will have collected from presenters.

Even a best friend makes mistakes, of course, particularly an extremely busy one. If you opt to use a travel agent's services, bear in mind that most agencies serve hundreds, even thousands, of customers. The tour manager must check and recheck every plane and hotel reservation, every car, bus, and van rental at least once before the company leaves home base, and again on tour prior to the time the service is needed.

Making Arrangements for Payroll

Before going out on the road, you need to make arrangements for smooth and orderly payroll disbursements (salaries and per diem allowances) while the company is on tour. Company members need cash to pay for meals, for incidental expenses on the road, and sometimes, for their accommodations. Most will also send money home to cover their regular bills. Monthly or semi-monthly disbursements would require people to carry too much cash, which can disappear quickly—even abruptly—on the road. Consequently, a weekly payroll is usually best.

During each week of touring, a specific day (preferably the same day of the week throughout the tour) should be designated as payday. The schedule of paydays should be determined well in advance of departure so that necessary coordination can be accomplished among presenter-administrators, local banks along the tour route, and the company's home bank.

Notify all the presenters whose bookings coincide with paydays that you may need their assistance. Generally, the presenter will be asked to vouch for whomever is responsible for picking up the payroll at a local bank (preferably the bank at which the presenting organization keeps its accounts). Beyond that, the nature and degree of assistance you need will depend upon the method you choose for receiving and disbursing payroll funds. Five of the most common methods are described below:

1. Some large, well-established companies wire payroll funds to local banks—where the presenter is known—and arrange to have the banks cash individual paychecks distributed on the road by the tour manager. On payday, each company member takes his paycheck to the local bank, where his signature is verified by a company-issued identification card. Company members may elect to receive all of their pay in cash, or they can arrange to have a portion sent via bank check to their personal checking account to cover bills at home.

2. The tour manager can carry several company checks—one for every week of the tour—each equal to one weekly payroll. The local bank will be asked to phone the company's home bank to verify that monies equal to the company payroll are being held in escrow specifically to back up the check, which the local bank then cashes. Of course, the escrow funds must be arranged prior to commencement of the tour, and the home bank must be prepared to receive confirmation calls. And advance notice of this procedure must be given to local banks and presenters.

3. The company can arrange for its home bank to wire the payroll to a local bank (as outlined above) in the tour manager's name as agent for the company. Prior to departure, the company notifies the bank

officer in writing that it plans to use this procedure; the local bank's acceptance of this arrangement should be confirmed by telephone. The presenter-administrator should be asked to notify the bank officer as to when the funds will be picked up and then to accompany the tour manager to the bank to vouch for the person collecting the cash.

4. The company can arrange with the presenting organization to have the fee (or a portion of it equal to the payroll) paid in cash. The tour manager, after making all required deductions (federal withholding, F.I.C.A., etc.), then distributes the cash among the company members, along with payroll slips explaining the deductions. These payroll slips are required for all the options described. And whenever payroll is disbursed in cash (the last three options), a receipt must be obtained from each company member.

5. One other option worth mentioning is to distribute per diems to company members for the entire tour before leaving home. The company then makes weekly deposits of salary checks directly into each company member's checking account. This option eliminates the hassle of payday on the road; however, its one drawback is that it requires the company to have a strong cash flow position.

Whatever option you choose, once arrangements have been agreed to, you should send a letter confirming these arrangements to each of the parties involved.

Plots and Crew

At the same time that the tour manager communicates with the presenter-administrator concerning scheduling, logistics, promotion, and other details, the stage manager works with the technical director responsible for the presenter's facility. Using the information received in the technical questionnaire, the stage manager or lighting designer sends the technical director a light plot and a hanging plot prior to the company's arrival. If the company carries its own lighting equipment or some supplemental equipment, instructions must be sent on this as well. The stage manager must also set up with the technical director a work schedule for the crew. After you have worked out the details these arrangements should be confirmed in writing. (See Chapter 12 for a more detailed discussion of this process.)

Program Copy

Presenters handle the printing of programs, and they need to receive your copy—legibly typed, exactly as you wish it to appear—approximately three to four weeks in advance of your engagement, and sometimes sooner.

Tours are programmed and cast by the company's senior artistic personnel, but in some cases other staff members should be consulted before final decisions are made and the program copy prepared. The choice of repertory for dance companies, for example, often depends upon technical considerations; the stage manager should be invited to a preliminary meeting to advise whether technical problems might preclude performing any particular piece. Theatre and opera companies will have been contracted by the presenter to perform a particular production, so casting is the only decision left to be made. Solo musical artists and chamber music groups usually choose their own programming unless they are playing with an orchestra or have been signed to perform an all-Beethoven program or the like.

Intermissions or pauses should be clearly indicated in the copy. Additions, inserts, and last-minute announcements should be kept to a minimum. The less time an audience has to spend figuring out who is doing what, the better.

Confirming the Arrangements

After all details of the engagement have been worked out and the materials have been sent to the presenter, two additional letters need to be sent to the presenting organization which confirm these arrangements: one to the presenter-administrator, the other to the presenter's technical director.

The technical letter states that the light and hanging plots and crew call information have been sent and asks the presenter's technical director to call the company's stage manager to confirm his receipt and acceptance of them.

The administrative letter confirms the performance and residency activities schedule, where and how the company will arrive and leave, pickup times if the presenter is providing local transportation, hotels, arrangements for after-performance meals, payday plans, etc. This letter should also spell out any logistical or programmatic details to which you and the presenter-administrator have agreed.

Tour Schedule for Company Members

Finally, company members should receive a tour schedule (shown in Exhibit 13) containing: a complete itinerary; detailed travel arrangements (transportation and accommodations) and schedule; a performance and rehearsal schedule; if necessary, a separate schedule for the technical crew, whose hours may be quite different from the artists; the repertory and final casting; time and location of press interviews and the names of company

EXHIBIT 13

The Tour Schedule

	HOTEL: The College Inn 300 South Thames Ann Arbor, MI 48104 (313) 769-2200
	THEATRE: College Center for the Performing Arts Huran & Fletcher Streets (313) 777-4343 backstage
DAY/DATE: Saturday, October 6 **HIGHLIGHTS:** Travel: Indianapolis to Ann Arbor, MI (275 mi.) Load-in _____ Performance: 8:00 p/Orchestra Load out _____	**PRESENTER:** University Musical Society (313) 555-1212 (office) (313) 555-1212 (home) **TECH CONTACT:** Greg Jones, SM (313) 666-6969
	DIRECTIONS: Indianapolis to Ann Arbor: I-69/I-94 To hotel: I-94 to exit 172-Jackson Rd. Jackson Ave. (east) 'til it turns into Huron Rd. about 2 miles. To theatre: 3 city blocks – E. Huron and State Street

TIME	ARTISTS	TIME	PRODUCTION STAFF	TIME	ORCHESTRA
7:45 a	Reporting time	6:00 a	Depart hotel to Ann Arbor	7:45 a	Reporting time
8:00 a	Depart hotel to Ann Arbor	1:00 p	Arrive Ann Arbor	8:00 a	Depart hotel
12:00 p	Lunch		(Eastern time + 1 hr.)	12:00 p	Lunch break
1:00 p	Break	1:00 p	Lunch break	1:00 p	
4:00 p	Arrive: Ann Arbor	2:00 p		4:00 p	Arrive Ann Arbor
	(Eastern time + 1 hr.)	2:00p	Load in		(Eastern time + 1 hr.)
	Break	6:00p			Dinner break
5:30 p	Reporting time, group #1	7:00 p	Crew call	7:00 p	Reporting time
5:45 p	Depart hotel to theatre	7:30 p	Half-hour	7:15 p	Depart hotel to theatre
6:00 p	Arrive theatre	8:00 p	Curtain	7:30 p	Arrive theatre
6:30 p	Reporting time, group #2	11:15 p	Load out	8:00 p	Curtain
6:45 p	Depart hotel to theatre	3:00 a		11:15 p	Depart theatre to hotel
7:00 p	Arrive theatre	3:00 a	Depart theatre to hotel		
8:00 p	Performance				
11:15 p	Depart theatre to hotel				

members on call; banks for check cashing; and any additional information which performers or crew might need.

Of course, the tour manager will carry not only the above information but also the file containing the signed contract, correspondence with presenters, and all the other materials reviewed in this chapter.

On the Road

The bus has pulled out on time; all performers and staff are on board; and the crew has gone ahead to set up the theatre. The tour on which you have worked so long and hard is under way.

The tour manager is the chief executive officer in charge of the tour. His performance is crucial to its success or failure. He is responsible for everything that happens on the road from the moment the company hits town to the "strike" at the end of the last performance. He is a policeman and fireman rolled into one—responsible for sorting out and solving emergency situations that might develop. Whether sitting at a desk in a backstage area preparing payroll receipts, meeting the presenter to solve a problem, or helping company members check into the hotel, wherever the tour manager happens to be, that is where the buck stops.

The tour manager's first line of defense when he is out on the road is the detailed, pre-tour planning that has just been described. If the logistical arrangements go as scheduled, the tour manager will have time to cope with the many difficulties that inevitably arise. No one can ever fully anticipate everything that will occur on a specific tour—each has a life and flavor of its own.

The Tour Manager's Responsibilities

The tour manager has a seemingly endless series of responsibilities out on the road. His office is makeshift at best, ranging from an empty office backstage in the presenter's facility, to a hotel room, an unused dressing room, a theatre's green room, or on travel days, his seat on the bus, plane, or van. He is the one who must make sure that performing and residency activities happen as scheduled.

In some respects the tour manager is even responsible for the artistic product of the company. If there is an overly long intermission or if there is a perception that the quality of production was not as high as antici-pated, he is the one to whom the presenter will complain.

The tour manager must also make certain that all of the logistical details—i.e., transportation, meals, lodging, payroll distribution—are arranged and function smoothly. If he does his job well, company members will treat such activities as so routine that they do not become sources of additional tension on the tour.

The tour manager's day is never done. Even when he has completed all of his administrative tasks, he may also have substantial non-administrative responsibilities. The tour manager may be in charge of wardrobe, setting up dressing rooms, overseeing the ironing of costumes, and more. In many small companies, the stage manager also acts as tour manager. The larger the company, and hence the larger the traveling staff, the more likely the tour manager will be strictly an administrator.

The tour manager is the company's spokesperson with the presenter, with everyone at the presenter's facility, with the people at each individual stop who provide services to the company, and with noncompany people, such as the bus driver, who may travel with the tour. He must make sure the artists and staff on the tour are comfortable and have what they need to do their best work. He must also work with company personnel to resolve any personal problems that arise which might threaten the cohesion of the tour.

To perform all these functions successfully, the tour manager needs to be a prodigious list maker and expert juggler. On tour there are always more balls in the air than meet the eye, and anything that is not written down can easily be forgotten.

Handling Emergencies

Emergencies and major snafus happen unexpectedly to the best tour manager: an artist becomes sick or is injured and needs to see a doctor, while his understudy must be told he is going on for the evening performance; the company bus breaks down one hundred miles from your performance site.

In emergency situations, the first thing to remember is to stay calm and under control; hysteria is contagious. The second is to communicate effectively with those who must be informed. As a general rule in emergencies, notify people on a "need to know" basis only. Why upset people or make them aware of problems unnecessarily?

When a situation creates a problem which involves the entire company, assemble the members to explain the circumstances honestly and discuss your plans to remedy the situation. For example, if the bus breaks down, discuss what each person can do when you finally arrive at the theatre to make the most out of the brief preparatory time you will have. In situations involving specific individuals, the tour manager should try to contain the number of people who have knowledge of the problem. If an emergency necessitates that the tour manager leave the company, he should always designate someone to take his place while he is away.

Communicating with Your Company

A tour manager's relationship with the members of the company is critical to the success of the tour. He must gain the company's confidence so that he can quickly, effectively, and tactfully handle any logistical and personnel problems that arise.

Many first-time tour managers often struggle with the difficult balancing act between a business and personal relationship with their company members. Most initially tend toward one of the extremes; either they attempt to become extremely close to the artists and technical staff, or they remain aloof and strangely separate from them. The best tour managers, however, strike a balance: honest and compassionate individuals who perform their jobs competently and professionally. By demonstrating a genuine interest in the welfare of the artists individually, and the company as a whole, the tour manager can build a reservoir of good will that will stand him in good stead when a real crisis strikes.

Dealing with the Presenter

Once his company has been settled in at the hotel or theatre, the tour manager's first priority is to meet with the presenter-administrator to review all plans and schedules. If a misunderstanding arises, never get angry. Rather, it is better to firmly but tactfully explain why something to which you both agreed some time ago must happen or why something unforeseen needs action.

Every good tour manager learns to spot situations where something cannot be fixed or changed. In such cases, he must be willing to negotiate the company's position. If, for example, you arrive at a theatre to find that the lights have not been prehung as per your instruction, what will you do about it? A screaming fit will help no one. It is more productive to calmly inform the presenter that the curtain is unlikely to go up on time if he cannot get an augmented crew to hang the lights immediately. The bottom line is to be reasonable and take the approach most likely to benefit your company.

The Call Board

An important part of a tour manager's job on the road is to communicate changes in schedule and important general announcements to company members. While it may be possible with a very small company to simply stick your head into the dressing room and announce "the van will leave at nine tomorrow instead of eight," a *call board* is necessary for larger groups.

A call board is a bulletin board, usually set up in a prominent place backstage, on which the tour manager promptly posts all changes and additions. All company members are instructed to check the board several times daily and note on their personal copies of the company schedule any changes, additional radio or TV interviews, or other information that has been posted.

Hotels and Food on Tour

Hotels. The tour manager should be at the hotel while the company checks in and for a specific period thereafter to oversee any problems that may arise. Send the hotel a company rooming list in advance and ask them to put keys for each room in envelopes marked by name. Upon arrival, these are given to the tour manager for distribution. Preregistration prevents the chaos which would undoubtedly occur in the hotel's check-in area should twenty weary travelers descend en masse on the desk clerk, all demanding to be checked in and shown to their rooms at once.

Sometimes there will be unsatisfactory rooms for which you will have to negotiate a change with the hotel's management. For instance, once in a while two people who normally room with one another will have had a falling out and not have bothered to notify the tour manager that they will no longer share a room.

Food. In addition to arranging late night meals for performers and staff in communities where there are no restaurants open after the performance, the tour manager must usually plan for those performers and crew who wish to eat something between the afternoon rehearsal period and subsequent performance. Some tour managers arrange for a simple buffet of light food and drink which takes into account the general preferences of company members. Others take specific food orders from individuals. The larger the company, the less likely this second option can work.

Complementary Tickets. A company receives a certain number of complimentary tickets to each performance as specified in the contract. These tickets are generally used by senior artistic staff to observe the performance. Companies also issue complimentary tickets to prospective presenters and to friends and family of company members. The tour manager must ascertain how many requests there are for complimentary seats from presenters and tour members and allocate seats accordingly, working with the presenter's box office staff to label the ticket envelopes with the appropriate names. He must be aware that changes inevitably will happen: someone for whom you were holding two tickets cannot come, someone else would like an extra, etc. The tour manager must also notify the box office when "comps" are not being used and can be released. This is very important to the presenter, especially if your performance is standing room only.

Money

The tour manager is responsible for all finances on tour. He prepares and disburses the payroll, pays for all expenses the company incurs while on tour, collects the company fee from the presenter, and maintains records of these transactions. Arrangements should have been made to pay major bills—such as hotel and transportation—by company check or credit card, which automatically produce records. When cash is used, receipts must be kept. Careful records should also be made of tips and other small cash expenditures for which one cannot expect a receipt.

Unforseen Expenses. Imagine this scenario: it is Sunday and your travel agency is closed. A snowstorm has begun in the city you are leaving, and your van will not be able to make it to the next destination. The airport is still open, and a plane is scheduled to depart for your next stop in an hour. Unless someone can pay for the airfare, the company will miss the evening performance—and forfeit the fee!

To cover all possible emergencies—large and small—as well as the countless incidental expenses that crop up on the road, a tour manager must have plenty of petty cash on hand at all times. Some crises, like the one described above, are not easily averted without a fistful of company credit cards.

Collecting the Check. The contract specifies the means (certified check, bank draft, etc.) and the time (before the performance, at the first intermission) when the company's fee must be paid. The tour manager must confirm these arrangements with the presenter both prior to the company's arrival and again once the company is on site to be sure that there is no misunderstanding. The manager must then be on hand to receive the check at the agreed time and place.

If the company's fee is based upon a split of the box office, the tour manager must arrange to get an up-to-date statement of sales from the box office upon his arrival. He also needs to be on hand on the night of performance: first to observe the presenter's box office staff as they sell tickets, and then to watch the ticket stubs and money be counted after the box office closes to ascertain the accuracy of the box office statement prepared by the presenter's staff.

Tipping. Tips can open a lot of doors. They can also save money. A good tip to a skycap can ease a pile of extra baggage onto a plane free of charge, when overweight charges might have been several hundred dollars. A bus driver, whose only official duty is to keep his vehicle out of the oncoming lane, may be willing to help load a weary dance company's luggage—if the tour manager shows some appreciation.

It is difficult to give advice on how much to tip. What is appropriate will vary depending upon the situation and the place. But good service always merits some sort of remuneration. In general, the amount should be based upon the relative importance of the service to the company.

Booking While on Tour

Touring is an excellent showcase for a company, and can result in new bookings for the following year. All prospective presenters on your booking list who are within a one-hundred-mile radius of a performance should receive a letter of invitation. Request an RSVP so that you can have tickets (complimentary if possible) set aside.

Following Up the Engagement

Within a few days after the event, the tour manager should call the presenter-administrator to ask his opinion about the company's visit. In addition, a follow-up questionnaire can be sent by mail so that he can provide a more detailed evaluation. In speaking with him, be sure to ask both what went well and where there were problems. Let him know you would appreciate candor. You can learn only from the truth, and constructive criticism can be most helpful. If the performance or residency went particularly well, ask the presenter if he will write a letter to that effect which might be quoted in a future booking brochure. If he is an APAP member, also ask that he send a report to the APAP *Bulletin,* a newsletter circulated to its membership.

In any case, after your follow-up phone call, the tour manager should write a note to the presenter-administrator, thanking him for his organization's hospitality. If the experience was a disaster, find something positive to write about anyway. "Although I know we had problems about the set up, I think you should know that we appreciate the wonderful dinner your organization provided for the company after the performance." Thank you's should also be extended to the person who hosted a reception for the company, to someone on the administrative staff who was especially helpful, to the owner of the restaurant which stayed open late to accommodate the company, and so on. Thanking people is something a company can never do enough of.

In the end, while touring can be difficult, it can be particularly rewarding as well. It provides opportunities for artists to perform before many audiences, affording them the possibility of touching people with a new or interesting experience. Whether the tour is a success or failure will rest in great part on the skills of the tour manager. It is his job to bring together all of the disparate pieces of the puzzle so that his company, the presenter, and finally the audience are well served.

❧

CHAPTER 11

Trends for the Future

The marketplace for touring and presenting has evolved in the years since *The Road Show* was first written. The shifts have been gradual, going almost unnoticed over several years. Recently the field has begun to recognize these shifts are not aberrations but represent new directions for touring and presenting. This chapter focuses on the most notable shifts and changes in the marketplace, so that you can incorporate the nuances of the new market patterns into your organization's strategy for touring.

In interviews with managers, presenters, and funders covering a wide range of organizations, art forms, and geography, the following shifts and changes were brought up most consistently (see end of chapter for list of interviewees):

1. Presenters and artists are more involved in project-based touring, including longer residencies during which an artist will spend several weeks in a community; commissioning of work by a presenting organization or several presenting organizations; long-term relationships between presenting organizations and artists.
2. Interest within the touring market is growing for work of artists of color and nontraditional artists, as well as for work outside the western European tradition, in recognition of the multicultural nature of U.S. society.

3. Marketplace opportunities are increasing for small and mid-size organizations, brought about by a significant reduction in touring by large national companies.
4. Fewer, less expensive engagements are being booked, and more accessible, salable, "popular" work is being presented as a result of economic pressure on both presenting organizations and performing companies.

These shifts in the field, largely caused by economic and social pressures, are nonetheless bringing about positive changes for artists, presenters, and touring in general.

Growing Interest in Project-Based Touring

There is growing interest by both artists and presenters in project-based touring—tours that put an artist/company into a community for an extended period, for repeat visits, and/or for commissioned work. Today, presenters and their audiences want an artist's time in their community to be more than fleeting, and artists are tired of running from engagement to engagement, hardly able to remember where they performed last week. Groups of presenters increasingly are working collaboratively to accomplish mutual goals. In addition, this new emphasis on project-based touring is being fueled by the monies that a variety of public and private agencies have invested in long-term residencies and commissioning as a better means to develop audiences.

Whatever the confluence of factors, the marketplace has become more project-oriented. The projects themselves vary: a consortium of presenters in a single state has a dance company tour for five weeks to highlight a particular culture; a rural presenter commissions a work from an artist to come out of the artist's interaction with members of the community; or an ensemble and a presenter come to an understanding that the presenter will bring the group back on a regular basis every two or three years.

Jackie Davis is responsible for arts presentation at the Lied Center of the University of Kansas. She describes the evolution in her own thinking, which has mirrored that of quite a few of her colleagues.

> As recently as ten years ago, many of my colleagues and I focused our discussions primarily on *marketing* performing arts events. We traded stories about successful promotional campaigns but rarely talked about what we did with artists when they dropped into our communities. The quick discussions centered on "Are they good?" and "Are they easy to work with?" In essence we were a passive delivery system in which artists entered our communities, performed, and went away without any real interaction. The artists were

usually "safe." Their names were recognizable. They were not controversial. In my case, they passed the "Midwest test." If ten friends had heard of the artist, I was safe to book him or her.

Then Philip Glass came to Lawrence in 1985. I knew little of him, but he was on the Mid-America roster and I had been encouraged to present this "cutting edge" artist. The morning after his performance, I went into the university fine arts building to teach, and there was an animation about the place I hadn't seen in the last five years. People were in corners and they were talking. They were talking angry or talking happy, but they were all very animated ... I went to my graduate class and said, "What's going on out there?" And they explained that everybody was arguing about the quality, the believability, the credibility of Philip Glass's music. Because Glass is a living composer, he did not have the universal stamp of approval like Mozart or Beethoven. People felt free to determine the quality of what they saw and heard. So instead of the usual dialogue in which students told me how nice the performance had been the night before, we spent the next hour in dynamic discussion.

This was an epiphany. I wanted people to start thinking about what they were [experiencing] without being told this is good and you have to like it, without being shoved in a direction. I wanted them to take the direction. The expanded role of the presenter was to give artists the freedom to create and to give audiences the equal freedom to respond. We determined that this could be accomplished only by creating a new program including less well-known, less safe, and more provocative artists. As a result, in 1987 we created a program called the New Directions Series. It is committed to new works created within the last five years. We do not promise the public that they will love these works. We simply ask them to have an open mind. The series has been very successful.

Then you come to the next part of the issue. You don't get people to understand any of this if you do things in a one-night stand through this passive delivery system. So we [evolved] the residency, [and the question has become] how long is long enough. At this point, we've gone from "two days would be nice" to "three days would be nice" to "a week is barely enough." ... In some cases we will present people for one night [but] eventually, I'd like to go to much longer residencies only.

With this new approach has come a new responsibility, which is to establish a relationship with the artist and to create an atmosphere with the community that is not intimidating. Sometimes this may mean that a presenter will commit to an artist over a number of years so that a community will see the breadth of that artist's work. Or it may mean long-term residencies. Whatever the case, the process of establishing an open dialogue between the touring artist and the community has resulted in an exciting collaboration. The artist has an expanded opportunity to communicate his work, and the audience has more ways to understand the artist's work.

What is so constructive about this shift toward an "open dialogue between the artist and the community" is that it is driven by mutual needs. The artist needs to stay longer in order to have a closer relationship to the community where he or she performs. The corresponding desire on the part of the presenting organization (and its audience) is to have a better understanding and appreciation of the artist's work and hence a closer relationship. Properly handled, longer residencies and ongoing relationships can have a positive impact on attendance and the overall marketing of performances.

Joseph Gresser, a presenter who worked in a rural Vermont community with limited financial resources, talked about how the shift toward residencies is being driven by both the artistic and marketing needs of his organization.

> It's not simple anymore. People don't feel obliged to go to a performance to get their dose of culture. Whoever used to feel that way has died. Now every audience we have is an ad hoc collection of people. We have to try to figure out what will work for our audience, and that involves bringing in people who will do things that you can't see anyplace else, or who have something very special that makes sense to our area. We make that connection wherever possible with residencies....
>
> My audience is not one you would think of as incredibly adventurous or sophisticated.... But we've been able to build an audience for some rather adventuresome things because of the connections we've been able to make between particular artists and the community.

Irene Namkung and John Ullman of Traditional Arts Management represent traditional American and world music artists and have always had to work hard to develop audiences for unfamiliar work. They point to funding programs which focus on audience development, such as Lila Wallace-Reader's Digest Arts Partners (see Chapter 3), as incentives for presenters and artists to collaborate in the form of longer residencies.

Janet Cowperthwaite, Managing Director of the Kronos Quartet, talked about the difference an ongoing relationship with a presenting organization can make for the Quartet and for the audience.

> Certain presenters have made a commitment to the group and bring them back over a period of time, whether it's every year or every three years, whatever is appropriate. You can absolutely see the growth in audiences. [The time frame differs from one community to the next,] but when presenters make that commitment to an artist over a period of time, it makes a huge difference in the artist's development and in what the artist can bring to the community. In places where we have been a number of times, we can now present a program that would be totally inappropriate for a first-time performance in that

community. That kind of development is what pushes the programming and pushes the group.

Andrea Wagner and Mark Murphy of On The Boards related how their organization has become involved in the commissioning of new work: "Involvement in the commissioning or co-producing of work has been really exciting because rather than just presenting an artist's work, we're able to play a role in helping them make it and validate it." They note the growing excitement, interest, and feeling of ownership on the part of their Seattle audiences as the organization has played a larger role in the creation of new work.

While the growing interest in project-based touring is being discussed throughout the field, single performances or short residencies remain a valid way to tour or present the performing arts. However, project-based touring is a very different type of touring, and such a tour cannot be conceptualized or sold to presenters as if it were "business as usual." If the booking person/agent/manager is seeking a dialogue about commissioning a work or a company residency of several weeks, she can't talk with that presenter in the same way she would about a "one-night stand." The language, and everything else that goes with this way of working, is different. It's not simply about "selling," it is about making marriages, partnerships, relationships. This is how it should be with any tour, really, but it's especially true in the case of project-based touring.

The relationship among the artist, the agent/manager and the presenter is not built on the supposition that the presenter pays a fee and the company comes in and performs. The implementation of the project often takes place over several years. During that time all of the parties involved work together in developing the project and in seeking funds from a variety of sources—foundations, public and private agencies—to make the project work. It is tough and time-consuming work.

Despite its growing popularity, project-based touring is still not the way most of the marketplace functions. Even presenters who do work in this fashion can't sustain more than a few project-driven residencies a season because they are so labor intensive. A presenting organization needs a large staff to run these residencies, more staff than would be needed to bring in several artists for single performances. Project-based residencies are simply a different way of working within the framework of the marketplace.

The Increased Share of Multicultural Work in the Marketplace

In recent years, especially in the field of dance, companies led by artists of color have received increasing recognition in the marketplace. This recognition has been fueled by the excellence of the work as well as the presenters' realization that they have a responsibility to present work that reflects communities diverse in gender and ethnicity.

Accompanying this increased awareness has been a growing interest in "traditional" or "world" music and other performing arts from different countries, especially those outside the European continent. Irene Namkung and John Ullman note, "Fifteen years ago, we were the only agency with a roster of various American and world traditions; now everyone has that [kind of work] on their roster. . . . There's a lot of interest now and focus on [touring] musicians from other countries."

Jackie Davis's community in Kansas is centered on the university. It is 90 percent Caucasian, but she feels strongly that "[i]f you are a presenter, then one of your obligations to your audience is to present diverse cultures so that they have an opportunity to see and understand those cultures."

Echoing similar thoughts, Andrea Wagner and Mark Murphy explain:

> One thing that's sort of exciting is that, since the beginning, On The Boards has always tried to have the season represent geographic and ethnic and aesthetic diversity. . . . In the last few years presenters at every level have tried to present a more diverse series of events. And it's great to see some of those artists become major touring artists. In general the dialogue in the field has really evolved. Now the idea of talking about an emerging artist on a larger level or talking about an artist working within a culturally specific area is just part of the ongoing dialogue of the field. You see it at the conferences now; people are more conversant with those kinds of artists and that kind of work. . . .
>
> That's reflected also in the media, which has changed and been a big help. Artists who were emerging when we first worked with them—Laurie Anderson or Mark Morris or Bill T. Jones—might be in *People* or *Vanity Fair*! . . . It's not just a dialogue within the arts field or the presenting field . . . it's in everyday culture . . . everyday life. People in this country are getting to understand the importance of that kind of work.

Kim Chan voices her concern and hope about the increased interest in work by people of color:

> Since I've been in this business these issues have been very important. They aren't issues that can be written into a grant and left on a desk so that you can go home and feel good about yourself. I'm really worried that people don't quite understand the nature of the transition that this society is going through. Trends that the presenters and artists are faced with are reflections of the larger society that we [people of color] are all a part of, and our intent to get an equal place at the dinner table with everyone else in the world. I would hope that as the issues we're dealing with—community relationships, being culturally responsible in a multiracial community—have begun to enter the mainstream, people would not simply attack them as being trends but [see them as] real issues that

profoundly affect people's thoughts and the way in which they're able to communicate with each other.

While some types of work have been getting more attention in the touring and presenting market, there has also been a disquieting decrease in the presentation of serious classical/contemporary music played by orchestras, string quartets, and solo recitalists. John Gingrich reflects:

> The market in classical music is certainly not the same. I think it has gone through a contraction . . . a series I can mention used to have lots and lots of classical music and it now has two out of 14 events.
>
> People [are] cutting, leaving [in] those things which will be less expensive to market. [It's] a reaction to either size or venue, dealing with "How many bodies can we get?" So if [there] are 12 instead of 20 [programs], we end up cutting recitals, we end up cutting chamber music. . . . There are colleges I visited on the road for Hurok in 1974 now saying, "John, I'd like to do some classical music, but we just don't anymore."

Janet Cowperthwaite indicates that the Kronos Quartet ". . . is touring more internationally and less in the U.S. . . . It has to do with the state of the arts in the U.S. and with Kronos's visibility in Europe in the last years. . . . I see less music all the time, less traditional music. Kronos is busy, but a lot of contemporary music groups are not."

Some individuals see a direct linkage between these two phenomena, and there is concern in some quarters that work by artists of color, non-Western music, and nontraditional work have replaced a significant percentage of the classical recitalists and ensembles in performing arts series across the country. Coupled with the decline in funding for touring and presenting, as well as a shrinkage in audiences and a decrease in the number of programs per series, the field is being forced to cut the pie into thinner slices, with fewer opportunities for more artists.

John Gingrich wonders whether audiences are having real input into what they want to see on performing arts series in their communities.

> The media, and our major universities and cultural centers, have abandoned serious western culture at about the same time. While I've been an aggressive proponent of cultural diversity and multiculturalism, I'm not sure I ever wanted to have it sort of mindlessly. . . . People who never understood string quartets are suddenly able to book groups from Indonesia or Sri Lanka or Bolivia with even less understanding of those musical cultures. It seems to be either a grantmaking deal or a last effort to be exotic and to avoid confronting the necessity of having the series be more a part of the community.

Ivan Sygoda says:

I remember when I first got into this business some fifteen or so years ago thinking that a lot of the market seemed to be going to artists who were mining the Cunningham turf, who were exercising dance intelligence along those particular lines. . . . I can see why many artists were paranoid; if you weren't doing that kind of work you didn't count. Now that's changed. There's a lot of attention to cultural pluralism, which is also a very good and important thing.

I was chatting . . . with a white choreographer from the Midwest who said, "Ah, diversity. That's the latest thing to include me out." Which is a very poignant, painful thing to have to hear someone say. But there is a kind of point there, because there isn't enough money to go around. Action always seems concentrated somewhere, but exactly what describes that action has changed over the years and will change again. There will be something else on the top of the list five or ten years from now.

Growing Opportunities for Smaller and Mid-Size Organizations

One significant marketplace shift is the increased opportunity for mid-size and smaller organizations to tour more widely. In large part, this is the result of a decision by many of the country's largest performing arts organizations to abandon the touring market partially or completely.

The Metropolitan Opera no longer tours, nor does the Houston Grand Opera's touring company, Texas Opera Theater. Resident professional theatre companies such as the Guthrie, Asolo, Missouri Repertory Theatre and others, which toured actively in the 1970s and 1980s, no longer do so. Larger regional ballet companies, including Pacific Northwest Ballet and San Francisco Ballet, do fewer touring engagements per season and only to major venues like New York or Los Angeles. Major symphony orchestras are in a similar situation.

Henry Moran, whose regional organization, Mid-America Arts Alliance, was central to the touring of major performing arts organizations throughout the mid-America region in the seventies and into the eighties, describes what happened in his area:

Coming out of the seventies there was a definable need for Mid-America Arts Alliance to foster the availability of high quality, name-recognizable programs for big ticket presenters because there were needs or demands for economies within that process. As that market matured, as more facilities came on line, as name-recognizable institutional dance companies, music companies, theater companies, opera companies, etc. began to become less available, have less interest in touring, or price [themselves] beyond the ability of presenters or agencies such as M-AAA to effectively intervene to make a difference, our programs began to change.

There are several reasons why these larger companies are touring less. As Moran mentions, the fees presenters can afford to pay these companies do not come close to covering the costs they incur on the road. With growing economic pressure on performing arts organizations, trustees are loath to raise money so that an organization can perform in another community, unless that venue has special significance and adds to the organization's cachet.

Many organizations have extensive seasons and obligations at home, and their primary artistic interest is in serving that community. Touring demands planning years in advance and puts intense pressure on staffing. In addition, many regional and national programs that used to exist to underwrite such touring have either disappeared or are so diminished that they can no longer make enough of an impact for company or presenter.

What resulted in Mid-America, as described by Moran, is indicative of what has happened around the country:

> We have continued and expanded a regional-based program—the Regional Touring Program, that's moved from thirty artists to double that number on the program. . . . That reflects several factors in the marketplace: the higher level of quality or perceived quality of producing companies that are within the region itself; [and] affordability on the part of presenters.
>
> Our flagship program—National Touring Program—has changed, has become less dependent on subsidy and more dependent on technical coordination of availability or cooperation among presenters. It has also taken on, in some ways, more adventuresome programming, less name-recognizable artists of a superior quality. . . . But they cannot necessarily sell tickets from a presenter's point of view.

Ivan Sygoda does think there has been a change in who tours in the dance field:

> Many presenters are [booking] fewer dance events, but . . . [dance touring] is spread around a lot more. If I add up all the companies that are out and around, [although] they're not at the mainline presenters, they're out there traveling, doing professional work. It's all less centralized, [and] consequently much of it is a lot less visible. Percentage-wise a lot more now involves non–New York companies, not major companies—people you never heard of. If you could put together all [that is] happening, it would be more than ever before. Local companies, regionally-based companies are filling in niches. I know some companies that are doing concerts for small fees, teaching, filling in the gaps.
>
> If you only think of the people who are on the lists, who go to conferences, that's only a subset of what there is. People find those other subsets from other networks. It turns out that their sister-in-law knows this [company], or they danced with that one. Real direct and personal connection. It has nothing to do with an in-house or out-of-house agent making calls.

With some larger national organizations leaving the field, there is perhaps more room for mid-size and smaller organizations. It is clear, however, that what presenters are looking for from those organizations has changed, mostly as a result of growing concern for "the bottom line."

Economic Pressures on Touring

As the 1980s have moved into the 1990s, touring has continued to be affected by a lingering recession. The National Endowment for the Arts and state and regional arts agencies have seen their funds cut significantly. There is ever-increasing competition for the consumer's discretionary time and money. A potential audience member today has a far wider choice of what to do with his leisure time dollar than even just a few years ago. The explosion of the cable television/home video industry and the growing number of families in which both parents work outside the home are but two of the social and economic trends that exacerbate the intense pressures on both presenters and companies. As a result, presenters are booking fewer or less expensive programs and are looking to more popular work or name-recognizable artists. To an ever-increasing extent, presenters appear to be driven by "the bottom line."

There seems to be no doubt about the increased interest in "popular" work—organizations or productions with a name. A theater company touring a Neil Simon play will generate more interest than one touring a play by Dylan Thomas. Or the interest might be in a concert with a big name soloist, a full-length ballet, a traditional opera, a company or artist that's known from television or has been featured in *People* or a similar magazine. These artistic products are different from what a university performing arts series might have booked five to ten years ago.

In the 1970s and 1980s the NEA and regional organizations played a major role in support of touring and presenting across the country; now, unfortunately, there is far less money available. Managers and agents also perceive that presenters are both downsizing their performing series and focusing on more popular work. And many are concerned. John Gingrich thinks that this trend is a consequence of the overwhelming role the electronic media plays in everyday life and the presenters' perceptions that only if a work or a performer has been validated on television will the prospective audience buy tickets. There is also the additional problem of whether such performers are affordable for the presenters.

> At a time when we have more and more varied work delivered to our homes
> via cable, what people can afford to bring to their local institutions, to their
> local auditoriums in the way of live entertainment, is probably less exciting than

it has been. . . . [Artists that] people can see on television and who are accessible to bring to their [local communities] . . . essentially come down to a rather large body of country and western performers . . . who are recognizable, small enough to appear on "The Tonight Show" and "Regis," but who also have reasonable enough fees.

But with jazz, once you get past Wynton Marsalis and the recently deceased, it's hard to come up with jazz names that the general public will recognize. It's hard to come up with names in classical music that the general public will recognize. In the days past, when I came to New York to work for Hurok, there were lots of concert series which could afford the then-famous Arthur Rubinstein, the then-famous Andres Segovia, the then-famous Van Cliburn. . . . [When you look for the] people whose names are automatic sells [today], the number shrinks.

Now someone [can] say, "I get to drive this far and spend $40 to see this company's Nutcracker . . . or I can spend $7 and see the film of New York City Ballet's Nutcracker on a wide screen." . . . [And he] realizes [that] "I can take all four of my kids and myself, buy popcorn, and still not have reached the cost of one ticket to a live ballet performance." . . . I think you have a squeezing of the market on the one hand, [as well as] a real problem of getting people out of their homes.

[Touring has become] harder and harder because of the electronic media. A big singer would rather sing and have it broadcast on PBS, [where] everybody can see it, than go through getting on the plane, schlepping off and mounting the performance, with chorus, getting back on the stage in another city or two or three or four. . . . It's just wonderful that the Juilliard and the Guarneri [string quartets] play as much as they do . . . I think it's wonderful that Itzhak Perlman and Yo-Yo Ma play as much as they do.

Janet Cowperthwaite comments on the tendency to present more "salable" events:

I have concerns about the kinds of things that people are booking. I also know they need to bring people into their theatres. It's a much larger problem than that of the people making the programming decisions. . . . People are reacting and having to cut back. . . . What is being booked—and this is a sweeping generalization—is not the most exciting work. I still see the typical fear of new work . . . but there is definitely some leadership that has emerged in the field.

We still have the same number of concerts a year, but many more of them are out of the country. People that could financially afford to take a risk—knew they were maybe going to lose money because they had a small hall, but felt it was important to have this component of programming—don't have that luxury anymore. The funding has [declined] and there are fewer opportunities for U.S. touring than four years ago.

I see numbers of presentations being cut down, which I don't see as a bad thing. Focusing and making a more specific artistic statement in terms of a whole season are important for presenters to do.

Jackie Davis agrees to some extent about the change in programming by some of her colleagues. "I've also seen a move to commercial programming, but by no means [is it] universal. Some presenters' boards emphasize the bottom line, others try to balance risk-taking events with 'safer' ones."

The artists that John Ullman and Irene Namkung represent have traditionally spent much of their time in performances and residencies in public schools and other community situations.

> We've seen [the level of touring] deteriorate. . . . Things that used to fill out the tour are drying up. . . . [Many] of the traditional ways we got into the community—commercial presenters and school presenters—[are] gone. . . . For example, in 1978 we did four weeks in the public schools in Portland, Oregon, with the Georgia Sea Island Singers. The public school programs that [sponsored] those kinds of residencies in Portland have been dead for a long time. The Washington State program to bring artists into the schools was decimated this year. So we've seen a deterioration of community-based residencies. We've seen a bit of a pick up in terms of one or two residency activities that a presenter might be [adding to a performance], but not [for] a week or two weeks and certainly not four weeks.

New Initiatives in Touring and Presenting

One positive thing about adversity is that it tends to bring out the best in most people. In the 1990s, presenters and artists are having to do more with less, and both groups are having to find creative ways to make what they do work for one another. With a diminution in resources, presenters, artists, managers, and funders seem to be taking a new look at collaborating with one another. There are too few resources for everyone in the field not to work together, and no room for adversarial relationships or an "us" versus "them" attitude. One symbol of this shift is the decision by the Association of Performing Arts Presenters and the Western Alliance of Arts Administrators to make artists and agents full voting members of their organizations.

Circumstances are pushing people to come up with creative ways to meet common problems. Presenters are banding together not only to commission works from artists but also to mount tours of major artists who could not tour without a joint effort. These tours are not being "booked" in the traditional fashion, but are being packaged in advance (often with presenters jointly reviewing work before deciding to participate) and preplanned with the presenters' involvement. The tour of an internationally famous theater company from Russia, for example, would be too complicated unless it were preplanned with a group of presenters.

There are other interesting developments as well. For instance, managers are taking on new and different roles. Along with a group of his colleagues, John Gingrich is helping to create chamber music series as his way of doing something about the decline he sees in the presentation of serious European music. He is not acting as an agent, he is acting as a presenter/producer:

> ... I think that those of us involved with classical art, whether it be dance or theater or music, need to work and ... pretend we're the World Wrestling Federation and create our own market.
>
> I am busy working with some colleagues in making sure that some more [chamber music] series start. What's interesting is to see where they end up, because there is a sincere and wonderful love of Beethoven among many people in this population. ... I would like those people to feel the same [about other composers] and embrace not only Ravel, but William Bolcom and Elliott Carter, too. One of the things we're now hearing from people is, "We live six miles from the university in our small town and we'd like to start a chamber music series." [When I ask] why, they say, "Well, the university has essentially abrogated their responsibility to do it, they're walking away from it. So we walk away from their series. We want to hear string quartets."
>
> And so I am trying to set it up [because we feel] there's an audience for this music, people desperately want to hear it. ... I have helped start two series in California, and each year I try to see if there isn't some productive way to work with enthusiasts out there to get chamber music started.
>
> [We] have just done our first concert [in one city], and they had to turn people away because there weren't enough chairs to seat all the people. It is a brand new series; they hadn't done a concert before. So someone says to me, on one hand, "We don't have a market for classical music," and yet they don't have enough chairs in this particular place. I think that's [increasingly] going to be the case.

Among the major impediments to presenters conducting residencies of any length is their cost, and the lack of income produced by the non-performance portion of the activities. Yet John Ullman/Irene Namkung think residencies are crucial to an understanding of their artists, and they are exploring new ways for artists to have a major impact on a community in a brief period of time.

> We're headed toward coining a word like "intensives" rather than residencies, where someone would come and in a relatively short period of time, by using community resources, make a real impact. ... A prototype for us would be bringing Obo Addy [an artist from Ghana and his troupe] into a community

. . . Obo's troupe knows about some great Ghanaian food, and in many places there are Ghanaians, who probably could be co-opted into cooking a stew. . . . Some [members of the troupe] could teach dance and some could teach drumming; some could talk about the social-political situation in Ghana. We would like to experiment with it. . . . The point is that Obo is a great musician, but he has all these [things]—political, social, cultural—to share; it is kind of a tragedy that he doesn't get a chance to tell people about them. So, we could construct a day, and it wouldn't have to be so much more expensive.

Neill Roan sees presenters taking on a new role as producer, as they commission work that reflects the specific needs of their communities.

. . . the line between the presenter and producer is blurring. . . . Some work that is critical to [involving] the community doesn't exist, which means the work has to be commissioned. And it also means the number of resources available for research and development for artistic growth and for the support of artists has to be enriched and enhanced.

The diminution of resources for the arts is changing the dynamic and the role [of presenters]. The ecosystem is changing, growing and becoming larger and more fragile at the same time. One good thing that has [resulted] is that public policy leaders, especially foundations and the Endowment, are really focusing on issues of context, community, and connection.

Looking to the Future

Speculation about the future runs the risk of seeming foolish in retrospect. Nevertheless, there are several important themes discussed here that can be expected to resonate throughout this decade and perhaps into the next millennium. Reviewing the ideas provided by the individuals interviewed, it is worth highlighting several areas.

The most crucial of these themes start with the recognition of a need to develop audiences for the performing arts and touch on creative solutions to cope with that reality.

1. We will have to continue to fight for audiences. The question is whether we will be able to fight on the same turf as everyone else: television. Most of the performing arts are light years behind MTV in performance on video, and our use of television technology for marketing is still rooted in the 1950s. So are we forever unable to compete on TV, even on the expanding cable channels? What do we have to offer that can translate the unique experience of a live performance onto the moving image of the video screen? Or do we concede and find some other way to reach audiences, such as through community involvement, as mentioned by many of the individuals

interviewed? Can either of these methods really succeed alone, or do we need both?

2. If audiences are telling us they don't want to come to the arts, maybe artists and presenters need to go to them on their own terms. These days, people are used to getting information in smaller pieces and in shorter amounts of time. People are used to switching channels as they sit in front of a television set, getting up to make some popcorn, and taping programs for later or repeat viewing. They may not want to devote two hours to a chamber music concert. Does requiring them to sit in remote buildings for two hours to see a complete concert make sense for the future? And if not, what are the alternatives? Might we have to move towards shorter performances, perhaps with artists interacting with the public before or after the performance, explaining what to expect or discussing with the audience what they have just seen?

3. People want to "get it"; they don't want to feel stupid. If they feel that way once, they may be unlikely to come back. This phenomenon can affect children viewing performances in school as well as adult audiences. Do we need to "demystify" the performing arts by telling audiences exactly how to go about looking at an artist's work, or is this too much of a radical step? If we want to do so, how do we make the performance personally significant to the members of the audience? What responsibility do artists have to demystify the work they make?

4. Whatever the direction for touring and presenting in the nineties, it will not be based on increased dollars but rather on people's initiatives and ideas. Most people involved with the arts believe that funding from the federal or state governments will not increase as other priorities take precedence. However, several major foundations are increasing their commitment to the arts, at least in specific areas, and there is some new private sector interest in making the arts function harmoniously with commercial interests. In general, however, the field cannot anticipate a huge infusion of capital from either public or private sources.

5. There are no universal answers. Some organizations have begun to rethink how they tour and how they present; others are being forced to do so. What seems clear is that there is no formula that will work for every artist or company or presenter. Although many artists (and presenters) will continue to succeed using past methods, the number of performers who will find success on this route can be expected to dwindle. For the most part artists themselves will need to decide whether, within the context of the work and the needs of potential

audiences/communities, to conduct "business as usual" or to make changes.

The process of change may be fraught with insecurity, but with change all around us, no one can stand still. After all, change, when successful, brings about renewal and growth.

Interviewees and Their Affiliations*

Presenters

KIM CHAN, Washington Performing Arts Society, Washington, D.C.

JACQUELINE Z. DAVIS, Lied Center, University of Kansas, Lawrence, Kansas

JOSEPH GRESSER, Northern Vermont Performing Arts, Morrisville, Vermont

NEILL ARCHER ROAN, California Center for the Arts, Escondido, California

ANDREA WAGNER and MARK MURPHY, On The Boards, Seattle, Washington

Managers

JANET COWPERTHWAITE, managing director, Kronos Quartet

IVAN SYGODA, Director of Pentacle, a not-for-profit service organization providing administrative and booking services for a group of emerging and mainstream performing artists

IRENE NAMKUNG/JOHN ULLMAN, Traditional Arts Management, managers of traditional and world music artists

JOHN GINGRICH, president, John Gingrich Management, an agency representing primarily classical music artists

Funders

HENRY MORAN, executive director, Mid-America Arts Alliance, one of the six regional organizations

* At the time of the interviews the individuals were working at the identified organizations.

What Presenters Need from Artists

by Susan Farr

What presenters want from the artists who appear in their houses is the same thing the artists want—an outstanding performance for a large and enthusiastic audience. Because the immediate goal is the same for both, the relationship between artist and presenter should be viewed as a partnership. The outcome of this partnership will be successful only if each partner meets the agreed upon obligations—a process which requires both mutual respect and understanding. It seems appropriate, then, to review some of the topics covered in previous chapters, focusing on the needs of the presenter.

Booking Timelines

The booking process is the search for appropriate partners—a search governed by timelines (the schedule within which a presenter works to plan a season). Timelines vary from one presenter to the next, depending upon the presenting organization's size and the length and timing of the presentation season. As you begin your search for prospective partners, it is important to understand their respective timelines so that your efforts can be closely coordinated with theirs.

In order to finalize all their bookings several months before the mailing date of promotional materials, most presenters begin to plan their series one to one and a half years in advance. College and university presenters, therefore, begin planning in the early fall for the following year and try to finish booking in the spring. Presenting organizations whose seasons occur during the academic year generally work within this same timeline. Even longer lead times—often from two to four years—are required by large producing organizations, such as symphony orchestras, opera companies, and festivals which sometime book major stars several years in advance.

Smaller presenters with shorter seasons often work on shorter timelines. These organizations are frequently a company booking person's best bet for filling in the gaps in an otherwise solidly booked tour. Any planning cycle will be influenced by current economic conditions as well as the size and type of organization.

Booking Brochures

Whatever promotional pieces you send to a presenter, she will assume they are the best your company is capable of producing, and this reflects directly on the presenter's perception of your artistic product. Most likely, a shoddy brochure will not even be read; yet a clear, negative impression will have been made in the presenter's mind—an impression which may be difficult to overcome in the future. On the other hand, a good-quality piece will almost always be read, and the result will be a positive first step toward a successful booking.

Once you have found a good design, stick with it, so that each time a presenter receives your material—in the mail or at a booking conference—your company's positive image will be reinforced. The booking process is a long one, and presenter recognition of your artist or company will help your many efforts to have a cumulative effect.

In a booking brochure, presenters look for information about key artistic personnel (choreographers, directors, conductors, etc.), highlights of the repertory, and a clear and concise description of the type of work in which your company specializes. If a presenter cannot tell right away whether you are a modern dance or ballet company, she is unlikely to read further or remember you.

Finally, a word of caution about including fees in booking brochures. It is true that many presenters like to have this information from the beginning. It is also true that if a presenter has sufficient interest in your company, he will call to inquire about fees and availability. The most important thing—particularly in the early stages of the booking process—is to initiate and maintain an ongoing dialogue with potential presenters, whether or not this results in an immediate booking. A printed fee might deny you the opportunity. Although you may have a vacant tour date for which you would be happy to negotiate an enroute fee, the presenter in that area may show no interest simply because she has been put off by what she considered a fee too steep for her budget.

Booking Conferences

Most artists and managers will tell you that their first trip to a booking conference was a nightmare. They knew no one; they had no idea how to work the conference effectively; they came home with few, if any, bookings. Interestingly, as a rule, presenters report the same discouraging results—the first time. Successive meetings, however, are usually more fruitful for presenters and performing companies alike.

Certainly, meeting presenters is one of the most important parts of a manager's job. Booking conferences are an excellent—and economical—way to begin building rapport with a number of prospects in a brief period of time. They also give you the opportunity to observe experienced managers in action. If, as a solo artist, you are trying to decide between managing yourself and hiring a professional, this can be particularly helpful.

Preview Books

The organizers of several of the annual booking conferences distribute a guide to exhibitors to presenters at the conference. The book is a compilation of materials describing the offerings of artists and managements signed up for the conference.

If you wish your company to be included in the exhibitors guide, be sure to meet the organizer's deadline, and stay within the prescribed single-page format. The copy should briefly, but interestingly, characterize the artists—highlighting what is special and distinctive about their work—and include the name, address, and phone number of the individual handling bookings, whether a company staff member or an agent from an outside management firm (see Exhibit 14).

The unique advantage of this piece is that it has a life of only one booking season and, therefore, can include information that the booking brochure does not, such as fees (or fee ranges), available dates, and the specific repertory being offered in the upcoming tour. If you are doing a special program for a Bach anniversary, for example, this is the place to mention it.

Presenters use these books before, during, and after meetings. Although the material you give them in person may be lost or misplaced, as long as your name and telephone number are included in the preview book,

EXHIBIT 14

Sample Preview Book Information

★ ★ ★ ★ ★ ★ ★ ★ ★ ★ ★

━━━━━ TONY AWARD-WINNING ━━━━━

THE NATIONAL THEATRE OF THE DEAF

You <u>see</u> and hear every word

"This is brilliant, engrossing theatre for any audience, with a style and emotional power all its own."
The Louisville Times

Performances • Workshops • Residencies

*For fees and availability call Roddy O'Connor or
Saundra Hall at (203) 526-4971
or write The Hazel E. Stark Center, Chester, CT 06412*

ALL NEW TOURS 1996-97
Western, Southern,
New England, Mid-Atlantic
Midwest & Mid-America States

CURIOUSER *and* CURIOUSER

NOW BOOKING

interested presenters will not lose contact. Furthermore, most presenters do not get to every booth in the exhibit hall, and the preview book provides them with current information about artists and managements they did not have time to meet. Considering how important the book can be, it is surprising how many companies fail to submit their material on time.

Booth Display

At some conferences, your booth display will be one among as many as 250 others competing for the attention of presenters. It is essential that your display be of the highest quality possible and that it be imaginatively and carefully designed to invite passing presenters to stop by. As with all visual representations of your company, presenter recognition is one of the most effective ways to attract attention. Thus, the same image your company chooses for the preview book and the booking brochure should be reinforced in the design of the booth display.

In addition to having plenty of press packets available, presenters also like to see the poster and flier you will be using on the tour. If you have samples and if they are of good quality, you will be an important step ahead of those companies who are not prepared to show their promotional tools to the people who will be using them.

Many managers bring or rent equipment so that presenters can listen to audio recordings or watch videotapes in the booth. At most booking meetings, however, presenters do not have the time to watch or listen with concentration. Still, some may ask to borrow a record or tape to take back to their offices, and the more of this material you can provide, the better—but only if it is of outstanding quality. Audio-visuals make strong, lasting impressions. The impression made by a dimly lighted, clumsily edited video or a scratchy, worn-out recording may prove to be indelible.

Gimmicks and giveaways, such as buttons, food, and helium-filled balloons, are favored by some managers as a way to attract presenters to their booths. Sometimes these efforts bring presenters to a booth, but you should quickly try to move the conversation to business. If gimmicks are not improving traffic in your booth, perhaps you should let your product speak for itself. It may take a couple of booking conferences, but sooner or later people will come to your booth and listen to what you have to say whether or not you give them a cookie.

Working the Exhibit Hall

Generally two kinds of presenters come into the exhibit hall: those who know what they want and have come to book it and those who are gathering information for future decisions. If you are new to a particular conference, most of the people who come to your booth will be among the latter group. (See Exhibit 15 for a sample of the type of information presenters gather.) Be friendly and outgoing with everyone who stops by. Learn as much as you can about the organizations they represent. Ask questions about their programming and their facilities. Try to ascertain if what your company offers relates to what they have presented in the past or are considering for the future. (At many conferences, there is a place for presenters to display copies of their own brochures. Pick up as many as you can and study them carefully.)

A presenter with dozens of companies to investigate will not want to spend a great deal of time at any one booth, so make the most of whatever time you have. Be sure each presenter leaves your booth with a booking brochure and any additional material he may specifically request. By the close of your conversation, you should have a pretty good idea of whether or not you are likely to hear from the presenter again.

If you have done a thorough job of promoting your artist or company prior to the conference, you may be visited by a presenter who already has some interest in a booking. If so, it is important to gauge just how serious the interest is. One of the most frequent complaints about presenters is that often they lead artists and managers to count on a booking, but then later, when the lead is pursued, the presenter fails to return phone calls or letters—leaving the manager wondering what happened.

Getting a commitment can be a delicate matter; you must not, in your eagerness, push so hard that you drive the presenter away. If a presenter comes to your booth and says, "We are definitely interested in booking your company," you should immediately determine whether she is ready to commit to actual dates for his upcoming series or is referring instead to some unspecified future season. Even in the latter case, you should not be discouraged. If the interest is serious, keep the connection open with phone calls and mailings in the months following the conference.

If the presenter comes to you prepared to commit to a booking, treat her as the full partner she is about to become. Begin by asking what she needs to know immediately. Before proceeding further, of course, for your own sake you should make certain that the presenter knows your fees and is willing to negotiate in the appropriate range. Interestingly enough, however, from the presenter's standpoint your availability on specific dates may be the more immediate concern. Many presenting organizations have limited access to performance halls and are able to present programs only during a set time period.

Be absolutely honest and forthright about availability. Whether you have severe limitations ("I can only offer you October 22 or 28") or none at all ("We have not yet set the tour dates. What would be best for you?"),

EXHIBIT 15

Sample Booking Conference Information Chart

UCSB Arts & Lectures

Management ______________________________ Date ______________

Artist/Company ______________________________
Availability ______________________________
Other Presenters ______________________________
Fees/Fee Support ______________________________
Notes ______________________________
____
____
____

Artist/Company ______________________________
Availability ______________________________
Other Presenters ______________________________
Fees/Fee Support ______________________________
Notes ______________________________
____
____
____

Artist/Company ______________________________
Availability ______________________________
Other Presenters ______________________________
Fees/Fee Support ______________________________
Notes ______________________________
____
____
____

Courtesy of UCSB

say so. Dating a tour is crucial to both the company and the presenter. If you add a date which requires too much travel time, the company is unlikely to perform at its best, which will leave everyone unhappy. Because booking conferences are held so far in advance of performance seasons, many of the presenters you meet will have a certain amount of flexibility. If your tour dates, likewise, are not yet set, get at least two time periods which work for the presenter and tell him that you will be in touch as your scheduling progresses. Ask the same of the presenter; he should contact you immediately if his plans change—if, for instance, he can no longer present you during the time periods which were available when you talked at the conference.

Other Conference Activities

Seldom are conference activities limited to what takes place in the exhibit hall. Often, there will be formal workshops or lectures, business meetings of the organization presenting the conference, or social activities. Many people have found that much of their most productive work is done in these settings. The marketplace tensions of the exhibit hall can be intimidating to presenters and managers alike, and the other activities offer a refreshing change of pace. By observing presenters in workshops or meetings, you can learn a lot about how they conduct business. If you meet a presenter at a cocktail party or a luncheon and have a pleasant, unpressured conversation, it is much more likely that he will stop by your booth in the exhibit hall.

Managers who spend their free time at conferences sitting by the pool commiserating with other managers about how badly things are going are wasting valuable opportunities to turn things around. No doubt their more skillful, more seasoned colleagues will be spending the same time more profitably, building relationships with potential partners. Apart from booking conferences, meeting presenters face-to-face can be prohibitively expensive and extremely time-consuming. During a conference, take advantage of every opportunity. Work hard; make every moment count.

Hold That Date: What To Do

The weeks or, more likely, months prior to the signing of the contract—during which time neither partner has a firm hold on the other's time and services—are nerve-wracking for everyone. In far too many cases, presenters have held dates open—dates which were terribly important to their series—only to find, when they called the manager to contract the engagement, that the date is no longer available. Perhaps even more often, managers who have planned tours around the dates given them by presenters find, when they call to confirm, that plans have changed and the presenter is no longer interested in the company. Both of these situations are avoidable through frequent, ongoing, honest communication between managers and presenters.

Once a presenter has actually placed a "hold" on a specific date, the tour manager should be able to count on the presenter's continuing commitment and his intention to contract an engagement. Be forewarned, however: not all presenters understand this. Nor do all managers, some of whom—because they are so anxious to book a date—merely compound the inherently complex logistics of tour scheduling by suggesting a tentative hold ("I'll just lightly pencil you in."). A manager who makes this mistake has only himself to blame for the frustrations which are almost certain to result.

If a presenter places a hold on a date, it is not inappropriate to ask when he thinks the date can be confirmed or what circumstances are preventing confirmation. This will give you a better idea of how likely the hold is to go to contract. The presenter may be having problems dating another performance around the same time; he may need to confirm the availability of his hall; he may be awaiting notification regarding a grant without which the organization will be unable to finance the performance. He might even be waiting for further information from you—about a special residency program, for example—which his organization requires before moving from hold to contract. This is another one of those times when viewing the presenter as a potential partner and keeping an open and honest dialogue going will be extremely helpful.

Negotiating Fees

As mentioned in Chapter 6, during negotiations one of the alternatives to accepting a reduced fee is agreeing to provide special services and activities in addition to performances. This can be very important to some presenters. If you have done your research, you should know which presenters are likely to be interested in residency activities.

An experienced presenter should respect your limits and not try to wring you dry during negotiations. Do not be afraid to refuse to go below a certain minimum on your fee, and never agree to more services than your company can comfortably provide. Explain your situation to the presenter. If she will not accept your reasoning, be prepared to forfeit the booking if necessary. The respect and understanding between partners must be equal.

In recent years, presenters have been seeking percentage agreements with increasing frequency. Negotiating percentages can be tricky. It requires careful attention to details, good judgment, and mutual trust. Young, unknown artists performing for the first time in a particular area should almost never agree to a percentage; it is unlikely that they will draw an audience large enough to return an adequate sum.

The most common reason for a presenter to request a percentage agreement is to reduce her financial risk. Most presenters are more than willing to share profits if the artists are willing to share some of the risk, in which case presenter and artist become true partners. Often, presenters feel that artists have little or no investment in the box office success or failure of a particular date. After all, with a set fee, the company gets paid regardless of how many or how few people attend, regardless of how much money the presenter might lose.

When a company enters into a percentage agreement, however, management and artists have an incentive to help sell tickets—by sending good publicity materials on time, by granting phone interviews, by coming into town a day or two early to do in-person interviews for the local media, and by getting program copy to the presenter promptly. Likewise, the presenter, in order to get the maximum return on the date—for the benefit of both partners—should work closely with the company to promote the event in using the resources the company provides.

If a presenter suggests a percentage agreement, give due consideration to the proposal, but withhold your consent until you are confident that your company has a reasonable chance to benefit. Be sure to cover all the bases. Before signing on the dotted line, consult someone who has been through the process before.

Contracts

In the contract, each party is seeking maximum protection against default. However, in many cases, the actual dollar amounts are so small that there is little likelihood of either party suing the other for breach. Therefore, while it is important to protect your interests contractually, you should think of the contract primarily as an informational document.

If you use your own contract form, it is likely that presenters will want to make changes. Before sending a contract, call the presenter to discuss any unusual clauses. Surprising him with a clause that requires his organization to provide extensive and expensive services for the artists is a sure way to make him angry and may endanger your booking.

A presenter should not receive a contract until all the terms have been negotiated verbally. When you send the document, ask the presenter to call you if he wishes to discuss any changes. If you do hear from him, be open-minded about his requests, and be realistic—and flexible—about compromising. If, for example, you have asked for an advance on your fee and the presenter's board or parent institution has a policy against advance payments, you would be wise to find another way to handle the matter. If, on the other hand, the presenter informs you that he cannot provide some essential service, such as an appropriate floor for a dance company, stand firm, even if it means sacrificing the date.

Some presenters are required, or choose, to use their own contracts, rather than sign a company's standard form. This is particularly common in educational institutions, and you will severely limit your touring if you refuse out of hand to use presenters' contracts. The practice presents no particular danger as long as you understand the terms and are able to agree to them.

If you wish to make changes in a presenter's contract, call to discuss them and come to an agreement over the phone. Most presenters respond negatively to getting their contracts back with major revisions that they have not accepted in advance.

The two contractual obligations which managements most often fail to meet have to do with timeliness. The resulting problems drive presenters crazy:

1. Do not agree to deadlines that you *know* you cannot meet. If the presenter's contract states that you will send posters no later than August 1 and your press run is set for August 15, inform the presenter immediately and suggest a deadline you can meet. Most presenters have some flexibility in promotional timelines, but they must be able to count on receiving materials by whatever dates you agree to.

2. Send and return contracts promptly. This is to your benefit as much as the presenter's. If a presenter has trouble getting his contract returned, he will begin to doubt your ability or willingness to perform in his series. Too many presenters have had the experience of sending a contract, not hearing from the artist or manager for some time, and then—at a point so late in their timelines that the situation is critical—learning from the manager or, worse, from a third party that the date has fallen through. Presenters are guilty of this lack of professionalism just as frequently as touring companies, but that is no excuse for you to handle your business badly. The entire touring industry would benefit enormously from an improvement in this area alone.

Programs

Presenters almost never get program information early enough, and artists almost always think they are required to provide it too soon. Yet, for some presenters, the programming is almost as important as the performers themselves, especially if a series includes more than one group of your type.

Presenters approach program development in several ways. Many presenters try to build a balanced season of different artists performing different pieces. If the presenting organization is a chamber music society, for example, it may not want to offer their audiences an entire season of works by a single composer or from any one period. The presenter of a dance series will most likely be uncomfortable if every company performs the same piece, or even different pieces of the same style. Other presenters may be planning a series within a specific genre or era. For example, a presenter may want to have the same piece performed by different ensembles to demonstrate various interpretations. Another presenter planning performances related to a specific time, place, or idea will want to know how all the works being performed relate to their chosen theme.

In any of these cases, a presenter may actually request a specific program. It is in your best interest to make every effort to give the presenter what she needs. The more satisfied she is with your performances—the more responsive her audiences are—the more likely she is to invite you back.

Another reason presenters need program material by a particular date is to meet printing deadlines. Some presenting organizations publish program magazines which include several events. If your concert is at the end of a series, the deadline for copy may seem early to you, but it is crucial to the presenter. If you are late, even by a few days, you will cause the publication to be late, or incomplete. Either way, the presenter is likely to incur additional costs which you may be expected to pay.

For most presenters, one of the more important components of this material is the program notes. Seldom will a presenter's staff include anyone trained to write this kind of copy. But presenters know that thorough and readable notes greatly enhance the audience's enjoyment of a performance. Surprisingly few companies seem to be aware of this. At least, few take the time to prepare the notes. If the cost of hiring a skilled program note writer is the problem, build the expense of developing this material into your fee and prorate it over the tour.

Program notes will not make the difference between getting a booking or being passed by. But, as in every other part of the presenter–touring company relationship, your willingness to extend yourself beyond minimum expectations will reflect positively on the presenter's overall perception of your company.

One final word about programming: do not make changes capriciously. If patrons have paid to see a particular piece or artist, they are likely to react badly to disappointment. Although most presenters publish a disclaimer regarding last-minute changes, it is always preferable to give the audience what it came to see. If you must alter the program, carefully explain to the presenter why you are doing so—a performer is ill or injured, your music went to Chicago and the concert is in an hour, the piece has not gone well on the tour and you would prefer to do something more promising—whatever. The important thing is to inform the presenter as soon as you know that a change must be made, and discuss how best to give notice of the change to the audience. Whatever you can do to make a change easier for the presenter will be much appreciated.

Promotion

Posters and Fliers. Your budget for posters and fliers is not the place to cut corners. For the presenter, these are essential selling tools, and they must be of the best quality that you can afford. In fact, it is better not to provide these materials if all you can come up with is an amateurish, hastily conceived, poorly designed piece. Presenters may choose not to use them rather than have their organizations associated with inferior visuals. If for any reason you are unable to provide posters and fliers, advise the presenter during the negotiation process, and be prepared to accept a lower fee to compensate for the presenter's costs of producing the materials himself.

Photographs. Poor-quality photographs are another frequent headache for presenters. Standard publicity shots should be eight- by ten-inch, black-and-white glossies suitable for newspaper reproduction. If you are uncertain whether your photos will reproduce well, take them to your local paper and ask. Action shots are generally preferable to head shots, and dance and theatre companies should be sure that their photos (clearly labeled) are of the works to be performed on the presenter's program. Some critics refuse to run photos from works other than those they are reviewing.

Some presenters also use color photos, videos, or slides. If you can provide them, your company or artist may well get more exposure than the performers in the same series who have only black-and-white glossies. It is perfectly reasonable, by the way, to ask that color slides be returned following the performance.

Communication. Ongoing communication between management and presenter is essential to effective promotion. If you have not heard from a presenter about specific materials, call to make sure he has everything that he needs. Some managers work directly with presenters to develop and schedule a promotional strategy or campaign. The manager has the advantage of knowing what has worked at other stops on the tour and may also have information about the company or performers specific to the particular date. The stop may be the hometown of a member of the company; it may even be an anniversary performance; there may be some personal angle which, although unrelated to the performance, could be of interest to the local public. For example, in an area with a large and active disabled population, an article about an artist's work to assist the disabled to live independently would be of interest.

It is important to understand that, even with your full cooperation and support, a presenter may be unable to attract a large audience for your performance. There may be a major competing event or the presenter may be in the process of building an audience for a particular art form, such as new music. Most presenters have some idea from the beginning, however, of the number of tickets they will be able to sell. Ask them what they are anticipating. It is best that you and your artists know what to expect before the curtain goes up—particularly if expectations are modest.

A presenter's choice not to mount a major promotional campaign for your performance is not necessarily reason to take offense. The presenter may know that your program is going to sell in his area without substantial promotion. In one case, when a musician complained that he had seen no advertising of his performance during the two days he had been in town, he was delighted to learn that, although a number of ads had been placed early on, the presenter had recently cancelled as many of them as possible because the performance had been sold out for two weeks!

At the opposite extreme, even with the most extensive campaign, ticket sales may be disappointing. If so, the presenter must decide when to cut his organization's losses. Under no circumstances, however, should a presenter request material from you which he does not intend to use.

Other Arrangements

Rehearsal Space. Rehearsal arrangements are often one of a presenter's most problematic concerns. Sometimes it is difficult enough to arrange for a company's full use of the theatre for technical installation and run-throughs, and full-company rehearsals. Providing additional studio space can be even more of a problem. At colleges and universities, the studios and rehearsal rooms are often in use by academic departments. Other kinds of presenters may have to go completely outside their own institutions to find space, and this can be expensive.

Dance and theatre companies should carefully review their rehearsal needs well in advance of an engagement and notify presenters immediately if the theatre will not be sufficient. Unless you can foresee your need for extra space early enough to make it a part of the contract, the presenter is under no obligation to provide this service. In any case, be prepared to pay for the space if your company's needs are unusually extensive.

Arranging rehearsal space for musicians would seem to be a simpler matter; actually, it can be very complex. Often the recital hall must be reserved for rehearsal time just as it is for a performance. In addition, the presenter must allow time for piano tuning. Again, you must determine precisely what you need as early as possible, and as soon as you know, inform the presenter. Be specific. Do not say, "We need somewhere to rehearse for a couple of hours before the performance," and expect to find rehearsal space ready and waiting for you. It is much better to say, "We need to rehearse in the hall Tuesday from 11 A.M. to 3 P.M."

If you have requested rehearsal space and later find that you will not be using it, be sure to let the presenter know right away. Many times she will have assigned a staff member to meet you at the hall, unlock the door, turn on the lights, and show you around. If you simply do not show up, you will have inconvenienced the presenter and may well have cost her money.

Transportation. This is another area which seems to be a problem more often than necessary. If you require any assistance from the presenter, discuss it well in advance. Be reasonable about your requests. Many presenters do not have the staff, volunteers, or vehicles necessary to provide this kind of service; they will need plenty of time to plan—and budget—for it. Large ensembles of any kind usually understand this and plan accordingly. Soloists and small groups seem to cause the most problems.

If you are traveling to an out-of-the-way place that has no public transportation, you will generally find the presenter eager to help. In more populous areas, however, where there are usually several alternatives, the presenter may expect you to take a cab or rent a car. If a presenter does agree to meet you at the airport, notify her promptly of any changes in your travel plans. If a busy presenter manages to arrive punctually and then, after a long, frustrating wait, returns to her office to find that the artist, at the last minute, asked his sister to pick him up, the residency will not be starting on a cheerful note.

Obviously, the presenter knows her own area better than you do, and it is always reasonable to expect her to provide transportation to any services you are providing away from the theatre. It is also reasonable to expect the presenter to be present at residency activities.

Coordinating Schedules. Before you depart for an engagement, call the presenter to confirm when you will arrive in town, where you will be staying, and when you expect to arrive at the theatre. It is also helpful to the presenter to know where to reach you during the week or so prior to your arrival, in case he has any last-minute questions. When you do arrive in town, call to let the presenter know where you are. He should not have to wonder if you made it.

Relationships. The extent and type of contact you have with the presenter will depend on your engagement. If you are playing a recital and plan to arrive in town two hours before the curtain rises and leave as soon as it falls, your only contact may be a quick hello before the concert and a brief chat afterwards. If you are in town for several days, however, you may spend a significant amount of time with the presenter, or with members of his staff. Experienced presenters will provide you with an itinerary and some information about the town in which you are staying. They will also give you a copy of the program and discuss the disposition of your complimentary tickets. Some presenters will be happy to provide you with temporary office space (a desk and a phone).

Both managers and artists should take advantage of any opportunity to get to know a presenter informally. If you are dissatisfied with some aspect of your stay, it will be easier to discuss your problem with a presenter with whom you have developed an easygoing relationship. Do not be afraid to ask for things that will make your stay more pleasant, but be reasonable in your expectations. Little things like parking permits, athletic facility passes, or specialty food may be more difficult for a presenter to provide than you think. But as long as your requests are reasonable, most presenters will appreciate the opportunity to make your visit as enjoyable as possible.

Performance Details. Sometime prior to the performance, consult with the presenter regarding house policies. Are latecomers seated at the end of the first movement or at the end of the first complete piece? Is there a policy about small children in the audience? Does the presenter expect a performance to start on time, or is it customary to start five minutes late? Will you be expected to receive audience members following the per-formance? The presenter may expect you to answer some of these questions; when to seat latecomers, for example, is quite often left up to the artists. Be prepared to help make the event run as smoothly as possible by sharing your preferences and then abiding by whatever is agreed upon.

After the Performance

The appropriate amount and type of follow-up will depend on how the residency goes. If you have the luxury of staying in town for a day or so afterwards, meet with the presenter to discuss your visit. Unless there has been some major disaster, most presenters will be reluctant to say anything at all negative, and you may have to read between the lines. It is a good idea to solicit comments with direct questions. "Did our technical crew do a good job?" "Were you satisfied with the master class?" "Were your donors pleased with the reception?" "Do you think the program was balanced, appropriate for the audience, too long or short?"

It is always better to find these things out directly from the presenter, rather than to have them catch up with you two stops down the road where word of the previous presenter's dissatisfactions may have preceded you. If you have to leave town immediately, follow up with a phone call or letter as soon as the tour is over, if not before. If the feedback is positive, be sure to ask the presenter if you can use him as a reference. This is also the time to ask if things look promising for a return engagement.

Whether or not you are diligent about maintaining a dialogue with past presenters, you can count on the fact that presenters do communicate with each other. In newsletters, at meetings, and on the phone, one of the most frequent questions is, "So how did the XYZ company's performance go?" Reports of your inability to meet deadlines, your inflexibility during negotiations, your betrayal of the presenter's good faith, or your lack of cooperation at the theatre will make future bookings more difficult. On the other hand, there is nothing as effective for clinching a booking with a presenter as an enthusiastic recommendation from a colleague.

Touring from a Technical Viewpoint

by M. Kay Barrell

The common goal of both the performer and the presenter is the best possible production, given the available time space and money.

The simplest and most inexpensive key to that end is accurate information. Facing the truth about a performer's company or a sponsor's facility can be painful, but for a successful performance the company and the presenter must assess their capabilities and limitations and share reality with each other.

Before a company can communicate real production information to a presenter, it must know where it stands in relation to the rest of the other similar organizations in the touring market. The quality of a company's production while touring may be very different from the same company's productions at home. It may have different equipment, different personnel, different repertory, and a completely different look.

Before a company can effectively commit to touring, it must take a long, objective look at a number of points, both philosophical and practical. Touring may often appear to be a financial panacea to a cash-strapped company, when in reality it can become a financial and artistic disaster. This chapter will deal with the technical questions and shy away from the philosophical ones. If after analyzing the needs and capabilities of your company you find that there are too many compromises required for touring, then touring is not an appropriate option.

The Need for Real Information

Communication is the key to successful touring. It has to come quickly and correctly from both parties. Before a company ever commits to tour it must decide what it is artistically, what it can supply from a production standpoint, what it requires from a production standpoint, and where it can be flexible from a production standpoint.

Taking Stock of What You Have

What equipment does the company have, and what will it take with it on tour? Different companies travel with vastly different amounts of equipment. Some large "four-wall" companies need nothing more from the presenter than an empty house of the proper dimensions and adequate electrical service. They travel with complete lighting and sound systems, their own draperies and floor, as well as full sets and costumes. At the other end of the scale are the many companies that climb on an airplane and put the entire production inventory (twelve costumes and nine sheets of gel) in the overhead bins. Oftentimes, traveling with as much equipment as possible makes life easier for both the company and the presenter, (it is often quicker to hang and focus your own lights than to learn the eccentricities of someone else's). There is, of course, an enormous cost involved; a company should travel only with what they cannot do without. Here, you must decide not so much what you want but what you *must have*.

Assessing What You Need

What does the company need from the presenter? First, the presenter must provide a space for the performance. In order to do a quality performance, the company will always ask for an adequate space, but the answer as to what constitutes an *adequate* space is a source of frequent argument and compromise. Once the absolute minimum acceptable dimensions of width, depth, height, wing space, and storage have been determined, the company will have to determine what will be required by the presenter in order to perform to a given standard.

Equipment needs vary drastically from company to company. Some companies have very few requirements because their production values are simple. Some have enormous requirements but travel with their own equipment. Still others have elaborate technical requirements and expect the presenter to take care of those needs. This is acceptable if all parties are familiar with the costs and compromises involved.

If the company will be counting on the presenter to provide a significant amount of equipment, both parties must know each other's limitations and ability to accommodate the other. Some items (lighting instruments and draperies, for example) are common to most theatres. Others are more specialized (i.e., special effects projectors, portable dance floors, wireless mikes) and may not only be unavailable in the theatre, but may be impossible to find in the vicinity. Often the stock stage equipment that the presenter may see as perfectly acceptable in the theatre, may not necessarily be acceptable to the touring company.

Crew size is linked to factors such as the amount of pre-performance time available in the theatre, local union rules, the capabilities of non-union crews (and for that matter union crews), and the specific repertory of the company. The company will need honest information from the presenter regarding schedule and crew competence before it can accurately determine the number of crew members required to prepare for and run the performance.

Amenities such as food and drink for performers or crew, special accommodations, and equipment specifications (i.e., the piano must be a Steinway nine-foot grand, or the lighting booms must be lag bolted to the floor) may not seem to be critical items to a presenter. They may even appear to be sheer foolishness. However, if the company considers them indispensable, these perceived amenities can become necessities, and they must be given the same consideration as the performance space, equipment list, and the crew call.

If something is important enough for a company to include in the contract, it is crucial for the sponsor to attend to. If the sponsor can't meet the letter of the contract and any associated riders then he or she shouldn't sign the agreement. Conversely, the company should only require items in the contract that it truly needs.

Flexibility

How flexible is the company willing to be in regard to performing space, equipment, time in the theatre, crew, and amenities?

A company must be very specific about what it is willing to live with or, more appropriately, what it cannot live without. A company that is absolutely inflexible will have a more difficult time getting bookings than a company willing to work with existing conditions, especially in the smaller (but more numerous) theatres. Traditionally, large companies are less flexible than smaller companies; often because they can afford to be.

If a ballet company insists on laying its own floor over an identical surface already installed on the stage, the company is being inflexible— not necessarily bad, just inflexible. If, however, the presenter does not have a dance surface, then the company's provision of one will mean a major rental savings. Another, smaller dance company, that travels without a dance surface and is adamant that the presenter not only rent a floor but insists on a specific brand name or a specific color, is inflexible. In this instance, if the specified floor is not readily available, the company's inflexibility will cost the presenter substantial rental money and possibly create ill-will if it is seen as an extravagance by the presenter.

Real Information Starts at Home

If a presenter is informed of, and has agreed to, the needs and critical production elements, and has still signed the contract, then all is well—assuming the presenter has comprehended what has been agreed to.

Everyone in the company, especially the artistic and production staffs and the booking management, must know and agree on what the company is really about, what it needs, and how much it can adapt on tour. Facing the realities may cost the company some booking dates, but may also save those presenters who remain committed thousands of dollars on the production, and avoid untold dollars of ill will in the long run.

Presenter Reality

Just as the company must face reality about production requirements, the presenter must face the reality of his or her organization's capabilities and the reality of the facility. The dilemma here is that the company cannot necessarily depend on the presenter's willingness, or ability, to do so. Once the company has arrived at the theatre, there is little that can be done do to address any misrepresentations that had been made by the presenter. Because time limitations are usually great, last-minute remedies will be slap-dash at best, and canceling a performance is catastrophic for all parties. In the end, the touring company must not only be responsible for their own preparations, but must do everything possible to see that the presenter fulfills his or her part of the bargain.

The Dangers of Misinformation

Receiving misinformation is very common and is often worse than receiving no information at all. The three common reasons why misinformation is passed between company and presenter are: (1) the wrong people are disseminating the information; (2) laziness; and (3) romanticism.

An uninformed person, be it a presenter, a booking agent, a secretary, or a volunteer receptionist, is the most frequent culprit disseminating misinformation. The safest path for the flow of technical information is directly from one technician to another. Every middle man simply offers another chance for error. The technicians from both parties that are ultimately responsible for the success or failure of a performance date, need to communicate the realities to one another.

The second culprit responsible for misinformation is laziness: Stock facility descriptions and equipment inventory lists are useful only if they are 100 percent correct. Sadly, this is seldom the case. Often, stated dimensions are only estimates correct to the nearest few feet, and the inventory list may have been compiled fifteen years ago when the theatre first opened. A stock facility packet should be checked and corrected yearly. If a packet is dated five years ago (or not dated at all), it should not be trusted as a source of reliable information. Out-of-date contracts and riders are equally useless.

Problem number three is romanticism; it may be appealing on stage, but backstage it causes disasters. Most presenters are extremely proud of their facilities, and many do not want to accept that their facility may be flawed or poorly maintained. A presenter may enjoy touting the merits of his theatre's marvelous dimming system. But,if the dimmer controller is not reliable or one third of the dimmers don't work the company that is depending on them will not be in serious trouble. Conversely, a company whose technical rehearsals traditionally take eight hours has no place claiming that they will need only half that time. Neither party likes, or needs, such surprises.

Gathering Information

The company has to learn as much as possible about the realities of the facility. It is critical to receive complete information well in advance of the company's arrival. Space limitations or eccentricities may well determine the choice of repertory or even preclude accepting an engagement. Decisions that must be made and designs that must be adjusted are better accomplished in the relative calm of the production office, rather than in an unfamiliar facility, with a performance deadline looming and a union crew standing watching the clock tick like a taxi-meter.

What Information Do You Need?

There are many kinds of information needed to intelligently assess an unknown performing space. Some are specific; some are intangible. The specifics should be included in a facility information packet supplied by the presenter.

Of first importance in the facility information packet are detailed dimensions and an overall description of the space. These should include the stage, fly space, wing space, electrical mounting positions, and dressing and storage areas. The more detailed the information available to a company—including accurate widths, depths, and heights—the better.

Second, is a listing of all stage machinery, including all fly systems, elevators, traps, and any other miscellaneous machinery. This should include detailed descriptions of these elements. A description of a fly system, for example, should include: type of system, single or double purchase, length of battens, spacing of battens, arbor capacities, maximum fly height of each batten, any permanently hung pieces, and any eccentricities or obstructions in the system. This is not simple stuff, but it is essential for most performing groups. Next, it is important to have an equipment inventory, a detailed listing of all lighting and dimming equipment, sound systems, and draperies. Again, these listings should be detailed, accurate, and describe any problem elements.

The most difficult elements of a theatre to assess, and the most deadly, are the eccentricities that have not already been made evident. Items such as columns in the wing space, electrical mounting positions that are totally inaccessible, or battens that can't fly since they're sandwiched between duct-work, may sound far-fetched; but these, and innumerable other oddities, are not uncommon.

All equipment and machinery needs to be evaluated qualitatively by someone. If equipment does not work properly, it is of little or no use. Such evaluation is particularly crucial for lighting, dimming, and sound equipment. To dance companies, the floor—its composition, its resilience, and its surface—is often the most critical element of a stage.

Finally, getting a sense of the crew's proficiency and attitude are critical to gauge the real time requirements for a production. These intangible factors are sometimes the most difficult to assess, but are often the most decisive in the success or failure of a production.

Paperwork

The prime tool used to gather the information needed by a company is the technical questionnaire. It is well worth the time necessary to compile it. A good questionnaire will be from one to fifteen pages, depending on the needs of the company. (See the example in Appendix C.)

The questionnaire, compiled by the company technician, should ask the telling questions most relevant to the company and its touring needs. An effective technical questionnaire will ask specific questions needed for a specific production. It won't necessarily ask the same questions as the facility packet supplied by the presenter. The specific information needed will differ very radically from company to company. It should be written in such a way that it remains a questionnaire and does not become a requirement sheet or technical rider. If a technical questionnaire asks too many general questions it may be glossed over by the presenter or the technical director. It should be the place where critical questions are asked and the intangibles are addressed.

Additional Paperwork

A company should request any stock information that the theatre may have. Any well-managed theatre should be able to supply a stock technical information sheet. The quality of the information is a telling determiner of the overall quality of the operation. This sheet should include a detailed line plot, or hanger log. A stock form may duplicate some of the information gathered in the company's technical questionnaire, but discrepancies noted in a comparison of the two can be a tell-tale of potential problems. If there are scale plans and/or sections of the theatre available, they can be very useful.

The Information Gathering Process

The earlier the company can obtain information about a facility, the sooner it can begin preparations. Basically, there are two ways for a company to gather information about a facility: (1) from the presenter; or (2) by its own advance man (I don't mean to be politically incorrect but that's the term).

The Advance Man

Sending an advance man is, theoretically, the most efficient and reliable means of gathering information. The company representative inspects the space personally and can verify the dimensions and check the amount and condition of equipment. He or she will also have the opportunity to get acquainted with the little peculiarities of the facility that are often the most troublesome aspect of producing in a new space.

Using an advance man is not without drawbacks, however. The first is money. Salary plus the extra expenses of travel and per diem make it very costly—and often prohibitive—to send a person out on the road for no other reason than to gather information about theatre spaces. Second (which also has to do with money), to do the job properly, an advance man must be a technician, preferably the same technician who will be supervising the company on tour.

Some companies try to economize by adding the responsibilities of the technical advance man to those of the p.r. person or booking manager. This has merit only if, in addition to his or her other skills, the person is a qualified technician. Although any traveling company representative should take every opportunity to examine prospective performing spaces, most are not qualified to gather the detailed technical information that is really essential, especially since the most important information (that regarding eccentricities and inadequacies) is often very subtle, or hidden by a well-meaning sponsor eager to make a good impression.

Gathering Information without Traveling

If a company cannot send an advance man (most can't), then it must gather information via the mail or over the phone. Since two-hour, long-distance phone calls can get expensive, the first step is to have the presenter's technician send any stock technical information available, then fill out the company's technical questionnaire. Some house technicians consider this a bother and a redundancy; often they are. Many stock forms are very good, but none can answer all relevant questions in advance. Many theatres use the same sheet several years in a row, and due to new purchases or—more often—attrition, the information is misleading or downright bogus. A company has the right to insist that a theatre fill out its technical questionnaire completely. The best leverage is to stipulate that the contract cannot be signed until the technical questionnaire is returned.

If the members of the theatre staff are qualified and know their space and equipment, completing the questionnaire will not be difficult. More importantly, if they are not qualified and do not know their facility, it will become glaringly apparent. This is a telling point in the information gathering process; it is as important to learn about the people that the company will be dealing with as it is to learn about the facility. It is as important to get a sense of the qualifications and attitude of the technicians as it is to know whether the connectors are stage-pin or twist-lock.

Once the company has received the technical questionnaire, it should be examined carefully by the company's technician. He or she should then note problems or obvious discrepancies, contact the presenter's technician by phone, and go over any areas in question. This is also the best time to go over theatre schedules and crew calls. Though tentative theatre schedules are often discussed in the initial presenter-booking manager conversations, they should not be finalized until the technical representatives of both parties reach an agreement.

The final way to gather information about a space that, although not formal, can be an invaluable supplemental aid, is discussion between technicians from other, similar, companies who have performed previously in the same space. Most theatre technicians love to talk to one another, especially if it concerns tour stories. Contact with another company's technicians can give insight into personalities, problems, and eccentricities that could never be gained any other way.

Transmitting Information: Plots and Riders

Among the final paperwork sent by the company to the presenter are several documents which transmit important technical information. These are the technical rider, the light plot, and the hanging plot.

Tech Riders

It is common practice to add a rider to the contract that specifies what the presenter must provide. Some companies require large amounts of support and equipment from a presenter; some are willing to use whatever is available; others require little more than a shell of a building. The rider is a means of restating and agreeing to what will be needed. It legally binds both parties to everything it stipulates and frees everyone from any obligations not specified either in the rider or the contract.

A technical rider should list, very specifically, all of the physical elements required by the company that the presenter must furnish. If a company knows the technical limitations of the theatre in advance, the rider can be written to reflect the reality of the space. Technical riders that are generalized tend to be no better than the out-of-date stock technical information sheet distributed by the theatre year after year.

Inconsistencies should be avoided. If the rider specifies that the proscenium must have a fifty-foot opening, and in the contract the company agrees to perform on a stage thirty-six-feet wide, the rider becomes a sham and the presenter will, often, disregard the entire document. Selectively agreeing to ignore portions of a technical rider without officially agreeing to them cannot only make the company look foolish, in some instances it will nullify the legality of the entire contract. To be most effective, a technical rider should be modified for each engagement and accurately reflect the company's true needs.

In addition to the company's physical requirements, addressing amenities and procedural requirements is just as important. Once agreed to in writing, these stipulations, too, must be enforced. If a presenter agrees to maintain the temperature on stage between 72 and 85 degrees and then disregards this responsibility, he or she is in breach of contract.

In writing a technical rider, a company should require only what is crucial and leave out the superfluous. If the company has optional requests, these should be communicated verbally and noted as such.

The other two pieces of information that come from the company, the light plot and the hanging plot, are often tied very closely to the technical rider. They are frequently merged into a single document, called a *light and hanging plot*, in some instances they are considered part of the tech rider. If so, the presenter should not sign the contract until he or she has received the completed light and hanging plot and had the appropriate technician scrutinize it thoroughly. This means that the company may have to create a final plot months before the tour.

More common is the practice of leaving the light and hanging plot separate from the contract and, therefore, open to negotiation between the company and the presenter. This is the more humane approach and gives both parties the ability to create the best product with the least waste. Plots that are designed with the specific theatre in mind tend to be more flexible, less expensive, less problematic to achieve, and more effective. But, to custom design an effective light or hanging plot for a space, a designer must have good, correct information about the theatre in advance.

Light Plots

A light plot is an encoded plan view of the stage that shows the electrical mounting positions with the lighting instruments drawn on them. Plots range from simple to complex, but their function remains the same—to inform. The light plot and the accompanying hanging plot serve as the guides for mounting the production.

There are basically three different types of light plots for touring theatre: the stock plot, the four-wall plot, and the custom plot. The company's size and circumstances will determine the type of plot used. The style is also influenced by the emphasis a company puts on production.

Stock Plot. The stock plot is for lazy designers, just as the stock technical information sheet is for lazy presenters. As the term implies, the stock plot is sent out to all theatres in exactly the same form, usually accompanied by a stock technical rider. The benefit of this type of plot is that it is cheap, since it requires that the company hire a designer only once. Companies that travel with little or none of their own equipment and that put very little emphasis on production are the most frequent users of the stock light plot.

The major problem with this type of plot is that it must necessarily be vague in order to accommodate a wide range of spaces and equipment inventories. Because the accompanying tech rider must then be equally vague in its demands, presenters often tend to disregard both. When the booking manager or the artistic director says, "Don't worry about the technical rider or the light plot," it is time for technicians for both the company and the presenter to worry.

Another problem with the stock plot is that it must be designed for the lowest common denominator, with the result that well-equipped theatres will suffer from under-utilization. In most cases, the presenter and the house staff will simply assume that the light and hanging plot are going to change once the company and the technicians arrive, and nothing of any import will be done in advance.

Four-Wall Plot. The four-wall plot is a rich man's version of the stock plot. The difference is that a company using the four-wall plot travels with its own equipment and executes the plot with their own equipment, exactly as indicated. Even so, the designer or technical director must do his or her homework to make sure the space can accommodate the installation. In this situation the presenter's main responsibility is to strike all of his equipment from the theatre in advance of the company's arrival; then, after the performance, the staff will have to restore the equipment.

Custom Plot. The custom plot, designed specifically for each performance space, requires more work from the designer than the other two types of plots. Not only must the designer gather immense amounts of information about the space, he or she must then adapt the production to fit and draft the plot to match the specifications of the theatre. Although this is a more laborious process than that required to devise a stock or four-wall plot, it optimizes the relationship between the company and the space and gives the best chance for a successful performance. Another plus for the custom plot is that, because it minimizes the chance of surprises and cost changes, it saves the presenter money.

Line or Hanging Plots. A hanging plot, often called a *line plot*, is a tool used to show the location of all hanging, or flown, pieces used by the company. The size of the production best determines how this is done.

The most elaborate form of hanging plot is a scale plan of the stage showing only hanging positions and the items on them. This is most often used in theatre and opera productions, where there is major emphasis on sets and other vertical elements.

A similar hanging plot is often drafted in section view rather than plan view. This can be very effective if there are large numbers of flown pieces and the trim heights need to be visualized to show the relationship of horizontal elements.

An alternative is to do a hanger log instead of a hanging plot. A hanger log is a listing of all the line sets with a description of what is hanging on each, including dimensions, weights, and trim heights. Often, larger productions require both a hanger log and a hanging plot to give the most complete explanation of the company's hanging requirements in the theatre.

Crews and Schedules

Variables. Crew size and time schedules are controlled by a number of factors, including the size of the company and the facility, whether the company and/or the facility has union contracts, the number of people in the company's traveling crew, and the size of the production.

Because the technical costs for a production incurred by a presenter are often equal to a company's basic fee, anything a company can do to keep crew size and working hours to a minimum will make it more attractive for booking. However, it can be suicidal to risk the performance in order to save a few man hours of crew time.

Crew calls and the time available in the theatre are the greatest variables with which a touring company has to contend, especially smaller companies which must deal with a wide range of facilities and crew types (i.e., student, volunteer, union, or a combination). At some facilities, student slave labor crews are virtually free and the adage "You get what you pay for," is painfully appropriate in such situations. The time required to achieve a decent production may be many times the norm if a presenter's crew is inexperienced or undisciplined.

There are no guarantees or constants by which to gauge crew quality. Some of the fanciest theatres in the country are among the most difficult in which to work, with self-important stage hands refusing to do traditional tasks. Conversely, some of the best-maintained and most efficiently staffed theatres in the country are in small, out-of-the-way college towns staffed with students or a mixed crew. Due to personnel changes, a theatre that was a pleasure to work in last year may have drastically changed by the time a company returns next year.

Tell-Tale Signs. One often-reliable indication of the quality of a facility and crew is the level of professionalism of the head technician (tech director, stage manager, or whatever the title). A well-qualified person in this position will do everything possible to keep the facility up to standards. If substandard conditions are forced on him or her, the conscientious head technician will be honest in representing the theatre's condition to touring companies. Also, in most cases, a quality head technician will have assembled a quality crew. This formula comes with no guarantees, but the odds for a technically efficient production are greatly increased if the person in charge knows the facility and the business of theatre.

If the qualifications of the head technician are so crucial, how does a touring company measure them? The quality of the technical information offered, the personal phone call, and contact with other companies which have worked in the facility are the best ways to gauge the quality of the technical staff.

The way a person fills out a tech questionnaire and answers specific questions over the phone will quickly give insight into both his knowledge and his attitude. Remember, however, that this process of gathering qualitative impressions works both ways: at the same time that the company is sizing up the facility and its technician, the presenter and the technical director will be applying the same scrutiny to the company. How well prepared is the staff? How much do they really know about touring? How easy, or how difficult, will the company be to work with?

There is a great interdependence between the company and the house staff and crew. If a crew likes and respects a company's touring staff, they will bend over backwards to give them the best possible support. If a company has had consistent problems with crews, it would be wise to examine the quality, preparedness, and attitude of its own technical staff.

Preparedness is the bottom line. If the company has gathered as much information as possible about the facility and crew, and if it has communicated as much information as possible about it's needs and scale of production, it stands the best possible chance of achieving a quality production with the least pain for everyone.

Schedules. Since crew types and qualifications vary greatly, the technicians representing the company and the presenter should discuss the crew situation and come to an agreement as to the number of personnel and the amount of work time as soon as possible. Union crews must be officially negotiated with the business agent of the local I.A.T.S.E., but prior discussion among the technicians will help give a more accurate picture of the crew and their relationship with the theatre. Once the schedule has been agreed to verbally, a written crew schedule should be prepared and added to the contract as a portion of the technical rider.

The schedule must be as complete as possible, listing not only the number of crew people, but the areas in which they will work, how many department heads will be needed, and any special talents that might be expected (i.e., riggers, pyrotechnicians, spot operators, or sound mixers). Time schedules should include call times, "go" times, and the lengths of each call, along with an explicit description of the work expected (i.e., load-in, focus, tech rehearsal, or performance).

Unions

The union with jurisdiction over crews for legitimate theatre is the International Alliance of Theatrical Stage Employees (I.A.T.S.E.), commonly called the I.A. There are a variety of situations where the I.A. becomes involved with touring productions.

Yellow-Card Shows

A touring company that requires a union crew is called a *yellow card* company. The term comes from the yellow card that is sent by the company's union steward to the business agent of the I.A. local with jurisdiction over the theatre. Companies that perform with union crews in their home theatres and have union employees as staff technicians usually require a "yellow card" union crew when they tour.

The touring staff of such a company must be composed exclusively of salaried union technicians. The company must travel with at least one union technician. For each union technician supplied by the company the local must supply at least one equal man (called *parity*). The different types of crew personnel that a company may need include: electrician, carpenter, fly man, prop man, rigger, sound operator, and wardrobe person.

The crew members will be supplied by the local union and paid at the prevailing local rate, which varies greatly around the country. The general rule of thumb is: the larger the city, the higher the rate.

If the union does not have enough available members to fill all the positions, the call will be filled out by permit workers. These nonunion personnel, hired by the union to work for a specific call, are paid the same wages as their card-carrying coworkers. Often in college theatre situations there is a mixed crew consisting of union and student members. These situations are negotiated between the union local and the theatre. In most instances of a mixed crew the students are hired as permit workers and paid at the prevailing union rates.

In some remote localities, a union local may have jurisdiction but insufficient members to fill the call, in this case the union's local business agent has the discretion to negotiate a compromise with the company and presenter. The union does not have the right to charge travel expenses when it supplies a crew from outside its home city, as long as it is still within its jurisdiction. If, however, a presenter or company wants specific union members badly enough, or crew members with special talents and is willing to pay for transportation, members can be brought in from another jurisdiction with the permission of the local business agent.

Once a company begins a tour as a yellow card show, it must maintain that status throughout the tour. On subsequent tours, however, the company may choose to go out as a nonunion show if it is going into nonunion theatres. If a company sometimes tours as a union show and sometimes as nonunion, letting the presenter know what to expect very early in contract negotiations is crucial.

Nonunion Shows

If a company is traveling as a nonunion show and goes into a theatre that has a union contract, the company may be obliged to work with existing agreements between the theatre and the union. Occasionally, a nonunion facility has a history of using union personnel although no formal agreement exists. In such a case, the union and the company or presenter can negotiate an agreement based on past precedents.

Right-to-Work Laws

Approximately three quarters of the states have right-to-work laws, the basic principle of which is that a nonunion employee cannot be displaced from his job by a union employee. This means that a nonunion house crew cannot be excluded from a call when a union company performs there.

Union Work Policies

Union work policies are dictated by the locals and vary from one area to the next. As long as there is no conflict with state or federal legislation, a local may set any policy it chooses.

Union rules cover minimum call time, hourly wages, overtime policies, break requirements, and various other working policies that affect the company and presenter, either of whom has the right to (and should) request the rules in writing.

Most union locals have different rate structures for different types of presenting organizations (i.e., standard theatrical, commercial, and nonprofit rates). These rates are based on the status of the presenting organization and not the performing company. If it is not known which union local has jurisdiction over a specific theatre, contact the international offices of I.A.T.S.E. (1515 Broadway, Suite 601, New York, NY 10036, phone 1-800-223-6872).

Working in a union theatre is complicated by the fact that there are often three, rather than two, parties involved in the negotiations: the union local that supplies the personnel, the company whose technicians have to work with them, and the presenter who will have to pay their wages. Still, union crews are—theoretically, at least—better trained, more experienced, and more safety-conscious than their nonunion counterparts, and in most cases, worth the extra cost.

The union is not generally a group of ogres, but disputes do sometimes arise. When they do, lack of communication is the typical cause. If a presenter can't deal with union crews, he should book only nonunion companies.

On the Road

When a company decides to tour, the primary technical consideration is one of scale: how much equipment and how many people to take along. The more you take the more it costs you, but economic considerations aside, it is also true that the more you take—both equipment and crew—the better your performance is likely to look. Working with your own equipment and personnel also means faster, more trouble-free set-ups. (It is much easier to hang your own fresnel than to rebuild the presenter's at thirty feet in the air.) A company that travels with nothing will often cost the presenter large amounts of money in equipment rentals and local labor. A well-equipped, practically self-sufficient company is likely to be seen by prospective presenters as worth a higher fee than a similar company that travels with nothing.

Tour Scale

Apart from money, the mode of transporting the equipment determines how much can be taken. The cheapest way to travel is on a bus, with everything the company needs for its production packed in suitcases. At the other end of the scale is a company with a fleet of semi-trailer trucks loaded with a complete pre-hung production. Between these two extremes is a series of modest progressions and major jumps.

The bottom rung is the small but growing dance company. The dancers travel to bookings by bus, carrying all of their equipment in their luggage: their wrinkled costumes, an iron, a few pieces of color media, a projector, and a tape deck.

The second rung: last season, because the company's repertory had expanded, it made its first quantum leap to a van. In this van (the small pick-up truck-based vehicle often used as a hauler of large families commonly called an econoline or cargo van), it was able to carry a portable dance floor, wrinkle-free costumes, a crate of projectors, a couple of fabric backdrops, a roll of color media, and two technician-drivers.

The third rung: due to great success, the company realized that it needed to carry more (i.e., a basic light and sound system), but the econoline had been absolutely loaded to the gills. It was time to graduate to a larger vehicle. The next jump is a U-Haul type, move-your-furniture-yourself vehicle, known as a bob-tail van. These trucks come with a cargo box ranging from twelve-feet to twenty-four-feet long. It has arrived at the point where a small- to medium-sized company can carry everything it needs, if not everything it owns, including a sound system, a dimmer board, crates of instruments, a floor, costumes, sets, and drapes. With a bob-tail van, even moderately sophisticated sets can be transported, provided they have been properly designed for touring. Costs have increased. The rental price is higher, the larger vehicle drinks more gas, and the company can no longer expect one of the performers to act as a back-up driver.

The fourth rung is a quantum leap: this is the tractor-trailer combination, or semi. Trailers range in size from twenty-seven feet to fifty-four feet. Since the cost of operating a large semi-trailer is very close to that of a small one, most companies use forty-five- to fifty-foot trailers. Semis are most often used by opera, ballet, and large theatre companies. A semi-trailer allows a company to travel with pre-hung light battens and larger set pieces than any other mode of transportation. This can make set-up time dramatically shorter. A semi usually requires a professional driver who does not act as part of the stage crew. If a company needs more carrying capacity than a semi, the next step is two semis, then three, then four, etc.

Special Tour Items

There are many technical items required for touring that are not crucial for a company that does all its performances in a home theatre. The longer a company spends on the road, the greater the number of these items that become indispensable.

Crates. Over-the-road travel is murder on equipment, and piggyback trailers on the railroads are even worse. Because technical equipment is so crucial—and very expensive—with very few exceptions, every item must be crated. To avoid wasted space, the crates are usually custom built for the items they store. A crate should be designed to hold as much as possible yet still be manageable for the smallest number of bodies who will ever be asked to move it.

Before designing the crates, many points must be considered: the kinds of passages the crates will have to fit through (doorways and stairs, for example), the type of truck to be used (height limitations, whether or not there is a lift gate), the crews available at different theatres to help unload (will there always be a crew, or will the two souls who have just driven five hundred miles have to unload the truck themselves?), the relationship of one crate to another (will the crates stack comfortably inside the truck?).

There are other design parameters that must be considered. The crates must be strong yet as light as possible, not only so that two people can move them, but also to keep the truck within legal weight limits. The handles must be designed so that they are accessible for carrying and lifting the crate by itself or as part of a pack. Multiple sets of handles are often needed for large crates, but unless they can be folded away, most likely they will be broken off. Wheels are essential. They can be permanently attached to the bottom of the crate or to wheel boards (four-wheel dollies) that are placed under each crate as it is unloaded. There are pros and cons to both approaches. Using a dolly requires that the crate be lifted onto it, but crates pack better and travel better if they are not on permanent wheels.

Crates must be properly labeled. They should have: the company's name, a thorough list of contents, the weight of each loaded crate, and any special notes as to how the crate should be handled, stored, or packed. Inside, the crate should have another list of contents, along with packing instructions if the packing technique is not self-evident. The people packing and unpacking the crates have never seen this equipment before. A company that tours regularly soon finds that the packing crate can be as important as the equipment itself.

Road Boxes and Rigging Crates. As soon as a company graduates to truck travel, it is vital to make a road box. Many companies travel with one or two for each department. A road box is simply a crate designed to carry small miscellaneous items (tools, hardware, rope, paint, tape, light bulbs, cues, pencils, needles and thread, spare parts, etc.) that do not have a specific crate of their own. Like the equipment crates, the road box should be well-organized and well-labeled.

As indispensable to the serious touring company as a road box, is a rigging crate. Any theatre, dance, or opera company must be prepared to rig certain items (sets, drapes, or electric) when they arrive at a facility. A rigging crate contains rope or aircraft cable and the attendant clips, clamps, clews, blocks, pulleys, and such, to hang equipment where no hanging point is available. Given enough time to rig, many companies can turn a junior high school gymnasium into a fully hung theatre, with borders, legs, back drops, and electric battens.

Special Equipment. The list of specialized touring equipment is endless. The number of these items which a company acquires will depend on the needs of the particular company and the depths of it's pocket book. There does come a point when it becomes worth the cost of designing and constructing special equipment in order to save time and insure production quality. The criteria is usually what the company needs most that theatres have least frequently.

Since most theatres are designed for legitimate theatre, additional equipment needs are most pronounced for dance companies. Some typical examples are: special resilient dance floors, portable dance floor surfaces, side lighting booms, on-stage spot towers, and unusual numbers of specialized lighting instruments. The side lighting alone for a dance production can require twenty-four to one hundred ellipsoidal reflector spotlights, the booms to hang them on, and cable to connect them to the circuits. Only the best-equipped theatres accustomed to producing dance events will have these kinds of items on hand.

Some companies will have extensive dimmer needs. Some will have unusually complex sound needs. Some will have special effect and projection needs. When any of these needs apply to a company, it will always operate more efficiently and more safely if it can supply the equipment. Although it may be expensive to procure and cart about, the cost will be justified by the improved quality of the performance. The rental and time savings for the presenter will not normally go unheeded.

Color Codes. One final touring tip, which can be a godsend for the crew and cost very little in comparison to the time savings, is color coding of equipment. A crew is usually willing to work, but needs an enormous amount of direction. If the equipment can be coded so that the crew can do many things without direct supervision, the set-up time will be greatly lessened.

Here are a few examples: if you have three lekos to be hung on a side-light boom and the instruments are coded red, yellow, and green, you can tell a crew to hang them on the color-coded boom like a traffic light. If the lekos, connectors, and the side-light cables (or twofers) that must be patched together are color coded, a novice crew member will be able to hang and connect an unknown system alone and correctly. A piece of webbing tied on an electric batten with colored marks that correspond to color-coded instruments will allow an electrician to hang, plug, and circuit the electricity perfectly without having to constantly ask questions. Flats that are color coded at each joint will be much easier to assemble into a set.

Crates that are color coded as to departments are easier to identify. ("The yellow crates go to wardrobe, the blue ones to electric, the black ones to sound.") Sets that have a secondary color code will be easier to group. ("The flats with the red stripe go stage right." "The pieces with the green stripe go on the truck first!")

Communication Again

Successful touring depends on communication. Unfortunately, this is not a skill that comes naturally to most theatre technicians. Yet, its importance is obvious the first time a designer or stage manager sets foot on a strange stage to begin the process of producing a performance in an alien environment. The more the company and the presenting organization know about each other before they attempt the collaborative effort of creating art, the better everyone's chance of success. If there is ever a hint of a question, ask it. If there is ever a chance that you have been misunderstood, volunteer an explanation.

CHAPTER 14

The Road Show Abroad

by Art Becofsky

It is logical that artists working in an era of increased global communication would view touring beyond their own country's borders as a valuable means of sharing artistic experiences and information.

The advice contained in this chapter is based on the assumption that sharing artistic resources and achievements internationally is important for everyone in the arts, that cultural differences are realities and that experiencing them challenges and, hopefully, sharpens everyone's way of thinking about his art and his life, and that political boundaries do not pose insurmountable problems to the global exchange of information. "The Road Show Abroad" is intended to help your company join the jet age by highlighting those variations in the processes of planning, contracting, and executing a tour which are specific to touring abroad. Except for the information discussed here, the basic principles and procedures relevant to domestic touring are directly applicable to foreign tours.

This material is based on twenty years of personal experience in securing and managing foreign engagements for artists—making contacts, drafting contracts, planning and scheduling the tours, and accompanying performers on the road. A truly complete discussion of all these components would require a companion volume to the one you now hold. Dozens, even hundreds of performers and managers would need to be consulted, and each would have a somewhat different story to tell, his own helpful hints to offer. Most likely, however, everyone would agree on certain basics, including: the importance of advance work; the need for consistent and clear communication among artists, managements, and presenters; the requirement that close attention (bordering on obsessive) be paid to all the daily details of life on the road; the edge to be gained from inventive responses to unexpected challenges; and the value of sharing experiences (the dilemmas as well as the solutions) with others who tour, or who wish to tour, abroad.

Needs, details, challenges—the exigencies of foreign touring may sound forbidding, but they can all be prepared for and accommodated. On the whole, touring abroad can be—should be—fun. If you plan carefully and stay on top of things, from departure to return, your efforts to present art that you value to audiences around the world will be successful.

There will be surprises, of course, and you are sure to encounter situations which never arise at home. After all, the promise of unique experiences is a major appeal of life on the road abroad.

The Decision to Tour Abroad

Everyone who faces the decision to tour or not to tour abroad has his own calculus for making a choice. Artists and managers choose to tour for a variety of reasons, including: the desire for a broader audience and for the prestige of international exposure; the need for more work for the performers and additional revenue for the company; a personal interest in having new experiences in unfamiliar environments; or sometimes simply because of an unsolicited offer for a foreign engagement. If you decide to embark on a foreign tour, you will need to reevaluate your decision periodically throughout the planning and booking process. Money is one of the first and most constant areas to be monitored.

Preliminary Thoughts about Finances

Everything that has been written in this book about the finances of touring is directly applicable to the financial considerations facing you if you decide to tour abroad. Before entering into talks with foreign presenters, however, there are additional considerations to be made.

Setting Your Fee. Assuming you already have a good idea about your domestic touring costs, you should also try to learn a little about the local economy in the foreign country where you hope to tour. This may affect virtually all the variable costs in your budget. You can incorporate certain safeguards into your contracts regarding fees, but even during preliminary budgeting, keep in mind that inflation rates and the stability, or instability, of governments may have their effects.

Budgeting per diem payments can be particularly difficult: if your engagement is in Argentina two years from now, for example, and you are giving your performers pesos for spending money, you might want to know whether or not the government is making any headway in holding down the current 500-percent-per-year inflation rate. Or, preferably, you might choose to budget and give your first quotations of fees in U.S. dollars. Be pessimistic in making projections about how many dollars you will need.

Travel. The costs of transporting personnel and freight will vary widely among performing groups of different sizes and types and will largely depend on where they are touring. In any case, these costs will be a large part of any foreign tour budget. Here, as in every other financial area, a little healthy pessimism is in order.

Researching ways to save money on travel can be well worth your while. Know the regulations and options regarding different carriers, fares, and routes. Special fares and discounts are available based on the duration of your journey, the number of stops you are making, and the number of people in your group.

On a tour to Austria several years ago, the Merce Cunningham Dance Company found it financially beneficial to stay for fourteen days (although only four days of performing were scheduled) in order to qualify for a special fare. Savings from the reduced fare easily covered all the needed per diem and salaries, and provided a paid vacation for everyone as well.

Seasonal fluctuations in fares can make a difference, too. Be sure to ask yourself (and a trusted travel agent): how much the air tickets and cost of air freight will increase before the tour begins; whether you might be able to qualify for a discount fare; if not, whether an alteration in your travel plans might make discounts available; and how much pressure the alteration would place on your performers and on your performance schedule. Note that not only do prices vary widely from one airline to the next, prices frequently change. Find out, and be sure to meet, the deadlines for paying for your tickets. Sometimes, being late only one day may mean missing out on a discount fare.

Programming. You may wish to begin your program planning earlier than you might for a domestic tour. Artists often wish to present their larger, costlier works abroad. This will affect your freight budget, and the number of performers may increase your travel budget. Also, lengthy or more demanding tours may require extra artists or extra support personnel.

Communication. The telephone and fax machine are important tools in all phases of foreign tour work. From initial contacts with presenters through contract negotiations, and throughout the time the group is actually on the road abroad, you will be spending more money than usual on communications. The money will be well spent. You should beef up your administrative budget for the hidden costs of long-distance telephone calls, as well as faxes.

Miscellaneous Expenses. In addition to communications, expect other hidden expenses to emerge. More often than not there will be costs involved with visas, inoculations, working papers, and airport departure taxes. A good rule of thumb for budgeting foreign miscellaneous expenses is to double the miscellaneous amount for a domestic tour of equal length.

Other parts of this chapter may also have financial ramifications for particular types of performing groups. Your own research, too, is important and often can mean savings. If nothing else, investigative work can spare you some of the worst surprises.

Booking Notes

Booking possibilities differ from country to country, from city to city within countries, and from theatre to theatre within cities. A number of towns and theatres have festivals for specific art forms, and certain presenting groups and theatres have affinities for one type of performance or another. *Musical America International Directory of the Performing Arts* and *PAYE (Performing Arts Yearbook for Europe)* are handy reference books containing: alphabetical lists of countries and available performing opportunities, facts about theatres, and contact names and addresses for further information. The particulars are ever-changing, however, and even the most current printed information available may be dated. The local information bureaus in the countries in which you are interested are often a more up-to-date source of initial contacts.

One of the soundest sources of timely data about foreign presenters is other American performers and managers who tour abroad. And contacts made at home can lead to contacts abroad, which is an excellent point of departure for getting the foreign booking process started. Sharing information among American artists is in everyone's best interests.

Be aware that politics plays more of a part in foreign booking than in domestic booking. Sometimes cities within the same country have deep-seated historical rivalries, or a dispute may have arisen out of current political affairs. The funds available to a presenter may be tied to the ascendancy of a particular national or local government.

These issues often come up during the first stages of booking. A presenter in Milan may say to you, "We want you to perform here very much, but not if you're giving shows in Rome first." A presenter in Rome might say, "We're ready to commit to your performances, but only if we are the only Italian city in which you perform." Or, "Let's proceed with our plans for your performance, but much of my funding depends on the Blue Party winning next month's elections." You may find yourself buying copies of the *International Herald Tribune* and studying election results.

Agents

Agents based abroad offer certain advantages: They are usually more adept at dealing with the language barrier (which can pose a problem from the outset for an American company); they presumably have a better understanding than the booking novice of the breadth of touring possibilities available abroad; and if they have been in the business for any length of time, they will have some readily accessible contacts with whom they have worked in the past. Hiring an agent also can be an efficient way of handling political and social factors of which your understanding may be limited. The agent can facilitate communications with presenters in order to get the most up-to-date information and choose the best travel options and performance spaces.

In general, profit is the motive behind the agent's helpfulness, with commissions ranging between five and twenty percent. If you are an established artist in America, a foreign agent might seek you out. Although he may be genuinely interested in your art, he may just as well be interested solely in your ability to make a profit. This in itself need not be a drawback. A foreign agent may work extremely hard to find performing situations for you, because his future commissions are directly linked to your success or failure. Like artists, agents have international reputations to protect and further. There are some fly-by-night operators, of course, and these could tarnish your own unsullied reputation, but with increasing global communications and the power of "word-of-mouth," it is becoming more difficult for unscrupulous agents to continue working.

Still, certain agents may not be the best spokespersons for your artists. They may be quick to accept a marginal performance venue with a difficult schedule because of the commission involved. They may represent such large rosters of artists that they will not be able to give your company the booking attention you feel it deserves.

Musical America lists international agents; you can also speak frankly with other American artists and managements about agents they work with or with whom they have worked in the past. Compare different agents as to the various services offered by each. Look at the lists of artists they represent, and call those artists to solicit their honest evaluations. Ask the agent himself for references, just as you would when interviewing anyone for a position in your organization. Be clear from the start about your touring needs, both financial and technical——and be as explicit as possible about what you can and cannot do.

Booking Yourself

Even if you have decided to give the bulk of your booking responsibilities to an agent, you may choose to supplement the agent's efforts by building your own network of foreign contacts, a combination which can be highly effective. Besides, no single agent is likely to have a truly global network of contacts, which means that there will be some areas where you will need to make your own.

Personal Visits. The importance of personal visits to presenters cannot be overemphasized. Although there may be considerable expense involved, presenters always appreciate such efforts, and there is no better way to get your points across about the distinctiveness of your group. You will also be able to gather essential information firsthand: spaces that look wonderful on paper can turn out to be unworkable; the "two-minute walk" from theatre to hotel may be closer to fifteen minutes; a satisfactory equipment list may prove to be misleading, with some pieces missing and others in disrepair; and some of the dressing rooms on theatre plans may have been turned into broom closets.

Try to budget for two sets of advance trips: during the booking stage, a personal visit is the best way to procure engagements; once a tour has been put together, a second visit to each site before your performers arrive will give you a chance to pick up technical information packets, refine plans, and cultivate friendships. From booking to following through with the details of the tour schedule, personal involvement on the part of management can translate directly into better treatment for the company.

Introductory Letters. Introduction letters to foreign presenters can be written in the same way you would compose domestic booking letters. In addition to the suggested dates of your coming visit, the letters might include an invitation to your next series of performances in your home city. Enclose any reviews you find particularly good (especially foreign ones), and ask to meet with the head of the presenting organization or with someone in administration. An initial mailing should go out three months before a personal visit.

After you have received enough responses to set up your booking trip, reconfirm your visit with each. Try to leave a little flexibility for changes in schedule, add-on meetings, or hunches that you find yourself following once your trip is underway. To save time, you may choose to limit your meetings to presenters who seem most committed to presenting your group, but it can be helpful to schedule meetings with people who may be less sure.

Making Contacts. Use all your time to make contacts: you never know who is going to switch positions or advance in his career. Underlings often know more about the internal workings of an organization than their superiors, and they might alert you to potential problems that the leaders of organizations do not acknowledge. Also, a supporting administrator might wind up being the next theatre or festival director, and you will have made an important connection for the future.

There is no foreign counterpart to the American booking conference *per se.* However, in Europe, making the rounds of the summer festivals (if money is available) is a good way to meet important presenters. Many regularly visit festivals to see what others are presenting; thus, an engagement at one festival means other presenters probably will see you, too.

This is not intended to imply that the process is simple. It may take years of sowing seeds with a hundred well-targeted presenters before your efforts bear fruit; but perseverance pays off, and in some cases, it is the only way to make inroads.

Funding for Foreign Tours

Philanthropic organizations offer support for cultural exchange to specific countries or continents. You can contact consulates, embassies or national information services for suggestions. The American government also makes available some foreign tour support through the United States Information Agency. Generally, however, if you want to embark on a foreign tour and your presenter has not made a specific request to the American Embassy in his home country for funding, you will probably have to manage with the fee from the presenter as your sole income.

The State Department is a good source of information about troubled areas in the world where the United States government suggests you avoid touring. For the most part, these are safety recommendations, not political judgments, and the information is straightforward and helpful.

About Foreign Presenters

In researching potential foreign presenting organizations, you should ask many of the same types of common-sense questions that you would ask in planning a domestic tour: Does the presenter have a long history of presentation? How has he treated artists in the past? Does the presenter have a good reputation in the arts world, or have there been chronic problems regarding treatment of artists, payment, or facilities? In addition, you will want to ask: What other foreign artists has he presented? Is his funding tied to the present government in power, and if so, are there elections being held shortly that might affect your engagement, or is the festival or theatre independent of local or national government support (a rare case, actually).

This information will help you to decide where you can afford to be flexible and where you need to be firm in contract negotiations. You can get answers to some of these questions through queries sent to your contacts at the presenting organizations, but checking with fellow American performers and managers can be even more enlightening. Look at presenters' brochures or advertisements from other engagements, and at the itineraries of other companies to find out the kinds of programming that have been presented by various presenters, as well as what they are planning for the future.

You should keep in mind that presenters abroad are constantly shifting positions—as different parties come to power, as government support changes, as new festivals and theatres are created and shakeups occur in administrations—so good information is sometimes hard to come by, or is quickly dated. Try to get an idea of when presenters' booking decisions will be made and how long in advance performances are booked. Keep track of which companies different presenters are contracting and—if the information is available to you—how much they are spending. Should your initial approach to a particular presenting organization be rejected, let them know that your interest continues, and keep in touch.

Throughout the entire process of foreign touring, from securing the engagement to setting the final itinerary, plan longer in advance than you would for domestic bookings. Festivals sometimes have their schedules set and contracts signed two years in advance, though one year of lead time is often sufficient. Overall, a healthy skepticism is in order in scheduling. Somewhere along the line, you can count on the date or time of your performance being shifted by a festival administration, or the flight schedule changed at the last minute by an airline on which you are dependent. Worst of all, cancellation is more common abroad than at home.

The Presenter's Expectations

The activities various foreign presenters request from visiting artists can differ widely. Be prepared for the unorthodox and be armed with ingenious responses. If the presenter's funding sources require an "education" element, your engagement may hinge upon teaching classes or offering lectures or seminars at the local university. If a powerful figure in local politics has been instrumental in securing financial support for your visit, your agreeing to do a high-visibility activity with political overtones, such as a ceremony at the city hall, might be of utmost importance to the presenter. This may hold no interest for the artists or tour manager, but it may be important to the success of your visit.

Contracts

Performing artists customarily use their own contract form for foreign engagements. This can be essentially the same form you would use for domestic bookings, with some additions.

Send the contract in English, no matter where you are thinking of performing. If the presenter chooses to translate your contract into the native language and requests that you sign the translation, hire a legal translator to make sure your original terms have been preserved. In addition, request that the presenter also sign a copy of the contract in English.

As with domestic presenters, you must be scrupulously honest and ethical in all your dealings with foreign presenters. Presenter networks transcend national borders, and word travels fast. Be conscientious and forthright even when you think a presenter is not.

Payment of Fees

When touring abroad, the bright manager quickly learns how to deal with money matters in a new way. The differences begin at the contract stage.

Taxes. When arranging payment of the performers' fees, be sure to ask about value-added taxes and other taxes that may exist in the countries you will be visiting. Your organization's nonprofit status may mean nothing to a foreign government. Even if exemptions are honored, reimbursement of government deductions from fees may require a lengthy procedure which should be begun as early as possible. Provide well in advance any necessary papers showing nonprofit status, or any other documents which will allow presenters to send payment in full. Include a contract clause that requires this on the part of the presenter ("Fees shall be paid in full, with no deductions of any kind."). If you know of any particular tax that a country levies, include a specific reference in this clause.

Advance Payments. Advance payments sometimes pose problems for foreign presenting organizations. A presenter may be telling the truth when he informs you that local regulations do not allow him to send any payments prior to the completion of scheduled activities. You may need the advance in order to send your freight prepaid to the engagement, or to purchase your airline tickets, but you will have to gauge for yourself how hard to push. Expect problems if you push too hard; the presenter may simply be short of cash.

You might decide that a fractional payment of the performance fee with the signing of the contract will be sufficient. In most cases, one quarter of the fee will cover airline tickets, and if you arrange for this payment to arrive early enough, you can qualify for discount airfares. The remaining three-quarters of the fee should be cabled to your home bank: one-half upon the arrival of the company and one-quarter on the day of the final performance.

Foreign Currency. Sometimes presenters demand that they be allowed to pay in their own currency. Although occasionally there are legal reasons why this must be so, protect yourself if it becomes necessary to agree to this sort of arrangement. Include a clause stating the currency value in relation to the U.S. dollar (pegging the foreign exchange rate of the dollar at the date the contract is signed), with a provision for renegotiation should the value of the foreign currency swing five percent or more in either direction. For example, if the fee is 50,000 French francs, to be transferred to your account at the rate of eight francs per U.S. dollar, and should the rate of exchange have risen or fallen by five percent on the date of the transfer (to either 8.4FF = $1.00 U.S., or 7.6 FF = $1.00 U.S.), the contract should state that the fee would be renegotiated.

Transferring Payments. Whatever the currency, have money transferred directly to your home account, which is safer than being paid in cash. Although cable transfers can incur delays, they are certainly more sensible than crossing borders with wads of currency shoved down your pants. Check with the local branch of your bank as to the method of transfer they suggest, and provide presenters with all the information they will need, including: your account name and number; the name of your bank and the branch address and code numbers; and the name and title of the bank officer to whose attention cabled monies should be sent.

Other Forms of Compensation. More often than with domestic presenting, foreign presenters may offer free airline tickets, free hotel accommodations, or full board, in exchange for a reduction of your fee. A presenter may have a connection with government-owned airlines, or he may have a special arrangement with a hotel or food establishment, and these kinds of fee reductions may mean the difference in the presenter's ability to offer an engagement or not. But proceed with caution.

These sort of arrangements must be exceedingly clear and explicit in the contract, and they should be checked and double-checked after the contract is signed. Otherwise, you may be unpleasantly surprised by food that is inappropriate to company diets (avoid fixed menus), or hotels whose policies prove inflexible or where living conditions are horrid.

Contributed airline tickets can cause the worst headaches of all. Your schedule may change after prepaid tickets have arrived, or your tour may be continuing to other cities and countries where prepaid tickets might be unusable or unexchangeable. Never accept standby tickets or charters. Once the contract is signed, you will have little legal recourse if these arrangements turn out to be inadequate or insufferable, and you may wind up spending lots of extra money to make the situation bearable for the company.

Presenters may offer you percentages of ticket sales as a way of covering your guaranteed fee (see Chapter 6). Again, be wary: it is difficult to know what you are getting into with foreign presenters, and it is hard to monitor sales; box offices abroad have different procedures, deductions, etc.

Signing the Contract

Try to sign all contracts for an entire tour at once. This is easier said than done, but do not put yourself into the predicament of having a single booking at a low fee because you were assuming more engagements over which you could spread the costs. Sign only when you are certain that what you have contracted is economically feasible.

Naturally, some presenters wait longer than others to sign, but those presenters who are ready to commit can be stalled only so long. No doubt, at some point in booking a lengthy foreign tour you will encounter a presenter who needs more time to raise funds or to secure performing venues. As with domestic bookings, it is best if these dates are scheduled for the beginning or end of the tour whenever possible. It is easier to change plane reservations for an earlier arrival or return than it is to sit in a foreign city handing out per diems from your earnings while you await the next paying engagement.

Preparations for Departure

Gathering Information. Unfortunately, sending technical questionnaires abroad is often a useless exercise (you can count on no more than a tiny percentage ever being returned), but it should be done anyway. Whenever possible, double-check the information you receive with other performing groups who have worked in the same facility. What some presenters tell you may be a gross misrepresentation of fact. Always, the most reliable and thorough information will come from technicians in American performing groups who have recently worked in the space. If you supplement this with telephone calls to the head technician at the facility, normally you will have enough information to make the necessary preparations.

By all means, send a clear and detailed list of your equipment needs as early as possible, and talk through the list line by line with the head technician. Be forewarned that in certain countries American equipment may be unavailable, and you may be asked if substitute foreign equipment is acceptable.

Unions. Union regulations differ from one country to the next. Be sure to ask questions at the earliest stages of negotiations about possible union-required royalty payments, overtime for crews, payments to unneeded musicians, and national dance, theatre or music society dues. Find out the union lunch and dinner hours and break times for crews (and the duration of these breaks). Otherwise, your schedule may be disrupted by the crew walking away unexpectedly during a technical set-up, a rehearsal, or a light-focusing session.

Translators. Be sure there is a clause in your contract requesting as many translators as you require. Often, only one translator will be assigned to each tour group. If he is working with the manager on administrative tasks or if an artist has enlisted the translator to help buy groceries, your technicians may have to resort to sign language.

Communicating With the Presenter

As you can surmise by now, a rule-of-thumb during the preparation period is to assume nothing, ask lots of questions, and be prepared to ask the same questions over and over again. Ironing out rough spots before the tour begins is always preferable to dealing with problems while far away from your home base.

Company Needs. Always assume that presenters are ignorant of the details of your particular needs on the road. Festival and theatre managements deal with many different performing companies, and they will have stories galore of the flexibility and cooperation of other groups. If you have particular, firm needs, you will have to make them very clear. If rehearsal hours, for example, cannot be shifted, or if there are certain other parts of your daily schedule that are unalterable, make sure these conditions are stipulated in your contract. Take the time and energy to discuss such details before your arrival with anyone who might need to know them. Refuse to budge when necessary, but do so politely, and be prepared to explain why you need to be firm on a given point.

Finding the Right Person. Do not assume that information is going to get through to all the right people with the mailing of one itinerary to a festival director or theatre manager. Frequently, prestigious presenters hold figurehead positions. Even if he makes programming decisions (most often, in consultation with a board of directors), there may be significant gaps in the presenter's knowledge of both the administrative and technical sides of your visit. The presenter may be working with more than one theatre and more than one staff, and his involvement with these personnel——who are key to the success of your engagement——may be seasonal. Also, the relationship between presenter and staff may be fraught with political or personal strains which you have no possible way of knowing about or understanding.

Seek the advice of other American groups who have worked with the same organization to find out where best to target your discussions at the various stages of arranging your tour. Ask the presenter about the chains of command. Find out which person or persons will be in charge of handling the details of your visit, and deal as often as possible with these people rather than with titular heads.

Audiences. Presenters the world over appreciate knowing that you care about the interests of their audiences and audience reactions to past seasons, about the other productions being presented, and about new approaches to publicity, subscription sales, or audience expansion which the presenters are testing. This friendly exchange of information may not aid you tangibly in preparation for your visit, but it may prove beneficial to have the presenter convinced of your sincere interest in the success of his efforts.

Schedules. When you are relatively certain about your company's optimum schedule and workload, run through the performer's daily schedule with both the administrative and technical liaisons. Often, these early conversations will bring to light information which would prove problematic for both you and the presenter if it had been unknown until your arrival. The less often this schedule changes, the better, but if there are potential changes make the presenter aware of them in advance. Personal visits are the best means of clearing up these scheduling questions, although the telephone can be an effective substitute. Be sure to confirm your discussions by sending letters or faxes.

Advertising and Publicity

Assume that your presenter has more of an understanding than you do of what methods will best advertise your visit to his country. Unless you hire a full-time foreign spy, it is impossible to monitor foreign advertising campaigns. This is one area where you have to have faith. Provide the clearest information and suggestions you can, and hope for the best.

Most likely, you will also have to trust your presenter's ability and thoroughness in dealing with the press. You will not be in a position to know good from bad reviewers, and you probably will not recognize the publications or television networks they represent. Although some of the promotional activities a presenter asks of your artists may prove to be a waste of everyone's time, on the other hand, most or all of what you are asked to do may be vital to the success of the engagement. There really is no way to know which is the case without major investigative work.

Accommodating the Presenter's Needs

Try to accommodate the presenter; obviously he will want as much press coverage as possible, and so should you. Decide what time the artists have available for interviews and other press activities, and let the presenter know of your interest and your limitations. Often, with tight tour schedules and the fatigue of long-distance travel, it may seem a nuisance to have any involvement whatsoever with the press, but try to see things from the presenter's point of view. The funding he has received may well be jeopardized in the future should the artists in his current program be perceived as inaccessible, remote, or haughty. Give more time to this than you might in a domestic booking. It will serve you well throughout your relationship with an individual presenter, and will enhance your reputation among other presenters.

Publicity Angles. An astute presenter will want to know the best publicity angles for your company, but you will need to take the initiative in focusing on your company's strong points and setting the overall tone and direction of the publicity. Assume, however, that an established presenter will know the best methods for implementing a campaign. Ultimately, ticket sales are the province of presenters, particularly in foreign tours, but the company must be willing to help by providing interviews and opportunities for television crews to shoot. (Be prepared that some of your promotional materials may not be useable. This applies most often to videotapes, because formats differ from country to country.)

Films and Videotapes. Ask about the possibility of filming and videotaping performances early on in your discussions. With the expansion of the video market, this is an issue of increased importance to certain performers concerned about protecting their video rights, and foreign presenters may be unaware of their sensitivities. If this is a major concern to you, put a clause in your contract. Expect, however, that in major urban areas abroad, requests for television coverage of your tour will be forthcoming. Naturally, it is easier to make these arrangements in advance than for your tour group to have to cope with the unexpected arrival of television crews at the theatre.

Activities

Some presenters know exactly what services or activities they want visiting artists to provide. Others look to management for guidance. What is beneficial to a foreign presenter's community may be very different from what you are asked to do at home, so be prepared for unusual requests.

Whatever is scheduled, be sure to spell out both your requirements and your limitations: the timing of activities, the space and equipment needed, the maximum number of participants, and the levels of proficiency required of students, along with any other limitations involved with classes or lectures. If you need any special equipment or personnel (lighting, microphones, accompanists, etc.), make this explicit from the first conversations about scheduling such an activity. Also, for performances, be clearer in your program notes than ever before. The words for "pause" and "intermission" are interchangeable in certain languages, so state the number of minutes in a program's break whenever applicable. Presenters will usually translate your artists' biographies. Some translations will be accurate; others will be horrendous. Most will just make you and your artists laugh. With any luck, you will not understand the translations anyway.

Technical Information

Often, the relationship between a presenter and the technical staff of a theatre begins and ends with each year's performances. While you should insist that the presenter communicate information to the proper authorized personnel at the theatre, you will want to develop your own separate communication channels with the theatre staff in some cases.

Equipment List. Get a list of available equipment from a presenter, and check the list with the technicians at the performance site. You might be including unnecessary poundage in your tour freight. Keep in mind, too, that you may be performing in old theatres. Remember to ask about the age of equipment and the rakes of stage floors. Find out what modernization of equipment and facilities has been done recently or is planned before your performances.

Customs. Customs difficulties arise for many reasons, the most frequent being that border officials suspect that your equipment is being brought into a country to be sold (to avoid import taxes), rather than to be used and re-exported. Contact the United States Chamber of Commerce for advice. Having the proper documents and paying the necessary fees to customs agents may mean the avoidance of hours, if not days, of delay in clearing your materials.

Freight Brokers. If you are traveling to more than one country, and if your schedule is tight (a requirement in most cases, if the tour is to be financially sound), you might want to enlist a freight broker or forwarder to prepare a carnet (a document which lists all tour materials and their values). For a fee, these companies take care of reserving and paying for the freight space necessary for your tour on air freighters or passenger aircraft, as well as for train and truck shipments. They prepare the papers necessary for border crossings and customs clearance, and they can set up ground transportation for your freight from venue to venue.

Questions to be considered in deciding whether or not this outside help is necessary include: Is your group on a cramped schedule with little margin for delay? Is the freight traveling with you, or does it need to arrive in advance of your personnel? Are you crossing a number of borders? Are some of the countries you will be entering known for strict, formal customs procedures? Do your tour effects include many items that customs officials might think you are intending to re-sell (new musical instruments and sound and video equipment fall within this category)?

Carnets. Remember that carnets of equipment must be filed ten working days before the anticipated departure of the freight from the United States. If your list varies from what is actually being transported, you may cause yourself a delay. This is a particular problem at the end of a tour, when surprising amounts and types of items "turn up" in road boxes. Caution your artists and other personnel that, though it may be very convenient to put their new sewing machines, bicycles, and other souvenirs into the freight, it is illegal (it will be seen as trying to avoid duty payments), and could hold up your equipment at the next border.

Traveling

Long travel times, airline delays, and time zone changes need to be taken into consideration in deciding on an activities schedule for your support personnel as well as for the artists. A one-week engagement in the United States might easily include seven performances. However, a group allotting seven days for a trip to Europe might be able to offer only three or four shows. In your programming suggestions to presenters, consider the amount performers can do given the extra strains of jet lag, strange diets, the pace of your tour, and the hours the technicians will need to be working due to theatre technical schedules.

Keeping Lists. Make a list of passport, visa, and airline ticket numbers, and keep a list handy of any other important information (the telephone number of your insurance company, lawyers, etc.) for emergencies. Your travel agent or airline representative might suggest the name of a contact should you experience any travel problems while abroad.

Ground Transportation. With few exceptions, you can assume foreign ground transportation will be much more comfortable and dependable than comparable services in the United States. Those who might be trepidatious about sending their artists out on Amtrak or into the New York City subway system have much less to worry about abroad. Do check the hours of operation of these services, and inquire about special fares for public transportation during a long stay in a single city. Prepare in advance, as much as possible, for the purchase of tickets or tokens. Maps with the best routes clearly marked and the fares carefully noted are an important aid to a performer trying to get to rehearsal on time.

Foreign Airports. Unlike most American facilities, foreign airports often charge a departure tax, a per-person fee which, as the term implies, you pay merely to leave the facility. If such a tax is levied at the airport from which you will be departing, try to get the presenter to pay it as part of his contractual agreement. Find out if there are any other departure charges or regulations (currency transfers, declaration of amount of currency taken out of the country, etc.).

Certain rules about baggage allowance on passenger planes vary from one airline to the next, and the rules may change from time to time. On transoceanic flights, you are allowed more weight than on intracontinental flights, and management may find itself liable for a surcharge on trips between engagements. Counsel everyone to pack lightly ("Yes, you can get toothpaste in Taiwan.").

Travel Arrangements. Check travel reservations as often as is humanly possible. The tour manager will have enough problems without having to spend hours at airline offices fighting obstinate computers for lost seats. Unless some members of your group are deviating from the company itinerary, arrange with the airline for group check-ins. Have the computer entry logged in the group's name with one official representative and a single computer reference number. Ask your airline representative about special group arrangements, such as first class lounges, for which your group may be large enough to qualify. This may not seem important until you find yourself delayed for ten hours in a crowded, noisy, overheated airport.

If some members of the company are deviating from your basic itinerary, be sure to handle the arrangements yourself. At all costs, you must avoid having an individual company member call an airline to change his own plans. Tickets will wind up being rewritten for the entire group, reservations will disappear from the computer screen, and the only person who will have the proper arrangements will be that single person who took the (improper) initiative! Check out each name separately with the airline representative. This may be tedious, but it will also be reassuring. Keep your computer reference number handy for confirmation calls.

Accommodations and Per Diem

Creature comforts can play an important part in keeping company morale high and in bolstering the stamina of performers and crew. More often than not, you will be at the mercy of presenting organizations for the arrangement of accommodations, but this need not be cause for dread.

Arranging Accommodations

Frequently, the presenter will have arranged a well-located hotel with a discounted rate for performers. However, if your visit is part of a festival or a large performance season, consider that a significant number of people may be coming from neighboring regions to see your performance specifically, and this could mean a rush for accommodations. If it is possible to make an advance administrative visit or consult with other American artists and managers, do not rely solely upon the presenter's suggestions. Do some investigating on your own about rates, distances from venues, the amenities offered to hotel guests, and the comparable value of various accommodations in light of what is available.

Even when you must rely completely on the presenter's arrangements, get as much advance information as possible about where the company will be staying, and pass along what you learn to your tour personnel. Try not to have hotel payments deducted from fees; rather, arrange to pay accommodation charges yourself or, preferably, give your artists a per diem and let them settle their own accounts (be sure to arrange this in advance). If hotel charges are deducted from fees, making sense of an establishment's accounting of room service charges, transoceanic telephone calls, and sundry other personal expenses can be a nightmare.

Crossing the Border

The procedure for border crossings differs from country to country. For the most part, it is a simple matter of showing a passport and (perhaps) a visa. Customs clearance can be more complicated, however, and you may wish to solicit advice from those who have previously made the same crossing. Certainly, it is wise to check with the consulate or information agency of the presenting organization's country regarding visas, health documents, papers necessary for currency when crossing borders, work permits, tax exemptions or payments, etc. Although the rule varies, there may be a fee involved for visitor's visas; consider this in your budget.

Speeding Up the Process. Find out if you would get special treatment at the border if you cross as a group or whether your artists should cross as individuals. Sometimes the process is speeded up by providing certain official (or at least official looking) papers from the presenter or from government officials. Check with presenters about procedures which have worked well in the past, and ask embassy officials for their suggestions. More often than not, the process in European countries is quite simple.

In many South American and Asian countries, lengthy delays can be expected as each company member's bags are inspected one-by-one, unless the presenter has enough government clout to cut through the red tape. In some cases, tour members have been strip-searched, boxes have been ripped apart, packages opened, presents unsealed, and four or five hours have passed before the entire group has gotten through the customs routine.

Working Papers. Ask your presenters about the need for working papers in each country you will be visiting. Some governments require proof that no money will be earned while on the country's soil. Others only check to see that you have a return ticket and a scheduled date of departure. In any event, it is usually the presenter's responsibility to make sure that working papers for your artists are requested of the appropriate government official and are in order for your arrival. But don't leave it to the presenter to fulfill his responsibility without prompting.

Inoculations. Consider the need for any inoculations that might be necessary for visiting certain countries. Even if health authorities do not require them, inoculations may be recommended by your doctor. You may be advised that company personnel will need several expensive shots or pills for a range of possible diseases. If so, these costs should be in your budget. (Pills for malaria and diarrhea on a recent Asian tour cost nearly $2,000 for a group of thirty.) An ounce of prevention is indeed worth a pound of cure when dealing with illness abroad: flying in a replacement or cancelling a performance because of sickness is not worth the risk if the risk can be eliminated by proper inoculations.

Setting Up Per Diem Payments

Before departing the United States, work out a system for making per diem payments to your tour group. When cash flow allows, try to pay per diem in advance, in dollars, so that company members can purchase travelers' cheques. Although major airports often have around-the-clock banking facilities, local currency may not be available to you elsewhere if you have strange arrival times and dates, but hotels will normally exchange travelers' cheques (or cash) in small denominations.

Even though you may have written into your contract the need for a cash payment from the presenter upon your arrival in order to cash salary checks and distribute per diem or advances, you may experience delays. Occasionally, the presenter will not be able to get cash from his account without your presence; consequently, it is advisable to enter a country with a small amount of the local currency. If possible, have someone precede the performers so that necessary cash payments can be made ready for their arrival. Be sure to check with presenters about these procedures in advance if having immediate cash is critical. Coordinate your plans with normal bank hours and bank holidays, and allow time for the sometimes exhausting procedures required for procuring cash on the road. (You would be amazed at the number of times a bank teller can rubberstamp, initial, pin, staple, unpin, unstaple, and further mutilate papers or currency during a single foreign transaction.)

These arrangements differ from presenter to presenter and from country to country. The sooner you know of your cash needs and communicate those needs to the presenter, the greater your chances of having your cash waiting for you when you arrive. When exchanging large sums of money from one currency to another, do not be misled by the apparent convenience of exchanging at your hotel. Although for small amounts (or in a pinch), your hotel will be an easy way of getting by, their exchange rates are normally not as good as a bank's.

Everything in your schedule can be thrown off by local or national holidays; be sure to inquire in advance. Travel schedules may change around a certain holiday; banks may be closed; restaurants may have different hours.

Distributing a Tour Itinerary

Managers should provide their tour personnel with a detailed, clearly presented itinerary well before departure. The itinerary becomes the tour "bible." Dates, times, venues with correct addresses, and personal contacts with phone numbers can help your company members avoid feeling disoriented, and they can be enormously helpful when the tour manager is swamped with work and is unavailable to answer questions.

Confirm and reconfirm the information you include, and make sure the presenter receives a copy as soon as the document comes out of the typewriter. If directions are needed because people are on their own to get places, provide a map. "Turn left at the corner in front of the hotel and walk right three blocks to the theatre" can be a nightmare in certain cities. Obtain maps in advance from a travel agent or from the national tourist office near you, preferably before you go.

Alert your touring party to any foreign customs that might be important for them to know. This will increase everyone's enjoyment and make the tour manager's job a lot simpler by forestalling the barrage of questions he is sure to encounter otherwise.

Ask your presenting organization about local performance customs. Do children throw flowers from the wings during performances? Are audiences accustomed to extra-long intermissions for chatting and for drinking coffee or wine? Do festival or public officials require special ceremonies that might throw off your tech crews or the timing of your performances? Will the presenter's photographer be shooting during a performance? Will there be any announcements made to the audience before the curtain goes up? Do shows begin with the playing of a national anthem? Is there any special protocol the performers should know about if royalty or other dignitaries are in the audience? What are the curtain times, and are curtains always on time or are they customarily late? Knowing these sorts of details will cut back considerably on opening night confusion.

About the Tour Manager

Your tour manager will be busier than on a comparable tour in the United States; he faces a wider range of problems which cannot be anticipated abroad. A high level of competence, a positive attitude toward work, the ability to be flexible in new situations, and sharp negotiating skills are critical to success.

Geniality is particularly important for smoothing out rough spots. You must be friendly even during the most trying times. Seek new solutions, exude charm and graciousness, and have a great deal of energy on reserve. Taking a presenter to dinner, buying flowers or a bottle of wine for the people working your box office, treating the theatre's public relations officer to a drink—all of these things foster an accommodating atmosphere which can be of enormous help when problems arise. Some of these niceties also add to your expenses, but they will be well worth the investment. Fluency in a second language is helpful; if nothing else, hire someone who is skilled at sign language.

Americans Abroad

There are places on this earth where Americans are unpopular. Strident, unaccommodating attitudes can reinforce prejudices and create a terrible working atmosphere. On the other hand, a friendly attitude can be an effective counter for whatever negative expectations may precede you. From your first introduction to the presenter all the way through waving from the departing airplane, you will be viewed as representatives of the United States of America. You may wish to return to a venue; you may want to solicit the advice and help of your presenter in cultivating future engagements. If nothing else, a presenter's helpfulness during your visit should be reason enough for courtesy.

Brief your entire tour group—artists, technicians, and administrators alike—on proper behavior in all the countries you will be visiting. They should know that they may be asked political questions, and they may find that recent political events or policy decisions in the United States have ramifications on the tour. (At a press conference for the Merce Cunningham Dance Company in Hong Kong, the executive director was asked to comment on American military action in Grenada.)

Social events for the performers take on a new importance in this light; meeting the community can be demanding. If handled well, it can also be fun and a promotional boon for all concerned.

As a tour manager, tuck into your touring bag a letter or some other kind of certification that you are the official representative of the touring organization and that you will accept the fees for the group. In addition, bring business stationery and a portable typewriter so that you can create bogus forms, and carry an official stamp of your organization. A stick of sealing wax can be used for decorative and impressive effect. Creating unexpectedly needed documents can be quite a challenge; in some countries (Italy and Portugal come to mind) it is a new foreign-tour art form.

Some More Hints about Money

Keep bank receipts from all transactions and know the currency regulations that apply to entering and departing all the countries you are visiting as well as the current American regulations for your return. Sometimes you cannot use currency outside a country's own borders (India, for example), or there may be limits on transfers or exchanges into other currencies. Again, assume nothing, ask questions, and reconfirm the answers.

Bookkeeping accuracy on the part of the tour manager is a must on a tour in which you might be using a large number of different currencies, each of which could change in value daily. Note the fluctuation of rates of exchange while on the road. You will probably want to use an average of the rates you have received when you do your final tour accounting. Be assured, however, that no matter how careful you are, there will inevitably be a mysterious miscellaneous amount missing and unaccounted for at the end of the tour due to currency exchange losses. A calculator with back-up batteries is, needless to say, a must.

Travel agents and tourist offices can give you information about tipping customs in the countries you are visiting. Check to see if taxes and tips are included in hotel charges or at restaurants. Most likely, tour managers will be obliged to tip in situations where gratuities might not be expected in the United States.

You may also be surprised by occasional, irksome situations that call for bribes. It is hard to provide counsel, but this does happen with enough frequency that it must be mentioned. Security guards and customs officials checking your freight at European or Asian borders may let you know in subtle but certain terms that you will get nowhere unless they are "taken care of." You may have done nothing illegal or even questionable, but if you feel a delay may jeopardize the performance, and if you get the signal, pay the bribe.

What happens if something involving your contract goes wrong while the company is abroad? Great diplomatic skill may be required on the part of your touring staff to cooperate with presenters, to be firm yet understanding, and when necessary, to compromise. It is important to remember that you are in a foreign land with its own system for adjudicating disputes. The chances are slim that an international court will rule in your favor on a contract dispute and that you will receive any unpaid fees owed to you. It is preferable that you be attentive to details in advance and hammer them out as early as possible, rather than harbor hopes that you can settle disagreements or unresolved questions on the road. Domestic contracts normally include a clause prescribing that contractual disputes be adjudicated under the laws of one's own state in the United States; foreign presenters will usually cross out these sections. The wisest course of action is to anticipate as many problems as possible, and find as many solutions as you can before the company gets on the plane.

Aftermath

The foreign tour does not end when the company arrives back in the United States. If you have finished a foreign tour and found it a worthwhile experience, you are probably entertaining the thought of another one. If so, consider the following suggestions. In various ways, they all deal with communication.

1. Say thank you. You can never do this too often. Write to your presenter, to important people in the presenter's administration, to technicians who were helpful, to translators who spent long hours with you and your artists, to the hotel manager who made your stay enjoyable, to anyone who hosted a party for your group, to an airline agent who made your travel plans easier, to contributors who donated money for your trip, to press agents, to American artists and managers who shared their insights and experiences with you. The list can go on. Besides being a courtesy, these little gestures might be remembered long after the annoyances and difficulties of a tour have faded.

2. Get a complete set of press releases, reviews, and feature articles about your visit. Good press coverage can be used to woo other

presenters on your next venture abroad. You should also send copies to those presenters who are already preparing to host your performers; reprints of favorable foreign reviews can be especially useful to them. Your performers may want reprints as well, and newspaper reviews often will not appear until after your artists have left for the next city.

3. Be prepared for lengthy waits for fees cabled to your home bank from abroad. This is annoying but not out of the ordinary. You may find yourself having to recontact presenters because cabled fees have not arrived. Ask for the number of the cabled transaction, the name of the bank and the branch number at which the transaction occurred, and the date of the transaction. Double-check that the presenter has used your correct account number and bank branch. These facts will help your local bank if they need to trace a cable.

4. Keep in touch with presenters after the tour is over. Let them know when you are planning to tour abroad again, even if your itinerary may not take you into their area. Keep them informed of your group's special events (new works, anniversaries, etc.). Perhaps you will be asked back, or the presenter may mention you to other presenting organizations. Ask previous presenters for suggestions about future possibilities. If a presenter has had a good experience with your group, he may be excited enough to help you in the booking process.

In short, if work and meticulous attention to details have resulted in a successful tour, you will have made some useful business contacts and some good friends. Keep those contacts and friendships alive.

Finally, the importance of sharing with your fellow American artists and managers the information you have derived from your experiences on the road abroad cannot be overemphasized. Your problems and your solutions may be comforting or inspirational to others.

Foreign touring is never dull. There is always something new to learn; there are always new problems and new solutions; there is always something to share.

CHAPTER 15

Touring: The Artist's Viewpoint

Administrative personnel book and set up tours, but it is the artists who ultimately bear the brunt if management has not done a good job. The artists—and the quality of their work—will suffer directly if performances have been booked too closely together, if the number of hours on the bus between engagements is excessive, or if no arrangements have been made for eating dinner after the performance.

Collectively, the four performers interviewed for this chapter—an actor, a dancer, an opera singer, and a pianist—have spent more than thirty years touring, in the United States and abroad. Although separate disciplines and individual temperaments give each a unique point of view, overall they share a great deal of enthusiasm about their experiences. There are frustrations, however, and it remains the responsibility of management to minimize the myriad pressures and inconveniences which can come between a performer's desire and his ability to do his best work on the road.

The four performing artists who participated in this interview, originally conducted in 1984, were Leon Bates, Richard Iglewski, Chris Komar, and Mary Shearer.

SHAGAN: *Has touring been beneficial to you as artists?*

IGLEWSKI: Without a doubt. You run on nervous energy and you're absolutely prepared to go on at any time—and that's stretching for an actor. You're always up for the performance, and being in that kind of physical state, you learn a lot about economy in your art. Your focus is on the art and filling the space, on relating in whatever way you have to.

SHEARER: I was with the Texas Opera Theater when I was just starting out, which gave me a chance to do the same roles more than one or two times. In terms of singing a lot, it was a chance to see what I was really made of—what I could do, where I could save, and what conditions I could sing under, like when you're feeling really awful. Now, it's doing anything, anywhere—as much as you possibly can—that you can feel good about. The more you do, the better you are going to get. It does no good to sit around and practice in your apartment or have coaching. You have to get out there and do it.

KOMAR: I think touring is beneficial to living, and being a human being, and being alive. The kind of travel I've done has given me the ability to take a problem and make it work for me. The more information you get from traveling, the better equipped you are to make decisions that will help things work. If you're only traveling around this one little area and you want to go further, you need information. And experience is information.

You also realize that people really are the same all over the world. They're striving for the same opportunities and ideals and aesthetics, and they want pretty much what you want out of life. And this is a very reinforcing, supporting aspect of touring.

SHAGAN: *Are there activities besides performance that are particularly satisfying to you?*

IGLEWSKI: The Acting Company offers workshops if we are in one place long enough. I taught an audition workshop. I got to meet a lot of local talent and had an opportunity to explain to them what auditioning in New York was like. It was also an opportunity to see what kind of acting training is being given across the country.

BATES: I love working with kids. It's particularly gratifying when I get to go into the schools and do a fifty-minute program I've put together. It started with people saying, "We'd like you to come to our high school and talk to the kids." I was only about twenty-one, not much older than the students, and I wondered why in the world they would want to talk to me. But it gave me an opportunity to express ideas about music—to say this is happening here, and that's going on, and this is what I like about the piece.

I really like to sell music to an audience made up of both musicians and non-musicians. You have to make it interesting, not only as a musician with the skills I've developed that way, but also verbally.

KOMAR: I love to teach anytime, anywhere, but it isn't always easy to find the time and energy. And it's hard to find and schedule space. If you have a dance space, everybody wants to use it.

It can also be a problem if the dancers you're trying to instruct are not at the same level. I taught recently in Hong Kong in an incredibly difficult situation. There were athletes who couldn't do anything but throw a ball into a basket, and then there were people who were members of a professional dance company. Once I found a way to work so that everyone could get something out of it, everything was fine, but it's not the most desirable situation. Still, the more teaching that can be made a part of touring, the more people will get out of it.

SHAGAN: *All of you seem to like touring, particularly the way it allows you to stretch artistically and to relate to audiences and to fellow artists around the country and around the world. What do you find most difficult on tour?*

IGLEWSKI: Lugging suitcases—you have to have one of those rolling carts—getting on the bus, getting off the bus. You learn to deal with the time you're confined in this little tin box—hours on end—and the inconvenience of not being in one place for more than a day. It's the actual physical part of touring that I dislike most.

SHEARER: I actually hate to travel. First of all you have to pack, figure out what to take, get the ticket, go to the airport. Then you get on the plane and you get all dried out. The air on the planes is dry for everybody, of course, but that can really be a problem for singers.

You have to be so concerned about changes of climate and food, time difference, water—you have to be careful about everything. You never eat like you normally do at home, unless you happen to be someplace for a long period of time and there is a kitchen. But most of the time it's eating out and trying to get something that isn't all starch. Any little thing can really be the difference between singing well or not singing well.

KOMAR: Always the bed in the hotel was too soft, there wasn't enough hot water, the room was too small, the stages were too cold, the dressing rooms were too dirty, the traveling was too long, and you were too tired. When you first start touring, those things weigh very heavily because they are so immediate that you can't think about dancing. You really do need to be taken care of. But the more I've traveled, the more I've found ways of dealing with these inadequacies. You realize that on tour you're just not always going to get what you think you need. So you find ways to accept that fact.

SHAGAN: *What was the single worst tight spot you have been in as an artist on tour, and how did you get out of it?*

BATES: For me it was probably my debut with the Philadelphia Orchestra. I was performing the Ravel Piano Concerto, and somewhere in the third movement I dislodged the face board on the front of the keyboard. When I struck it, it jumped up in a crooked way so that I only had access to the lower half of the keys.

I had a break of a couple of measures and I was trying to get this piece of wood back into position before my next entrance. People were watching me and trying to figure out what in the world I was doing. Finally, I yanked it off and slid it under the piano, and came in at my next entrance. But it was hairy. I didn't have time to do anything except deal with the situation. I didn't have time to think about it or panic. I just knew it had to come off.

KOMAR: After years of touring, we all have our stories. Recently we were performing in Copenhagen in a building that had been a gasworks—a huge, round, brick building—and they made it into a theatre. The day of performance it poured—a torrential downpour all day long—and by the time of the evening performance, the water started dripping through the roof. There were puddles of water here and there upstage, and it was so dark you couldn't see them, so people were falling. Three dancers actually hit the deck.

One of the stagehands had to crawl along the stage with a towel and wipe it up and crawl back, and then come out and do it again. Fortunately, a remarkable thing about Merce's and John's work [choreographer Merce Cunningham and composer John Cage] is that it allows for these sorts of situations to happen. It's so practical that you can have something that is totally outside the work and still include it.

Of course, Merce didn't want anything like that to happen unless it was really necessary. But when a situation becomes unsafe, anything might happen, and you have to deal with it.

IGLEWSKI: One of the tightest spots I was in happened just a short time ago. Alan Schneider [artistic director of The Acting Company] died. We were informed after one of our shows that he had been in a very serious accident, and two days after that he died.

As a company, we were able to deal with all the pain and regret, with the loss of someone we'd been close to on the road, by drawing more closely together than we had been before. Sometimes you don't want to be too close to people when you're with them twenty hours a day, seven days a week.

SHAGAN: *What's the biggest single difference between performing in your home city and performing on the road?*

IGLEWSKI: People have different perspectives on the work. A New York audience is a New York audience. You know that they probably know the plays that you're doing, if you're doing something like *Merry Wives of Windsor* or *Pericles*. And if you're playing somewhere else, they may not know the play. So there are things you have to do in terms of dealing with the text and language of Shakespeare that are simply actors' tasks. The task of a performer dealing with his audience is to establish communication, and that becomes refined on the road. The Acting Company is a classical company; we do a lot of Shakespeare. Outside of New York, a line of text that may be highly convoluted will need, perhaps, a little bit more energy, or a little bit more focus on image in order to relate the full meaning of the text.

BATES: I think there can be problems sometimes playing in your home town. I've played with the Philadelphia Orchestra and on some concert series in my home town of Philadelphia, and I've been aware of feeling like I really had to be on my toes, to make sure that my playing was really top-flight—-there as opposed to somewhere else. It wasn't that I was going to play with any less fervor or abandon elsewhere, but somehow or other it was more crucial. I felt that obligation to my friends and family to really be on top of the game. But interestingly enough, I find that I play less well because of the added pressure. Somehow people in Philadelphia think of me as a local; they don't look at me in the same way as if I came from somewhere else, and that can have negative effects.

SHEARER: I've performed with the New York Philharmonic and other groups in the city. It's wonderful working at home: all your stuff is there; you're really self-sufficient. If you get ill, you know who to call or where to go. It's familiar territory. Your voice teacher is there, your coach—

everyone you might need to call upon while you're singing. But from an artistic point of view there are wonderful things going on outside of New York, and you work with wonderful singers and musicians.

KOMAR: If you're here in New York, the situation is known—especially since we've been performing at City Center for so many years, and we perform at the studio. For the most part you know what to expect in New York.

SHAGAN: *It's interesting to me that only Richard mentioned that his performance—as an actor—might be different in New York than on tour. Do you sense a difference in the audiences or between different types of presenters from region to region?*

IGLEWSKI: It seems to me that there are two major categories of presenters our company performs for—colleges and universities and downtown theatre centers. The college audiences are different: they're younger; they respond more quickly. They may or may not have read the play, but when it's a full house of young people, you don't have to work very hard to get them into the cycle of responding. That kind of environment does have an effect on a company like The Acting Company. In a downtown theatre it can be more difficult. They don't seem to be as close to the material.

BATES: I've run into differences, but basically I'm used to getting a very warm response from the audiences. Generally the New York audience will be very knowledgeable. Some of the West Coast audiences would be too, I think—and Chicago. I don't play differently from one *place* to another. As far as approaching things differently, I'm more interested in how I'm feeling from one *concert* to the next, and what I want to express. So I don't really give in to playing to a specific audience.

The one thing I will do is I might be adventurous in trying some things in places where the people are more knowledgeable. But generally speaking, I try not to be affected by that. All audiences deserve a certain quality, regardless, and I don't like to try to predict the way people will react.

A college or university audience might be more receptive to contemporary music—some things that are a bit more off the beaten path—particularly if they have a big, strong music department. You come out with the Eighth Sonata of Scriabin, and they're more inclined to know it. You might find a community series where the people won't know a lot of the literature and might not respond as well to certain things you might have done otherwise. In those cases, a little forewarning on the part of the presenter might be valuable.

SHEARER: I find that in some cities people sit on their hands. Maybe they really liked it and that's their way of showing appreciation. Some of the best receptions I've gotten have been in Europe, but most of that has been singing modern, contemporary music. In general audiences for opera tend to be rather polite.

KOMAR: There's no difference between how we're received here in New York City and elsewhere around the world. We get the same kinds of comments about the dance and the music, and a basic, general enthusiasm about the work whether we're in Japan or India or St. Louis or San Francisco. I think that's because people are becoming more and more the same. They're getting more and more of the same information.

Also audiences are traveling themselves. We find people will come and see the company in Lyon and in Paris and then show up in other cities in Europe. I suppose there are differences, but I would hate to generalize as to what they are.

SHAGAN: *What should presenting organizations know about your needs?*

KOMAR: Probably the most important thing is to have a theatre that is comfortable, that is equipped with some decent dressing rooms, some shower facilities, some place where you can be warm, a decent floor, some light. I think the theatre situation provokes dancers more than the hotel situation because the theatre is where you spend most of your time. It's hard if the theatre is cold from the time you get in until you leave, if you can't walk down the stairs in your bare feet without picking up six inches of dust, or if you can't go to your dressing room and at least feel comfortable and wash your hands and face in a basin.

We're living in a theatre for at least ten hours a day—the crew is there at least twelve hours a day—but it's very hard for presenters to understand that every part of every day is as important to us as the time we spend on stage after the curtain goes up. If the class has to be done in a cellar or on a stone floor and its freezing cold—but it happens to be a free space—then they feel they're covered. If they have all the equipment in the world, the most modern computer boards, and what have you, they think they've done their job. But if the dancers have to warm up on a cement floor, then what have they provided? Very little. They've also cheapened the performance, denigrated what the dancers have to do.

Basically what we're doing is living in their theatre, so we have to have some kind of living facilities—a green room with couches and maybe a refrigerator, some food, any kind of little machine where you can get a soda or juice. Anything that provides you with these normal things that you could get yourself if you weren't in the theatre is helpful, because the problem with dancers is that we're stuck there. We can't leave until we're let go. You can usually deal with small bedrooms or other inconveniences at the hotel because you know that next week you're going somewhere else. But the theatre is where you have to perform, and that's what you're concerned with. If it's uncomfortable and inadequately equipped, it starts everything out wrong.

BATES: Dressing rooms with no heat are the bane of a pianist's existence because you cannot walk out on the stage with cold hands. And if there's no hot water, you can't even warm your hands by running water over them. Is there a piano in the building, other than the one on the stage, where you can warm up your hands before the performance? Or at least let me have the hall early enough so that I can spend a half hour doing my exercises.

Another thing is that a lot of times people are very reluctant to tell you what they think about your playing. It wouldn't be so bad if these same people didn't so often become completely and totally openmouthed when they get with someone else. For instance, in a couple of cases, a presenter said, "Oh wonderful, wonderful concert." Then to some other presenter they said they didn't think the playing was this, that, or the other, or, "I thought he could have done this." I don't see where this benefits anybody.

If there is a problem, I would prefer they express it to me, instead of just being polite, instead of giving you the same face they put on for any artist that comes through. What that does is breed mistrust. The presenter who is less than frank with you may not catch it, but maybe the next presenter you work with does, because you don't feel relaxed, don't feel you can establish an honest rapport. You come to feel that they're not interested in that. "They only see me as a saleable commodity. They're always checking me out, watching every single thing I'm doing." You begin to develop a certain professional facade and you use up a lot of energy making sure they don't get beneath it. That's when it gets to be kind of grueling to go out and play.

SHEARER: I've been places where they want to entertain you perpetually. You just can't do it. Your first obligation has to be to your performance. I've also been places where they invite you to a party, and you get there and they rip out the piano and expect you to sing. Supposedly you were invited there to have dinner and relax. And even though it's only at someone's house, you really feel you have to sing well.

SHAGAN: *How difficult is it for you to adapt as you go from space to space?*

BATES: The halls themselves are no real problem, but the pianos can be. Sometimes you might find the pianos are very stiff. There may be problems just in terms of physically playing the instrument. Or the action may be very uneven so that moving from one note to another can be very different. You have to make subtle adjustments.

Say you're trying to get a very even melodic line, but you're playing on a part of the piano that's uneven, because the action has not been regulated recently. You have to be aware of the notes that are going to stick out so that you can back off of those. You have to think of what your presentation is about.

I've come close to having to perform on pianos that were unplayable. Sometimes it's a situation where a presenter is not even aware of how bad an instrument is. You're telling them about this and they say, "Oh, really?"

SHEARER: The hall can affect you, but there's nothing you can do about it so you can't let it get you down. If it's too big, if it's dead, if it's very live, you just have to know how to handle it. But you can't adjust your voice to a hall. Sometimes, if it feels as if the hall is dead, you can bring your voice up a notch if you were singing something soft—but no, you don't push. A conductor can help a lot if voices don't carry well. He can keep the orchestra down. Maybe a stage director can keep everybody downstage and not have anything back in the set. But your instrument is your instrument, your voice is your voice. You can play with it to a certain extent but not a lot.

IGLEWSKI: It's difficult playing one night in a house where you have a hundred lights and a computer dimmer board and the next night playing in a high school auditorium with ten lights and a manual board. It shakes you, but you have to learn—our *responsibility* was to learn how to deal with that kind of change. You have to retrain yourself to be aware of the lighting all over again, where the entrances are, where the floor creaks.

One night you play in a 6,000-seat house with 3,000 people in the audience, and you have to learn how to project in that space without ruining your voice. Then you go to a 300-seat house, and you have to pull back or you'd blow them out of their seats. You have to learn fine tuning.

SHAGAN: *What about the people who book and manage tours? What would you like them to know in terms of what's important to you on tour?*

IGLEWSKI: It's good to be told how many miles you are going to have to travel in a day. Sometimes the itinerary doesn't tell you, and that's annoying. You have it set in your mind that it's two and a half hours to the next stop and you figure that you can go to the bank, get to the drugstore, and have dinner once you get in, and then take the bus to the theater. Then suddenly it takes three and a half hours and all your plans are shot. Of course, every once in a while things happen.

Another thing is checking into hotels. Sometimes they make you sign in, and there are seventeen people in line who have just gotten off the bus—it's chaos! Also, booking hotels that have restaurants and bars and laundromats—that's important.

And it's nice to have days off in larger cities.

It's very important to have a complementary relationship between performers and management, and you have to be aware of how difficult the road is when you're choosing people for the company. If you have one rotten apple, it can affect the entire company, and it can affect the work. If someone is basically unstable and you put them in an environment where they have no security, you are only inviting them to release the behavior that expresses their insecurity.

KOMAR: To me, a single room is very important—my own space that I can deal with in whatever way I want. If I'm jet-lagged and wake up at 2 A.M., I want to be able to listen to music, or turn on the light, or take a walk—or do whatever I want.

A lot of dancers in our company share rooms because they need to cut down on expenses. But for my own particular needs, the money isn't the point. There has to be some kind of individual control over one's private existence.

BATES: My airline should be booked well in advance, so there's never any question about "Will I make that flight today?" Everything should be planned and set out in advance so that my mind can be clear to think about the music.

What is really very nice is for a representative from the series to come and meet me at the airport and get me to my hotel room, someone who has the itinerary for the time I'm going to be there. They can give me a schedule for when the rehearsals will be, if there is a party or reception after the performance, and so forth. If there is any media, radio, or television, let's have it in advance.

I like to have my schedule confirmed as soon as I get there, so if there are any changes, I'm immediately aware and can write them in. And I have to get practice time in the hall at least twice before the performance, once the evening before and then again on the day of the performance.

It's nice if you can have a number of engagements arranged one after the other in a single geographical area as opposed to bouncing around the country. That's pretty crucial, especially in terms of money. I know you can't always prevent this if it's a matter of getting a booking or not getting it.

SHEARER: Managers should be aware that it's very hard to sing several performances close together. I've sung a Saturday night and a Sunday matinee. Sometimes you get into a situation where you have the dress rehearsal the morning of the performance. Sometimes there's a rehearsal on a Saturday morning, performance Saturday matinee and then again Saturday night. You need time between performances to recoup your voice, especially if you're doing something really big, like a Verdi Requiem.

Someone should meet you and take you to the hotel, rehearsal, or wherever you need to go, but what you must have is a decent place to stay. And always try to get a decent rate on a hotel, a good price on a flight—because we're paying for it. The artist needs to come back with something.

SHAGAN: *What do you enjoy about touring?*

IGLEWSKI: There are lots of things I enjoy, some of them more so in hindsight than when I was out on the road. I saw a lot of new places—150,000 miles of this country, big cities and small towns—from a bus. There's a German expression for this period in a person's life that I've just come through. It sort of translates as "the wandering years."

Artistically it was a period when I was able to focus exclusively on my work as an actor, because I was removed from a lot of things that we deal with living in one place.

BATES: It's exciting in terms of how I feel about myself. There's something terribly professional and uplifting about having this ability, this skill, about people hiring you to come in and do your work.

You spend your whole life getting to the point so that you can be out there from time to time. In the beginning I would make one trip, do a concert, and then come back. Then I got to the point where I was doing two engagements, and then three, and now I'm out three or four weeks at a time. In terms of being able to make the necessary growth, to continue to improve, to reach new levels of excellence, you have to stay out and play your programs time and time again and see what it feels like when you're tired, when you don't want to play. You have to play on different stages and get the responses of different audiences—the good ones *and* the bad ones. Everything I do revolves around that.

KOMAR: What I've been finding out about touring over an eleven-year period is that it can provide a very positive influence not only on the performer as a performer but on the performer as a human being, as a member of society. I joined Merce Cunningham for the experience, and traveling is one of the most enlarging experiences I've come across.

Touring with this company has presented me with so many different situations, and the more difficult the situation, the more enlightening and educational it is. You have to learn about yourself and other people. You learn things about working and performing that you'd never be forced to find out about if you were at home under controlled conditions. You find out there are things you can do that you didn't realize before.

Of course, Merce's work is unique, and when you reach an audience, even when only a few people come backstage afterwards, if they're ecstatic about what they've seen, it's thrilling—to be able to touch people that way, to give them that experience.

The Artists

LEON BATES is a pianist who has toured since 1969 throughout the United States, Europe, and Africa and has won numerous major awards in artists' competitions.

RICHARD IGLEWSKI is an actor who has traveled for several years on the road with The Acting Company and has performed in a broad range of plays—from the classics to experimental works.

CHRIS KOMAR, a dancer with the Merce Cunningham Dance Company, has also served as assistant to the choreographer and has mounted works for both domestic and European tours.

MARY SHEARER is a lyric soprano who started her career with Texas Opera Theater and has performed with opera companies and orchestras both in the United States and abroad.

Contracts

Sample Contract with a Technical Rider

AGREEMENT made this _____ day of _____ 19_____, by and between the _____ company (hereinafter,the "COMPANY"), New York, N.Y., and

_____

_____

_____

(hereinafter, the "PRESENTER") engaging the artistic services of the COMPANY, pursuant to the terms hereunder:

1. ENGAGEMENT
    A. _____ performance(s), at _____ o'clock on _____, 19____
    B. _____ week(s) residency, to include _____ activities, on _____,
       19___ of the following nature:

2. COMPENSATION

A COMPENSATION of _____ dollars ($ _____) for the services shall be paid to the COMPANY on the DATE OF THE PERFORMANCE AND PRIOR TO THE TIME OF THE PERFORMANCE. THE COMPENSATION shall be by certified check, made payable to the _____. The date and time of payment are understood to be of the essence of this agreement. The Company shall not perform if they have not received above mentioned compensation. The check shall be given to the Company Stage Manager.

3. TECHNICAL REQUIREMENTS

The technical requirements described below are essential to the COMPANY's performance and residence activities and are understood to form an integral part of this contract. The PRESENTER agrees to notify the COMPANY in writing of any special or other arrangements, or changes in agreed arrangements at least 6 weeks in advance of the performance-residency dates to determine if such alternations are acceptable to the COMPANY.

A. MASTER AND REPERTORY CLASS REQUIREMENTS

1. The dancers need a place to dress, preferably private, one hour before the Master Class.
2. The space being used for the Master Class or an adjacent area must be available to the company to warm up *one hour* prior to the class.
3. The floor must be smooth and without obstruction. Its surface should be neither splintery, varnished, nor waxed. The floor should be either linoleum or wood *not laid on concrete*. It should be dry prior to the class.

B. PRODUCTION REQUIREMENTS

Unless otherwise specified, production requirements pertain to Full Performance, Narrated Performance, and Lecture Demonstration.

1. TECHNICAL DIRECTOR

   The PRESENTER must designate a Technical Director with decision making authority to be present, responsible to, and accessible for consultation with the COMPANY at ail crew calls.
2. FACULTY AND EQUIPMENT

   The PRESENTER must provide the following:

   A. *Proscenium Stage* performing space of 36' width (proscenium opening) by 27' depth (curtain line to cyclorama or sky drop)
   B. *Floor* The floor must be either linoleum or wood *not laid on concrete*. Its surface must be neither splintery, varnished, nor waxed. All nails and staples must be removed, holes filled or taped, and unused floor packets covered. If the floor surface is not safe for barefoot dancing, a dance floor covering—Marley or Tarkett dance floors or battleship linoleum—must be provided. The floor and wings must be clean (mopped and swept) prior to rehearsal and performance.

C. *Draperies*

1. House curtain
2. 3–4 borders (black velour preferred) to provide complete overhead masking
3. 4–5 pairs of legs (black velour preferred) to provide complete side masking
4. black backdrop or traveller (velour preferred) or black scrim
5. white or light blue cyclorama or sky drop
6. all draperies to be hung prior to the arrival of the COMPANY stage manager

D. *Lighting Equipment*

Full Performance, Narrated Performance

1. 30 dimmers, 3KW capacity or greater
2. 10 6" × 12" (two plano-convex lenses) lekos-750W
3. 45 6" × 9" (two plano-convex lenses) lekos-750W
4. Cyclorama lighting (scoops or strip lights) in red and dark blue
5. 8 10' high booms with 50-pound bases
6. Cable as necessary to hang the COMPANY plot
7. 1 ladder, scaffold, or cherry picker tall enough to allow an electrician to safely focus instruments 23' off the stage floor
8. Plot hung accurately, circuited, and patched prior to the arrival of the COMPANY Stage Manager

Lecture-Demonstration

1. General illumination

E. *Sound*

1. Theater sound system of good quality that has:
   a. stereo tape deck, 7½ ips, reel-to-reel
   b. amplifier(s)
   c. house speaker system
   d. two backstage monitor speakers
2. Headset intercom system with stations for the Stage Manager, Light Board Operator(s), Sound Technician, and, if necessary Curtainman

Lecture-Demonstration only (in addition to 1. and 2.)

3. 1 microphone and floor stand located downstage right
4. 1 lectern, 4'–6' maximum height, located next to microphone

F. *Heat*

1. The performance space must be heated to a minimum seventy-four degrees (74°) by noon on the day of performance or three (3) hours prior to a Narrated Performance or Lecture Demonstration.

3. DRESSING ROOMS

The PRESENTER must provide two clean, private dressing rooms for dancers allowing non-public access to the performing area. Each room must have makeup lights and mirrors, chairs and tables, costume rack, and nearby lavatory and sink.

The PRESENTER must also supply a steam iron and ironing board.

4. CREW AND WORK SCHEDULE

The PRESENTER must supply all theater personnel and schedule adequate time for setup, rehearsal and performance.

A. Crew

1. 2 stage electricians
2. 1 sound technician
3. 2 stagehands
4. 1 wardrobe mistress
5. All personnel must be the same persons for both rehearsal and performance

Lecture-Demonstration

1. 1 stage electrician
2. 1 sound electrician
3. 1 stagehand

NOTE: The COMPANY is a Non-Yellow Card attraction. IATSE stagehands are not required. If local rules specify their use, all necessary negotiations with the local and all expenses incurred remain solely between the PRESENTER and the local and will not affect the COMPANY.

B. Work Schedule

Full Performance. The performance space and adjacent areas must be scheduled for uninterrupted COMPANY usage from 12 noon until 12 midnight on each performance day and for a maximum of eight (8) additional hours prior to 12 noon the first performance day for use by the COMPANY Stage Manager for COMPANY load-in, focusing of lighting instruments, cueing, etc.

Narrated Performance, Lecture-Demonstration. The performance space and adjacent areas must be scheduled for uninterrupted COMPANY usage for two hours prior to the Narrated Performance and for a maximum of six (6) additional hours prior to those two hours for use by the COMPANY Stage Manager for COMPANY load-in, focusing of lighting instruments, cueing, etc.

It is further understood that the exact crew and work schedule can be finalized only after the PRESENTER has returned the COMPANY Technical Questionnaire and residency activities have been scheduled.

4. HALL AND HOUSE PERSONNEL AND EQUIPMENT

The PRESENTER agrees to provide a suitable and appropriate hall for the performance of the COMPANY, cleaned and heated to the satisfaction of the COMPANY's representative. The PRESENTER further agrees to supply a House Manager, all ushers, ticket sellers, doormen and all other personnel reasonably necessary to permit the presentation, and all printed programs, tickets and other printed materials necessary at the expense of the PRESENTER.

5. PROGRAM

The COMPANY will provide for the PRESENTER all program information to be reproduced in full and exactly as offered to the PRESENTER in all printed programs. All references to the COMPANY in paid or unpaid advertising, announcements, houseboards, flyers, posters, publicity releases and any other promotional materials for the services above shall be as follows:

The COMPANY shall have the right to alter the program sent to the PRESEN-TER at any time up to and including the performance.

6. REPRODUCTION

The PRESENTER shall not authorize or permit, and shall take all steps necessary to prohibit and/or enjoin the recording, photography, reproduction, transmission, and/or broadcast, or any other use whatsoever, by any means or through any media whatsoever, of any portion of any performance or its rehearsal or of any portion of any service scheduled above by any means whatsoever.

7. LIABILITY

The COMPANY shall be under no liability for failure to appear or perform in the event that such failure is caused by or due to the physical disability or illness of the COMPANY, or acts or regulations of public authorities, labor difficulties, civil tumult, strike, epidemic, interruption or delay of transportation service, or other similar or dissimilar cause beyond the control of the COMPANY.

8. TRANSPORTATION

The PRESENTER agrees to provide adequate directions to the scheduled place of residency and performance. The PRESENTER agrees to provide transportation for the COMPANY to and from all activities including performances, master classes, lecture-demonstrations, narrated performances, and informal discussion.

9. COMPLIMENTARY TICKETS

The PRESENTER shall supply the COMPANY upon its request, with 4 (four) complimentary tickets to each performance.

10. SUBCONTRACTING RESIDENCY ACTIVITIES

The PRESENTER shall not sub-contract the COMPANY's services to any other institution, school, or other organization except with the *written permission* of the COMPANY.

11. The person responsible for scheduling details of the residency for the COMPANY is:

The person responsible for scheduling details of the residency for the PRE-SENTER is:

_____

THIS AGREEMENT sets forth the entire understanding between the parties with respect to the subject matter hereof and no modification, amendments, or waiver of this agreement or any provision thereof shall be binding upon either party unless confirmed in a written document signed by both parties. The validity, construction, and effect of this agreement, and all extensions, modifications, and amendments hereof, shall be in accordance with the laws of the State of New York.

IN WITNESS WHEREOF, the parties have executed this agreement as of the date first written above.

PRESENTER

by   _____

_____

COMPANY

by   _____

_____

Sample Contract with a Separate Technical Rider

THE CLASSIC THEATRE COMPANY
666 West 16th Street
New York, NY 10000
(212) 555-6789

CONTRACT

AGREEMENT, made this _____ day of _____, 19_____, by and between THE CLASSIC THEATRE COMPANY, (hereinafter "Company") and hereafter "Local Manager") whose address is:

_____

_____

1. Company will present at _____ the following program:

_____

_____

2. The total fee for this engagement herein is the sum of payment by accepted draft payable to the order of The Classic Theatre Company as follows: twenty-five (25) percent ($_____) deposit to be mailed no later than _____ _____. (Deposit refundable if engagement cancelled through sole fault of Company.) The balance ($_____) due and payable no later than _____ after completion of the first public performance.

   In the event that payments are not made as herein provided, Company shall, at its option, have the right to refuse to perform, and Local Manager shall remain liable to Company for the agreed price herein set forth.

3. Company travels with full sets, props and costumes. The Local Manager is required to furnish a fully equipped stage capable of accommodating Company; dressing rooms which meet the "Safe and Sanitary Code" of Actors' Equity Association; sufficient lighting instruments and dimmer boards to meet the needs of Company's lighting plot with the equipment therein contained as specifically described in Exhibit A ("Technical Requirements"), hereby incorporated into and made a part of this agreement as though fully set forth herein. Lighting instruments to be prehung according to Company lighting plot, prior to Company arrival, and all sides and overhead masking and sound equipment when required. It is agreed that Company shall be guaranteed exclusive and uninterrupted access to the full stage auditorium area and dressing rooms from arrival time to departure time. The specific needs of Company will be sent to the Local Manager at least two weeks prior to the performance. Some plays

require a piano, in tune, for the performance. If a piano is required, Company will inform Local Manager at least two weeks prior to the engagement. If company carries its own piano, Local Manager agrees to provide and pay for the services of a piano tuner.

4. Local Manager agrees to completely fill out a Management and Technical Questionnaire of the facility in which Company is to perform and return it to Company or its agents no later than one month after contractual agreements are signed. Local Manager agrees that Company shall not be required to perform the program until this Questionnaire has been returned and approved by Company. Company will endeavor to design all productions to fit on most stages. However, certain productions cannot be put on stages with restricted space and/or limited technical facilities. Therefore, failure to return said Questionnaire promptly will make it difficult for Company to guarantee the choice of play.

5. Local Manager agrees to furnish at its own expense an eight (8) member stage crew, as more specifically described in Exhibit A ("Technical Requirements"), hereby incorporated into and made apart of this agreement as though fully set forth herein, to assist Company in unloading scenery and costumes, in setting up the production(s), in running the production(s), in "striking" the production(s), and in loading the scenery and costumes onto the trucks and buses. The crew members who set up and run cues must be the same individuals who run the performance(s). Should the Local Manager fail to provide the required personnel, it is agreed that the Local Manager will be responsible for paying to Company's representative a sum in the amount of thirty-five dollars ($35.00) for each person under the required number of personnel each time the Local Manager fails to supply the required crew. This crew will be responsible to the Technical Director and/or Production Stage Manager provided by the Company.

6. Local Manager also agrees to furnish at least two (2) dressers/wardrobe personnel, one male and one female, to help the artists and costumiere before, during and after the Performance(s). These dressers/wardrobe personnel will be responsible to the Wardrobe Supervisor and/or Production Stage Manager provided by Company.

7. If the theatre at which Local Manager is to present Company has other minimum requirements regarding stage crews, etc., including requirements of various unions, Local Manager agrees to provide and pay for these requirements.

8. Local Manager agrees to carry general liability, theft, and property damage insurance in amounts sufficient to provide coverage for personnel employed by, and scenery, costumes, and equipment owned and/or rented by Company. Further, Local Manager agrees to defend, indemnify, and hold Company harmless from any claims, suits, demands, actions, proceedings, judgements, costs, and expenses with respect to any accident, injury, damage, cost, and expense in connection with Company's performance(s) as described in this contract.

9. Local Manager shall be responsible for insuring compliance with and shall perform at its sole cost and expense all local, state, and federal governmental rules in regard to this presentation.

10. Company will furnish Local Manager with copy for the program to be performed at each performance and Local Manager agrees, at its own expense, to print and distribute a sufficient quantity of house programs conforming with the program copy furnished by Company. Local Manager agrees to allow Company to insert performance programs with the Company newsletter and informational materials.

11. All programs shall include in bold face type on the credit page the following note: "The taking of photographs or operating of recording devices during the performance is strictly prohibited."

12. Local Manager is not the agent for Company and has no authority to commit or bind Company.

13. Local Manager represents that it has a lease for the theatre, hall or auditorium, covering the dates of this engagement, which lease will be shown to Company upon request.

14. In the event that Local Manager refuses or neglects to provide any of the items hereinbefore stated, Company shall have the right to refuse to present the program, and the Local Manager shall be liable to Company for any damages on account thereof.

15. If before the date of any scheduled program, Company finds that Local Manager has failed, neglected or refused to perform any contract with another for an earlier engagement, or if Company finds that the financial credit of Local Manager has been impaired, Company shall have the right to cancel this contract.

16. Company shall be under no liability for failure to appear or perform in the event that such failure is caused by or due to "Acts of God," including, but not limited to, acts or regulations of public authorities, labor difficulties, civil tumult, strike, epidemic, interruption or delay of transportation service, or any other cause beyond the control of Company.

17. This contract cannot be assigned or transferred without the written consent of Company, and contains the complete understanding of the parties respecting the subject matter hereof.

18. All notices to be given and communications to be addressed to Company in connection with this contract and program shall be in writing, addressed to: The Classic Theatre Company, 666 West 16th Street, New York, New York 10000.

19. This contract shall be deemed entered into the State of New York and shall be construed under the laws of the State of New York.

20. Any dispute or controversy arising under this contract shall be submitted to binding arbitration in New York, under the then prevailing rules of the American Arbitration Association.

21. It is understood that this contract is an offer of services by Company, and is not binding on either party until both Local Manager and Company have signed and initialed any changes. To accept this contract as binding, Company requires that Local Manager sign and return it to company within ninety (90) days of the contract date.

22. Company affirms that it has the performance rights for all plays in the touring repertory and Local Manager will not be liable for any claims, suits, or judgments by Playwrights or their representatives.

23. Company will supply Local Manager with all available publicity materials such as Posters, flyers, press kit materials, the amount to be determined by the length of engagement, and choice of repertory.

24. If Local Manager has discount priced tickets (i.e., for students, etc.), Local Manager agrees to grant such discounts to those persons who present proof that they are National Members of The Classic Theatre Company.

25. Local Manager agrees to make available to Company eight (8) complimentary tickets to each performance in good locations unless the performance is sold out. If the performance is sold out, Local Manager agrees to hold eight (8) tickets until noon on the day of performance which may be purchased by the Company. Furthermore, Local Manager agrees that, subject to local fire ordinances, or availability, seats or standing room will be made available for all performances contracted herein for those Company personnel not performing. Company agrees to provide Local Manager upon request a list of Company personnel in this regard by noon on the day of performance.

The Classic Theatre Company:

by _____

_____

Local Manager:

by _____

_____

Technical Rider

CLASSIC THEATRE COMPANY
EXHIBIT A – TECHNICAL REQUIREMENTS

The following equipment and personnel ar required for the company's production of _____

LIGHTING EQUIPMENT. All available equipment, including, but not limited to the following:

24 2k Dimmers with A/B switching *or*	48 2k Dimmers (preferable) 2 scene preset
6 6"×9" 500w Lekos	17 6"×9" 750w Lekos
7 6"×12" 750w Lekos	9 8" Fresnels: 500–750W
7 Barndoors for 8" Fresnels	5 6" Fresnels: 500W
5 Barndoors for 6" Fresnels	7 Beam Projectors: 500–750W
2–3 Colortran Farcycs (or other instruments suitable for washing cyc evenly)	1 Followspot
	Houselights
	3 8' Booms and Bases
Gel frames, cable, twofers	4 Adapters (if necessary)

SOUND

1 Mixer (4 inputs, 3 outputs)	2 large proscenium speakers
3 Channels of amplification	1 Open reel tape deck, 7½ ips, ½-track stereo
1 Cassette deck	Head sets as necessary (up to 5)
Cables and plugs as necessary	

SOFTGOODS

Scrim (if available)	Cyc (white)

PERSONNEL

1 Sound	4 Electricians
3 Carpenters	2 Costume Personnel

I have read this Technical Rider and agree to provide the equipment and personnel required above.

Presenter's Signature _____

Letter of Agreement

This shall serve as a binding agreement between Classic Theatre Company (hereinafter referred to as "The Company") and

Organization: _____

Representative: _____

Address: _____

Telephone: _____

(hereinafter referred to as "The Presenter").

1. The Company agrees to present _____ performance(s) on the date(s) of:
   _____
   at _____ o'clock, in: _____

   The Company agrees to perform the following residency activities:
   _____ on _____ 19____
   _____ on _____ 19____

2. The Presenter agrees to pay to the Company, without any offset or deduction whatsoever, the amount of:

3. It is further understood that a full contract including all technical and publicity requirements will be executed to supplement this Agreement.

IN WITNESS WHEREOF, the parties hereto have caused this Agreement to be executed as of the day and year herein below mentioned:

For Classic Theatre Company:

Signature: _____
Name: _____
Title: _____
Date: _____

For: _____

Signature: _____
Name: _____
Title: _____
Date: _____

Tour Manager's Resource Kit

Performance/Residency Checklist

PRESENTER: _____

Address: _____

Office Phone: _____ Home Phone: _____

TECHNICAL DIRECTOR: _____

Address: _____

Office Phone: _____ Home Phone: _____

	MAIL DATE	BY	DATE RET.	COMMENTS	COPY TO	DATE
Letter of Agreement	____	____	____	_____	____	____
Contract	____	____	____	_____	____	____
Tech Questionnaire	____	____	____	_____	____	____
Perf/Res Packet:						
1. Info Sheet	____	____	____	_____	____	____
2. Questionnaire	____	____	____	_____	____	____
3. Calendar	____	____	____	_____	____	____
Request Form (Promo)	____	____	____	_____	____	____

Initial Promo Materials
 & Glossies   ___ ___ ___ _____ ___ ___
Travel Confirmations:
 1. Inter-Perf. Trans.   ___ ___ ___ _____ ___ ___
 2. Local Trans.   ___ ___ ___ _____ ___ ___
 3. Accommodations   ___ ___ ___ _____ ___ ___
Posters, Flyers   ___ ___ ___ _____ ___ ___
Complete Promo Kit   ___ ___ ___ _____ ___ ___
Payroll Letter   ___ ___ ___ _____ ___ ___
Light Plot   ___ ___ ___ _____ ___ ___
Crew Confirm. Letter   ___ ___ ___ _____ ___ ___
Program Copy   ___ ___ ___ _____ ___ ___
Tech. Confirm. Letter   ___ ___ ___ _____ ___ ___
Admin. Confirm. Letter   ___ ___ ___ _____ ___ ___
Sched. for Co. Members   ___ ___ ___ _____ ___ ___
Follow-Up: Call   ___ ___ ___ _____ ___ ___

HOTEL INFORMATION

Name: _____

Amenities: _____

Address: _____

Phone: _____

Price: Singles: _____ Doubles: _____ Triples: _____

Company Rooming List:

TRANSPORTATION ARRANGEMENTS:
 A. Inter-performance:

 B. Local:

AFTER PERFORMANCE MEAL ARRANGEMENTS:

BANKING AND PAYROLL INFORMATION:

CONFIRMED SCHEDULE:

PERFORMANCE REPERTORY AND CASTING:

Performance/Residency Information Packet

To: *Presenter's Name*
From: *Company Manager*

The following is IMPORTANT INFORMATION regarding the performance/residency by the company for your community. Please read all of the information carefully. PLEASE FILL OUT THE INFORMATION FORM ATTACHED TO THIS MEMO AND THE RESIDENCY ACTIVITY CALENDAR IF YOU ARE HAVING RESIDENCY ACTIVITIES AND RETURN THEM BY:

Date:_____

To: *Company Manager*
    Address
    Phone

The following is some important information we think you should have regarding the company's stay in your community before you fill out the Presenter Information Form.

1. We ask on the information form for suggestions as to which hotel/motel the company should stay at while in your community. The company prefers to be as close to the theater as possible. Bathrooms need to have bathtubs. If you have a special reason for suggesting a specific hotel/motel, please note it on the form.
2. Dancers cannot eat a meal before a performance, so normally by the time our company's performance in your facility is over they have had nothing to eat for 10–12 hours. They need to have a good dinner at that point but in many communities there are no restaurants open past 10:30 P.M. If this is the case in your area, we ask your help in arranging for a local restaurant to stay open late. If no restaurant can accommodate us, we ask that you see that the dancers get dinner at someone's home.
3. The company is happy to attend a reception after the performance if you schedule one. However, the reception must include dinner food for the company members. We cannot ask our dancers to eat cheese and crackers or punch and cookies for dinner as we're sure you can understand.
4. The company holds daily class while on the road as well as some rehearsal sessions. We need approximately 2 hours per day in a dance studio, gymnasium, stage, or other space large enough for this purpose.
5. The company is always available for press interviews, TV programs, etc., but these activities need to be scheduled well in advance and should be a part of the schedule.

Activities Information Sheet

The following is information we think you should have before filling in the
RESIDENCY ACTIVITY CALENDAR.

1. _____ company is a dance company which puts
   its emphasis on performing. The company is with your school/community for
   a short period of time. Within this time frame the company feels that it can give
   a dance experience to more people through performances, lecture demonstrations, etc. than through activities involving smaller numbers of people. We
   do, however, try to tailor each residency to the particular needs of each presenter.

2. The company can do activities during our stay with you. Please put together a
   list and schedule of these activities. Or if you have any uncertainty about what
   activities would be best or their scheduling, contact our office.

The company offers the following activities from which you can choose.

ACTIVITY	TIME ALLOTTED	REQUIREMENTS/NOTES
Performance	2–2½ hours	See contract for complete Tech specifications. No other activities scheduled on day of performance, unless performance is not the first day of residency and takes place in same theatre.
Narrated Performance	45 min.–1 hr.	For children, utilizes costumes, available lighting. Minimum set up time 3 hrs. depending on equipment.
Lecture-Demonstration	1–1½ hours	For high school, college, adult audience. Stage, gymnasium, large space. 2 hour minimum set-up time.
Master Class	1½ hours	Modern dance, advanced, intermediate, beginners. Dance studio, stage, gymnasium, large space, accompanist if possible.
Repertory Class	1½ hours	Same as above.
Movement for Actors	1½ hours	Same as above.
Technical Aspects of Dance Theatre	1 hour	Stage or Technical Workshop.
Open Rehearsal	2–2½	Space where performance will take place.

PLEASE NOTE THE COMPANY CAN PERFORM NO ACTIVITY ON A CEMENT FLOOR OR ON A FLOOR OF WOOD OR LINOLEUM LAID DIRECTLY OVER CEMENT. THE COMPANY CANNOT DANCE ON RUGS. Please, we really mean this ... There can be *no exceptions* as our dancers' professional lives are at stake. Let us know well in advance if you have a floor problem. There are several inexpensive ways of fixing a floor and we can advise you of same. If upon arrival we find that you have scheduled the company into a space with the above problem(s) we will not be able to perform that activity unless it is rescheduled in an acceptable space.

Dancers' muscles tend to cramp when they are dancing in cold or drafty places. Please see to it (as per contract) that the rooms, stages, etc. where dance activities take place are well heated before an activity begins. We ask that the heat be 75 degrees for two hours before an activity begins.

When figuring out your schedule for the company please keep in mind:

1. It takes dancers ¾ hour to 1 hour to warm up before an activity begins. Please be sure to include adequate warm-up time in your schedule. If you are scheduling two activities on the same day in the same place, you might schedule them back to back with a short break. This way the dancers will only have to warm up once.
2. If the company has activities to perform on the day following an evening performance, please do not schedule these activities before 12 noon without prior consultation with the Company Manager.

On the next page is a blank schedule. Using the information given earlier in this material, please fill in the activities you would like the company to perform, on what day they will take place, time, place, and participants as well as any other comments you might have. After receiving the schedule, the company will inform you as to any changes it might need to make or suggestions as to schedule or programming it might have. We will work with you to provide a schedule that is mutually satisfactory. Once an agreement on schedule is reached and confirmed the schedule cannot be changed without notifying the Company Manager.

Residency Calendar

DATE/DAY	ACTIVITY	TIME BEGIN/END	PLACE BLDG./ROOM	STUDENTS/AUDIENCE NUMBER/AGE/LEVEL
Day 1				
Day 2				
Day 3				
Day 4				
Day 5				
Day 6				

Please return this form to: COMPANY MANAGER: _____

ADDRESS: _____

PHONE: _____

Presenter Questionnaire

Presenting Organization: _____ Tour Dates: _____
Mailing Address: _____

Presenter: _____ Office Phone: _____
(Mailing address if
   different from above): _____ Home Phone: _____
Residency Activity Contact: _____ Office Phone: _____
(Mailing address if
   different from above): _____ Home Phone: _____
Contact when company
   arrives: _____ Office Phone: _____
Home Phone:
Technical Director: _____ Office Phone: _____
(Mailing address if
   different from above): _____ Home Phone: _____
Technical information
   and plot to: _____ Office Phone: _____
Mailing Address: _____ Home Phone: _____

Name of Theater: _____ Office Phone: _____
Exact Street Address: _____ Home Phone: _____
Box Office Phone: _____

What is your deadline for program and publicity materials?
Publicity: _____
Program: _____

HOTEL/MOTEL INFORMATION
Hotel/Motel Closest to Theater or Campus: _____
Address: _____ Phone: _____

Distance to Theater: _____ Rates for singles: _____
   doubles: _____
   triples: _____
Is a special rate possible? _____
Is that reflected in rates quoted above? _____
Does hotel/motel have:
Restaurant: _____ Hours open: _____
Phones in rooms: _____ Switchboard open 24 hours: _____
TV in rooms: _____ Pool: _____
Bathtubs: _____ other: _____

Hotel/Motel 2nd closest: _____

Address: _____ Phone: _____
_____

Distance to Theater: _____ Rates for singles: _____
doubles: _____
triples: _____

Is a special rate possible? _____
Is that reflected in rates quoted above? _____
Does hotel/motel have:

Restaurant: _____ Hours open: _____
Phones in rooms: _____ Switchboard open 24 hours: _____
TV in rooms: _____ Pool: _____
Bathtubs: _____ other: _____

Is there a courtesy car between any of these hotel/
motels and the local airport or bus station? _____
Do any of these hotel/motels have a courtesy car? _____

OTHER INFORMATION ABOUT YOUR COMMUNITY

Please enclose a map of your city and directions to the theater with this form.

Local Physician: _____ Phone: _____
Local Emergency Room: _____ Phone: _____
Address: _____
_____

Laundromat closest to theater: _____
Dry cleaner closest to theater: _____

The company may need to use a local bank in order to facilitate its weekly payroll.
Which bank does your organization use: _____
Address: _____ Phone: _____
Officer to whom you are known: _____

Local restaurants open after 10:30 P.M.

NAME	TYPE OF FOOD	ADDRESS	PHONE
_____	_____	_____	_____
_____	_____	_____	_____

Nearest airport to your city: _____
Which airlines serve this airport? _____
How far is airport from theater? _____
What touring theatrical or dance companies have performed in your theater in the
last 2 years? _____

The Tour Schedule

	HOTEL:
	THEATRE:
DAY/DATE: HIGHLIGHTS:	SPONSOR:
	TECH CONTACT:
	DIRECTIONS:

TIME	ARTISTS	TIME	PRODUCTION STAFF	TIME	ORCHESTRA

Request for Promotional Materials

PRESENTER'S NAME
PRESENTER'S ADDRESS

Dear (Presenter's Name):

The company offers presenters the promotion and publicity materials listed below. You should already have received one company press kit and 10 8" x 10" black-and-white glossy photographs.

Please indicate on the form below the quantity of each item you are requesting, tear off the form and *return it immediately.* All requested materials will be sent not less than 12 weeks prior to the company's arrival, unless you advise our office otherwise. The materials are free and delivered postage paid except as indicated.

We do not put a limit on the amount of materials a presenter can request; however, please order only materials and in quantity you can put to good use.

Cordially,

Company Manager

— —

Presenter's Name: _____

Mailing Address: _____

ITEM	NUMBER REQUESTED	MAIL DATE	MAILED BY	COMMENTS
Press Kit				
Glossies (8" × 10")				
Posters (16" × 18")				
Flyers (9" × 12")				
35 mm slides				
Video spots				

Please return this form to: COMPANY MANAGER: _____
                                 ADDRESS: _____

Technical Information Questionnaire

Typical Dance Theatre

NOTE: This "Technical Information Questionnaire" is considered a part of TDT's contract with you. The contract cannot be signed until this questionnaire is received. Please provide all requested information and return to: Typical Dance Theatre, P.O. Box 222, Paris, Idaho 20202, Attn: J. Fred Muggs, Technical Director.

Typical Dance Theatre (TDT) is a repertory company and its touring engagements draw from approximately twenty active dance works. The questions that we ask on the following pages are important in determining which works can be done to provide the best program for your performance space. While this questionnaire may be more complete than others you have received in the past *we need all the requested information as accurately as possible* to be able to adapt to your specific circumstances in the limited time we will have in your theatre.

Since this questionnaire is being completed by persons with a wide range of technical expertise many items and terms have been greatly simplified. If this questionnaire tends to be speaking down to you, we apologize.

Please return this questionnaire by _____.
If you have questions or need assistance, please call J. Fred Muggs at (202) 555-1212. Thank You.

MEASUREMENT REFERENCE POINTS: To describe stage measurements and locations please refer to, and measure from, two standard reference points:

1. The Center Line (CL): This is the line which runs through the center of the performance area from the front to rear of the stage separating stage right from stage left (the performer's right and left).

2. The Plaster Line: This is the line forms the opening of the proscenium at the upstage (back) edge of the proscenium arch. (This is similar to the curtain line, but is a more precise measurement.)

In addition to the information requested please include any additional information regarding your theatre that may be available:

- ☐ Ground plan of the stage
- ☐ Line plot or hanger log of the stage
- ☐ Stock inventory sheets
- ☐ Theatre policy sheets
- ☐ Map to locate the theatre building

If there is anything unusual, special, or "bizarre" about your facility or equipment that we do not ask about in this questionnaire, please volunteer the information. We hate surprises ...

TDT Technical Information Questionnaire

SPONSOR CONTACTS

Name of performance space _____

Address _____

City_____ State _____ Zip Code _____

Name of institution college or organization _____

Please describe how to locate the performance space (street address, campus location, etc.) Include map if needed. _____

_____

Person responsible for this engagement:

Name: _____ Position: _____

Office Phone: _____ Home Phone: _____

Person to whom the light plot should be sent:

Name: _____ Position: _____

Office Phone: _____ Home Phone: _____

Person completing this questionnaire:

Name: _____ Position: _____

Office Phone: _____ Home Phone: _____

I. GENERAL INFORMATION

   A. Auditorium capacity: Main floor_____ + Balcony_____ = Total_____

   B. Load-in point: ☐ Directly on stage ☐ Scene shop ☐ Other

Describe _____

C. Is loading area? ☐ Above stage level (dock height) ☐ Stage level ☐ Other
Describe _____

D. Comments on load-in problems: (Stairs, narrow doors, etc.)

_____
_____

E. Is a union crew required? _____

II. DRESSING ROOMS

A. Total number of dressing rooms:_____
How many: Principal_____ Soloist_____ Chorus_____

B. Where are the dressing rooms? (NOTE: Dressing rooms for six men and eleven women are required.)
☐ Stage level ☐ Above stage level ☐ Below stage level
Describe distance and path from stage to dressing rooms:

_____
_____

C. Are there page monitors in each? _____

D. Are they equipped with? ☐ Mirrors ☐ Make-up lights ☐ Sinks
☐ Showers ☐ Wardrobe racks ☐ Adequate heat

E. Can quick-change booths be set-up backstage with lights and mirrors?

_____

III. STAGE DIMENSIONS

A. Stage
1. Depth from plaster line (upstage edge of proscenium wall) to back wall:

_____

2. Depth from front of apron to plaster line: _____
3. Wing space stage right: _____
4. Wing space stage left: _____
5. Height from stage floor to grid (or ceiling if dead hung): _____
6. Usual trim height (floor to bottom of borders or teasers): _____
7. List all usable entrances to the stage (with dimensions): _____
8. Comments on stage space (columns, permanent set storage, permanent piano storage, permanent stage managers booths, etc.): _____

_____
_____

IV. FLY SYSTEM

A. Do you have a fly system? ☐ Yes ☐ No

B. If you have a fly system:
1. What type is it? ☐ Counterweight ☐ Hemp ☐ Electric winch
2. How many line sets (battens) are available in the total system?_____
3. Describe lines that are unavailable due to permanent storage: _____

_____

    4. How high will lines fly? _____

    5. How close to the floor will the pipes come in? _____

    6. Is the fly system?　☐ Single purchase　☐ Double purchase

  C. Act curtain (house curtain):

    1. Does it?　☐ Fly　☐ Draw

    2. Is it?　☐ Manual　☐ Motorized. If motorized, what is the cycle time _____

    3. What is its colors? _____

    4. What material is it made of? _____

    5. Additional comments: _____

V. MASKING (CURTAINS)

  A. LEGS (side, vertical masking drapes)

    1. How many pair of legs are necessary to mask the stage? _____

    2. How many pair of legs do you have available? _____

    3. What are their hanging dimensions? _____ × _____

    4. What material are they made of? _____

    5. What color are they? _____

    6. What is their condition? _____

    7. Are the legs permanently hung? _____

    8. If the legs are permanently hung, or if there is a usual leg hang, list it below: (distance from plaster line)

      a. Set #1 _____

      b. Set #2 _____

      c. Set #3 _____

      d. Set #4 _____

      e. Set #5 _____

  B. BORDERS or TEASERS (overhead, horizontal masking drapes)

    1. How many borders are necessary to mask the stage? _____

    2. How many borders do you have available? _____

    3. What are their hanging dimensions?_____ × _____

    4. What material are they made of? _____

    5. What color are they? _____

    6. What is their condition? _____

    7. Are they permanently hung? _____

    8. If they are permanently hung, or if there is a usual border hang, list it below: (distance from plaster line.)

      a. Set #1 _____

      b. Set #2 _____

      c. Set #3 _____

      d. Set #4 _____

      e. Set #5 _____

  C. BACKINGS

    1. Do you have a curved cyclorama?　☐ Yes　☐ No

      a. What are its dimensions? _____ × _____

      b. What material is it made of?_____

    c. What color is it? _____

    d. What is its condition? _____

    e. What is its distance from the plaster line? _____

    f. Is there a cross-over behind the cyclorama? _____

    g. Can the cyclorama be moved or struck? _____

  2. Do you have a flat sky-drop? ☐ Yes ☐ No

    a. What are its dimensions? _____ × _____

    b. What material is it made of? _____

    c. What color is it? _____

    d. What is its condition? _____

    e. What is its normal distance from the plaster line? _____

    f. Is there a cross-over behind the sky-drop? _____

    g. Can the sky-drop be moved or struck? _____

D. Additional comments: _____

_____

V. LIGHTING SYSTEM

A. DIMMERS

  1. Brand name of dimmers: _____

  2. Type: ☐ Solid state (SCR or Triac) ☐ Auto-transformer ☐ Resistance

  3. Total number of dimmers: _____

  4. List dimmer numbers by wattage capacity:

    _____ dimmers at _____ watts capacity each

    _____ dimmers at _____ watts capacity each

    _____ dimmers at _____ watts capacity each

  5. How old is the system? _____ years

  6. In what condition are the dimmers? (How reliable are they?) _____

_____

B. CONTROL BOARD

  1. Is it? ☐ Memory ☐ Preset ☐ Manual

  2. List brand name: _____

  3. List model name if known: _____

  4. If it is a memory board:

    a. Is it programmed by? ☐ A keyboard ☐ Potentiometers ☐ Both

    b. Does it have sub-masters? _____ If so, how many? _____

    c. Does it have assignable control channels? _____ If so, how many? _____

    d. Does it have soft patch capabilities? _____

    e. Describe back-up system, if applicable: _____

_____

    f. List any unusual features: _____

_____

    g. How reliable is it? _____

  5. If it is a preset board:

    a. List the number of presets: _____

    b. Describe the kind of presets (cards, pots, wheels, etc.): _____

   c. Is there a grand master controller? _____
   d. Are there sub-masters? _____ If so, how many? _____
   e. Is the fade controller? ☐ Crossfade ☐ Splitfade ☐ Pileon ☐ Timed
  6. What is the location of the control board? _____
  7. Is there a remote control station? _____
C. PATCH PANEL
  1. How do you patch circuits to dimmers? ☐ Dimmer per circuit
     ☐ Pin and plug, patch panel ☐ Quick connect ☐ Hard wired
  2. Brand name of patch panel: _____
  3. Where is it located? _____
  4. Total number of circuits in system: _____
  5. Is there a F.O.H. disconnect in the patch panel? _____
D. POWER SOURCE
  1. Is there a company switch for tieing-in road boards? _____
  2. If there is a company switch:
     a. Is it three phase or single phase? _____
     b. What is the amperage per leg? _____
     c. Where is it located in relation to the stage? _____
  3 If there is no company switch:
     a. Where is the closest source of electricity to the stage?
        minimum ☐ 400 amps. 120 VAC of single phase per leg OR
        ☐ 250 amps. 120 VAC of three phase per leg
        _____
     b. Describe source (power panel, transformer, existing dimmer buss bars,
        etc.): _____
     c. Do you require your electrician to tie into this power source? _____

VII. LIGHTING EQUIPMENT
   A. LIGHTING INSTRUMENTS. Please list all lighting instruments available for
      use during the time of TDT's performance.

QUANTITY	TYPE	LENS DIAM. X	FOCAL LENGTH	SINGLE OR DOUBLE LENS	WATTAGE	BRAND
	Leko*	6" X				
	Leko*	6" X				
	Leko*	8" S				
	Leko*	X				
	Leko*	X				
	Fresnel	6"	######			
	Fresnel	8"	######			
	Scoop**	###	######			
	Beam Projector	###	######			

   * Ellipsoidal Reflector Spotlight   ** Ellipsoidal Reflector Floodlight

B. STRIP LIGHTS: Do you have strip lights? ☐ Yes ☐ No
   1. How many sections? _____
   2. Length of each section: _____
   3. Number of circuits in each section: _____
   4. Wattage of each lamp: _____
   5. Are strips permanently hung? _____
   6. If permanently hung, list distances from plaster line:_____
C. CONNECTORS: What type of connectors are used in your lighting system?
   1. Pin connector: ☐ 2 pin (ungrounded) ☐ 3 pin (grounded)
      ☐ 3 pin locking (Hargelock)
   2. Twist lock: ☐ 2 prong (ungrounded) ☐ 15A ☐ 20A ☐ 30A
      ☐ 3 prong (ground OUT) ☐ 15A ☐ 20A ☐ 30A
      ☐ 3 prong (ground IN) ☐ 15A ☐ 20A ☐ 30A
   3. Parallel blade (household or Edison):
      ☐ 2 prong (ungrounded) ☐ 3 prong (grounded)
   4. Other: ☐ Stage plug (slip plug) ☐ 20A ☐ 30A
      ☐ Other (describe and diagram)

VIII. LIGHTING POSITIONS
   A. ONSTAGE LIGHTING POSITIONS
      1. First electric or bridge:
         a. Distance from plaster line: _____
         b. Number of *different* circuits: _____
         c. Does it fly? _____ If no, list height: _____
         d. List any permanently mounted instruments: _____
      2. Second electric:
         a. Distance from plaster line: _____
         b. Number of *different* circuits: _____
         c. Does it fly? _____ If no, list height: _____
         d. List any permanently mounted instruments: _____
      3. Third electric:
         a. Distance from plaster line: _____
         b. Number of *different* circuits: _____
         c. Does it fly? _____ If no, list height: _____
         d. List any permanently mounted instruments: _____
      4. Fourth electric:
         a. Distance from plaster line: _____
         b. Number of *different* circuits: _____
         c. Does it fly? _____ If no, list height: _____
         d. List any permanently mounted instruments: _____
      5. Cyclorama lighting:
         a. From what pipe do you light the cyclorama?_____
         b. Distance from this pipe to cyclorama:_____
         c. Do you have a cyc pit or trough? _____
         d. If yes, list distance from plaster line: _____

    e. What kind of instrument do you light the cyc with? _____
       Type of instrument: _____
       Number of instruments: _____
       Wattage of each lamp: _____
       Number of units required to get an even wash: _____

6. Tormentor or cove position:
    a. Distance from plaster line: _____
    b. Distance off-stage from center line: _____
    c. Height range from floor: _____ to _____
    d. Number of *different* circuits: _____

7. Side booms or ladders:
    a. How many do you have? _____
    b. Describe their locations: _____
    c. How many *different* circuits does each have? _____

8. Floor pockets:
    a. How many do you have? _____
    b. What type of connectors? _____
    c. Number of separate circuits in each floor pocket: _____
    d. Are they ganged side to side? _____
    e. Are these pockets the source of circuits used for side lighting? _____
    f. Describe the location of all floor pockets: _____

B. FRONT OF HOUSE LIGHTING POSITIONS:
1. Beam slot #1 (ceiling slots or ports):
    a. Distance from plaster line: _____
    b. Height above stage level: _____
    c. Number of *different* circuits: _____
    d. Describe all permanently mounted instruments: _____

2. Beam slot #2:
    a. Distance from plaster line: _____
    b. Height above stage level: _____
    c. Number of *different* circuits: _____
    d. Describe all permanently mounted instruments: _____

3. Beam slot #3:
    a. Distance from plaster line: _____
    b. Height above stage level: _____
    c. Number of *different* circuits: _____
    d. Describe all permanently mounted instruments: _____

4. Balcony front (balcony rail):
    a. Distance from plaster line: _____
    b. Height above stage level: _____
    c. Number of *different* circuits: _____
    d. Describe all permanently mounted instruments: _____

5. House booms (vertical pipes or ladders in the house):
    a. Distance from plaster line: _____
    b. Height above stage level: _____

c. Number of *different* circuits: _____

d. Describe all permanently mounted instruments: _____

IX. SOUND SYSTEM

A. Do you use your sound system for the reproduction of music recordings?

_____

1. How would you objectively rate the sound created by your system? _____

_____

2. How reliable is your sound system? _____

B. Amplifiers:

1. Brand name: _____ Model: _____

2. What is its (their) age? _____

3. What is its (their) condition? _____

4. Is the system stereo? _____

5. What is its rated wattage per channel? _____

C. Pre-amplifiers (mixers):

1. Brand name: _____ Model: _____

2. What is its (their) age? _____

3. What is its (their) condition? _____

4. How many channels are available? _____

5. Are bass and treble adjustable? _____

6. Where is control board located? _____

D. Speakers:

1. Brand name: _____ Model: _____

2. What is its (their) age? _____

3. What is its (their) condition? _____

4. Describe the house system (sizes, numbers, and locations): _____

_____

5. Describe the stage monitor system (sizes, numbers, and locations): _____

_____

E. Reel-to-reel tape deck:

1. Brand name: _____ Model: _____

2. What is its (their) age? _____

3. What is its (their) condition? _____

4. Is it stereo? _____

5. Number of tracks ☐ One ☐ Two ☐ Four ☐ Eight

6. What speeds does it run? ☐ 3¾ ☐ 7½ ☐ 15 ips

F. Other equipment: Describe any other types of additional sound equipment available (Dolby, DBX, equalizers, etc.):

_____

G. Communications:

1. Do you have a communication system? _____

2. How does it operate? (head-sets, biscuits, phone handsets) _____

3. Brand name: _____ Model: _____

4. What is its age? _____

5. What is its (their) condition? _____

6. How many stations are there? _____

7. Where are they located? _____

X. MISCELLANEOUS ITEMS

A. STAGE FLOOR

1 Is the floor resilient? _____

2. Describe floor surface (materials and condition): _____

3. Describe the floor support structure (if known): _____

4. Are there traps or elevators in the floor? _____

5. Do you have access to a portable dance floor? _____

6. If so, brand name: _____ condition: _____

B. WARDROBE

1. Is there a dry cleaners nearby that you would recommend to clean costumes?

☐ Yes   ☐ No. If yes, then:

a. Name: _____

b. Address: _____

c. Phone number: _____

d. Hours: _____

2. Is there a laundromat nearby that you would recommend?

☐ Yes   ☐ No. If yes, then:

a. Name: _____

b. Address: _____

c. Phone number: _____

d. Hours: _____

C. LADDER. Do you have a ladder, cherry picker, or rolling scaffold high enough to reach the on-stage electrics when they are at their trim height? _____

D. COMMENTS. Please make any other comments about your performance space which will be helpful to us. *Thanks again for your time.*

Date _____

Technical Glossary

General Stage Terminology

On The Stage

DIRECTIONS. In the theatre, directions are *always* given in terms of *stage left* and *stage right*. This is the *Performer's* left hand and right hand as he faces the audience. *Upstage and downstage* are terms that originated in the time of raked stages when the back of the stage floor was slanted higher than the front. Thus the portion of the stage closest to the audience is downstage and the back of the stage is upstage.

PROSCENIUM ARCH. The opening in the downstage wall separating the audience and the stage.

FLY LOFT. The space directly above the stage where draperies and lighting instruments are hung. Ideally, the height of the fly loft is three times as high as the proscenium arch.

GRID. The metal framework at the top of the fly loft just below the stage roof. Everything that flies is suspended from the grid.

WORK LIGHTS. Lights that fully illuminate stage and wings, used primarily during rehearsals and mid-performance set changes.

FLY SYSTEM. A series of cables, pulleys (called sheaves and pronounced shivs), and counterweights that enable scenery, drapes, or lighting equipment to fly in and out. There are two basic types of fly systems. The *hemp system* uses ropes to support the battens, and the counterbalance is a large sand bag. This is a very old system but works well in the hands of a competent fly man. The more modern system is the counterweight system. The battens are supported by metal aircraft cable, and the counterbalances are steel or iron counterweights held in a large metal arbor.

LINE SET. A group of three to seven lines used together to lift a batten.

BATTEN. A metal pipe attached to the cables of the fly system on which all scenery and lighting equipment is tied or clamped.

TRIM. A mark designating the height of a batten in relation to the stage floor, when it is in a working position.

SECTION. A side view of the stage, drawn to scale, drawn through the center line of the theatre. Usually used to show relative trim heights of flown pieces.

PLASTER LINE. A line drawn across the stage at the upstage edge of the proscenium. It is at this point that all measurements up and down stage are made. This is one of the two major points of reference used in measuring a stage.

CURTAIN LINE. The line on the stage where the act curtain (see masking) falls. Used as a measurement point for up and down stage much like the plaster line. It is not as accurate a measurement as the plaster line, since the curtain can shift and the curtain's fullness is often forgotten in measuring.

CENTER LINE. The other major point for measurement on the stage. It is a line running directly down the middle of the stage separating stage left from stage right. All measurements on the stage are made from the plaster line and the center line.

GROUND PLAN. An aerial view of the stage drawn to a specific scale (usually one-quarter inch equals one foot or one-half inch equals one foot) showing all the pertinent elements of the stage.

LIGHT PLOT. A ground plan of the stage with all the lighting instruments drafted on, showing where each lighting instrument is hung, what type it is, what dimmer it is patched into, what circuit it is plugged into, and what color it is gelled.

Masking

MASKING. Any drapery or scenic piece used to define the stage or hide the view of the audience.

BORDER OR TEASER. A horizontal masking piece used to hide anything in the fly loft such as lighting equipment and scenery.

LEG. A vertical masking piece hung at the sides of the stage used to hide the wing spaces.

WING. The offstage space between the legs.

GRAND DRAPE. The first (downstage) border often called a teaser. It is the visual determiner of the height of the proscenium opening (called the trim height). It is not the main curtain that opens and closes.

TORMENTOR or TORM. The first (downstage) leg. It can be a soft drapery but is often framed and solid. This is the visual determiner of the width of the stage.

HOUSE CURTAIN or ACT CURTAIN. This is the curtain that opens and closes separating the audience from the stage. It is usually hung directly upstage of the grand drape.

ASBESTOS. A fire-resistant curtain located at the proscenium opening. Recently replaced by a fibreglass material called Zeetex.

CYCLORAMA. A very large fabric drop rigged at the back of the stage and wrapping downstage in the wing space. Its primary use is to give a feeling of great depth. Usually not very applicable for dance as the downstage curved portion provides a barrier that makes exits and side-lighting very difficult.

SKY DROP. A fabric drop at the back of the stage used for sky effects without wrapping downstage like a cyclorama.

SCRIM. A transparent gauze material used for ghosts, clouds, and any effect requiring something to appear and disappear. When lit from the front, it becomes opaque; when lit from behind, it becomes transparent. Often used in front of a skydrop to give more sense of depth.

Instrument Mounting Positions

ELECTRIC. A batten with cable and connectors mounted on it specifically used for hanging instruments.

BRIDGE. The term for the first downstage electric when there is a large trusswork instead of the simple batten. The bridge was originally designed so a stage hand could move about to adjust the carbons of early carbon-arc spotlights.

BOOM. A vertical pipe used for mounting instruments. On stage booms are usually portable. When mounted in the audience, they are usually a permanent fixture. The terms tree, tower, and ladder are often used for a portable boom.

HOUSE BOOM. A permanent boom mounted in the house.

BOX BOOM. A boom mounted in a box seat.

BALCONY BOOM. A boom mounted in the balcony.

BALCONY RAIL. A mounting position on the front edge of the balcony. Very popular for musical comedy but rarely used for dance lighting.

BEAM SLOT. A false beam mounted in the ceiling of the auditorium used for a mounting position. Beam slot has become the term for any horizontal ceiling mounting position.

F.O.H. Front of House. Any mounting position in the auditorium.

A.P. Ante-Pro. Any mounting position in the auditorium.

Courtesy of Western States Art Foundation.

Resources

FEDERAL GOVERNMENT
National Endowment for the Arts
Presenting and Commissioning Program
1100 Pennsylvania Avenue, NW
Room 710
Washington, DC 20506
202/682-5444; FAX 202/682-5612

REGIONAL ARTS ORGANIZATIONS
Arts Midwest
Hennepin Center for the Arts
528 Hennepin Avenue, Suite 310
Minneapolis, MN 55403
612/341-0755; FAX 612/341-0902

Serves the states of Iowa, Minnesota, North
Dakota, South Dakota, Wisconsin, Illinois,
Indiana, Michigan, Ohio

Consortium for Pacific Arts and Cultures
2141-C Atherton Road
Honolulu, HI 96822
808/946-7381; FAX 808/955-2722

Serves the territories of American Samoa,
Northern Mariana Islands, Guam

Mid-America Arts Alliance
912 Baltimore Avenue, Suite 700
Kansas City, MO 64105
816/421-1388; FAX 816/421-3918

Serves the states of Arkansas, Kansas,
Oklahoma, Missouri, Nebraska, Texas

Mid-Atlantic Arts Foundation
11 East Chase Street, Suite 2A
Baltimore, MD 21202
410/539-6656; FAX 410/837-5517

Serves the states and territories of Delaware,
District of Columbia, Maryland, New Jersey,
New York, Pennsylvania, Virgin Islands,
Virginia, West Virginia

New England Foundation for the Arts
678 Massachusetts Avenue, 8th Floor
Cambridge, MA 02139

617/492-2914; FAX 617/876-0702

Serves the states of Connecticut, Massachusetts, Maine, New Hampshire, Rhode Island, Vermont

Southern Arts Federation
181 14th Street NE, Suite 400
Atlanta, GA 30309
404/874-7244; FAX 404/873-2148

Serves the states of Alabama, Florida, Georgia, Kentucky, Louisiana, Mississippi, North Carolina, South Carolina, Tennessee

Western States Arts Federation
236 Montezuma Avenue
Santa Fe, NM 87501
505/988-1166; FAX 505/982-9307

Serves the states of Alaska, Arizona, California, Colorado, Hawaii, Idaho, Montana, New Mexico, Nevada, Oregon, Utah, Washington, Wyoming

PRESENTERS' ORGANIZATIONS

The Association of Performing Arts
  Presenters (APAP)
1112 16th Street, NW, Suite 400
Washington, DC 20036
202/833-2787; FAX 202/833-1543

International Society for Performing Arts
  Administrators (ISPAA)
4920 Plainfield NE, Suite 3
Grand Rapids, MI 49505-1010
616/364-3000; FAX 616/364-9010

National Association of Campus Activities
  (NACA)
13 Harbison Way
Columbia, SC 29212-3401
803/732-NACA; FAX 803/749-1047

Pacific Northwest Arts Presenters
  (PNWAP)
P.O. Box 55877
Seattle, WA 98155
206/365-4143; FAX 206/365-8618

Western Alliance of Arts Administrators
  (WAAA)
44 Page Street; Suite 604B
San Francisco, CA 94102
415/621-4400; FAX 415/621-2533

PRESENTER CONSORTIA

Current information about local presenter consortia is available through the NEA and regional arts agencies.

SERVICE ORGANIZATIONS

Alliance of Resident Theatres/New York
131 Varick Street, Room 904
New York, NY 10014
212/989-5257; FAX 212/989-4880

American Arts Alliance
1319 F Street, NW, Suite 500
Washington, DC 20004
202/737-1727; FAX 202/628-1258

American Symphony Orchestra League
777 14th Street, NW, Suite 500
Washington, DC 20005
202/628-0099; FAX 202/393-7228

The Association of American Cultures
1704 West Kings Highway
San Antonio, TX 78201
210/736-9272; FAX 210/736-6921

Theatre Bay Area
657 Mission Street, Suite 402
San Francisco, CA 94105
415/957-1557; FAX 415/957-1556

Chamber Music America
545 Eighth Avenue, 9th Floor
New York, NY 10018
212/244-2772; FAX 212/244-2776

Colorado Dance Alliance
P.O. Box 356
Boulder, CO 80306
303/443-2100 or 333-4643

Dance Theater Workshop
219 West 19th Street
New York, NY 10011
212/691-6500

Dance/USA
777 14th Street, NW, Suite 540
Washington, DC 20005
202/628-0144; FAX 202/628-0375

Hospital Audiences, Inc.
220 West 42nd Street
New York, NY 10036
212/575-7676

Los Angeles Theatre Alliance
3540 Wilshire Boulevard, PH 1
Los Angeles, CA 90010
213/380-3378

Meet The Composer
2112 Broadway, Suite 505
New York, NY 10023
212/787-3601

National Assembly of Local Arts Agencies
927 15th Street, NW, 12th Floor
Washington, DC 20005
202/371-2830; FAX 202/371-0424

National Assembly of State Arts Agencies
1010 Vermont Avenue, NW, Suite 920
Washington, DC 20005
202/347-6352; FAX 202/737-0526

National Association of Artists'
   Organizations
918 F Street, NW
Washington, DC 20004
202/347-6350; FAX 202/347-7363

National Association of Performing Arts
   Managers and Agents
c/o Ingrid Kidd, President
Main Stage Management Int'l., West

3532 Katella Avenue, Room 111
Los Alamitos, CA 90720
310/493-5690; FAX 310/430-7897

National Jazz Service Organization
P.O. Box 50152
Washington, DC 20091
202/347-2604; FAX 202/638-3460

Opera America
777 14th Street, NW, Suite 520
Washington, DC 20005
202/347-9262; FAX 202/393-0735

Theatre Communications Group
355 Lexington Avenue
New York, NY 10017
212/697-5230; FAX 212/983-4847

Volunteer Lawyers for the Arts
1 East 53rd Street
New York, NY 10022
212/319-2787; FAX 212/223-4415

STATE ARTS AGENCIES

Current information about state arts agencies is available through the NEA and regional arts agencies.

APPENDIX F

Selected Bibliography

American Theatre. Monthly. New York: Theatre Communications Group.

Andreasen, Alan R. *Expanding the Audience for the Performing Arts.* Washington: Seven Locks Press, 1991.

Anschell, Bill. *Jazz in the Concert Setting: A Study of the Barriers to Presenting Jazz in the Concert Hall.* Washington: APAP, 1987.

Brecher, Charles. *A Portrait of the Financial Condition of Presenting Organizations in the United States.* Washington: APAP, 1987.

Chamber Music. Quarterly. New York: Chamber Music America.

Confronting Crisis, Creating Change. Washington: APAP, 1991.

Controversy and Collaboration. Washington: APAP, 1990.

Dance Magazine. Monthly. New York: Dance Magazine. Subscription information: 33 West 60th Street, New York, NY 10023.

Fisher, Rod and Huber, Martin, eds. *Performing Arts Yearbook for Europe 1994.* London: Arts Publishing International Ltd, 1993.

Forging Alliances. Washington: APAP, 1989.

Inside Arts. Quarterly. Washington: APAP.

Katz, Jonathan, ed. *Presenting, Touring and the State Arts Agencies.* Washington: National Assembly of State Arts Agencies, 1992.

Lewis, Cathy, ed. *Music, Opera and Dance in Canada and the United States of America.* London: Arts Publishing International Ltd, 1993.

McDaniel, Nello and Thorn, George. *Workpapers I: Rethingking and Restructuring the Arts Organization.* New York: Foundation for the Extension and Development of the American Professional Theatre (FEDAPT), 1990.

Melillo, Joseph V., ed. *Market the Arts.* New York: FEDAPT, 1983.

Morison, Bradley G. and Dalgleish, Julie Gordon. *Waiting in the Wings: A Larger Audience for the Arts and How to Develop It.* New York: American Council for the Arts, 1993.

Musical America International Directory of the Performing Arts. Annual. New York: K-III Directory Corporation.

National Task Force on Presenting and Touring the Performing Arts. *An American Dialogue.* Washington: 1990.

Niemeyer, Suzanne, ed. *Money for Performing Artists.* New York: American Council for the Arts, 1991.

Opera America Newsline. Bimonthly. Washington: Opera America.

Rhodes, Naomi. *21 Voices: The Art of Presenting the Performing Arts.* Washington: APAP, 1990.

Roan, Neill Archer. *From Wary to Wise: Winning Strategies for Presenting Risky Events.* Washington: APAP, 1989.

Stern's Performing Arts Directory. Annual. New York: Dance Magazine.

The Technical Production Handbook: A Guide for Performing Arts Presenting Organizations and Touring Companies. Santa Fe: WESTAF Publications, 1995.

Turk, Frederick J. and Gallo, Robert P. *Financial Management Strategies for Nonprofit Organizations.* New York: American Council for the Arts, 1984.

Wolf, Thomas. *Presenting Performances.* New York: American Council for the Arts, 1991.

Index

Rena Shagan

Rena Shagan is president of Rena Shagan Associates, Inc., an organization which markets performing arts companies for touring in the United States and abroad. Her company also develops funding for commissions and tours. Clients include dance and theatre companies as well as music ensembles, with work ranging from contemporary to classical.

Rena Shagan is from time to time involved in special projects and partnerships related to touring and has served as consultant to numerous companies and presenters. She has been a consultant and lecturer on booking and tour management techniques and has planned conferences on the subject for organizations across the country, including the Mid-America Arts Alliance, Southern Arts Federation and Mid-Atlantic States Arts Consortium. In addition, she has written numerous articles on the subject for a variety of publications.

A former modern dancer, Rena Shagan has been general manager for several dance companies. She served as chairman of the Task Force for a National Dance Organization which created a new national service organization for the professional dance field, Dance/USA. Ms. Shagan currently serves on the board of the International Society of Performing Arts Administrators (ISPAA) and has been a board member for both Dance/USA and the American Arts Alliance. She has also been a grants and policy panelist on the Dance Advisory Panel of the National Endowment for the Arts and has served on panels for several regional organizations.

ALLWORTH BOOKS

Allworth Press publishes quality books to help individuals and small businesses. Titles include:

The Performing Arts Business Encyclopedia by Leonard DuBoff
(softcover, 6 × 9, 320 pages, $19.95)

Stage Fright: Health Hazards in Theater by Monona Rossol
(softcover, 6 × 9, 144 pages, $16.95)

An Actor's Guide—Your First Year in Hollywood by Michael Saint Nicholas
(softcover, 6 × 9, 192 pages, $16.95)

Writing Scripts Hollywood Will Love by Katherine Atwell Herbert
(softcover, 6 × 9, 160 pages, $12.95)

Arts and the Internet by V. A. Shiva
(softcover, 6 × 9, 208 pages, $18.95)

The Business of Multimedia by Nina Schuyler
(softcover, 6 × 9, 240 pages, $19.95)

Licensing Art & Design, Revised Edition by Caryn R. Leland
(softcover, 6 × 9, 128 pages, $16.95)

Legal Guide for the Visual Artist, Third Edition by Tad Crawford
(softcover, 8½ × 11, 256 pages, $19.95)

Business and Legal Forms for Fine Artists, Revised Edition by Tad Crawford
(softcover, 8½ × 11, 144 pages, $16.95)

Business and Legal Forms for Authors and Self-Publishers by Tad Crawford
(softcover, 8⅞ × 11, 176 pages, $15.95)

Immigration Questions and Answers by Carl Baldwin
(softcover, 6 × 9, 176 pages, $14.95)

Please write to request our free catalog. If you wish to order a book, send your check or money order to Allworth Press, 10 East 23rd Street, Suite 400, New York, NY 10010. Include $5 for shipping and handling for the first book ordered and $1 for each additional book. Ten dollars plus $1 for each additional book if ordering from Canada. New York State residents must add sales tax.

If you wish to see our catalog on the World Wide Web, you can find us at Millennium Production's Art and Technology Web site:
http://www.arts-online.com/allworth/home.html
or at
http://interport.net/~allworth